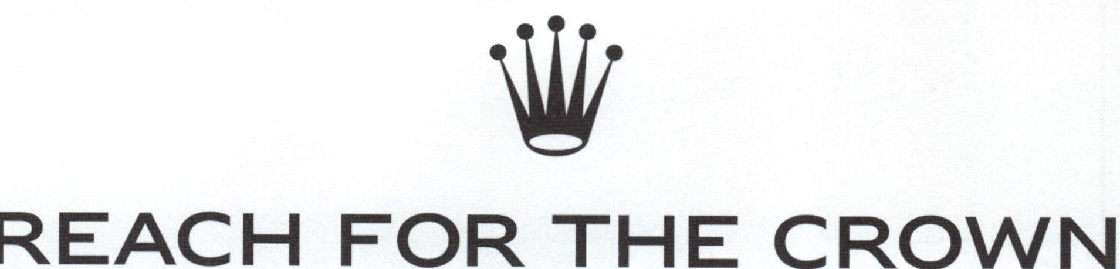

REACH FOR THE CROWN

THE DATEJUST

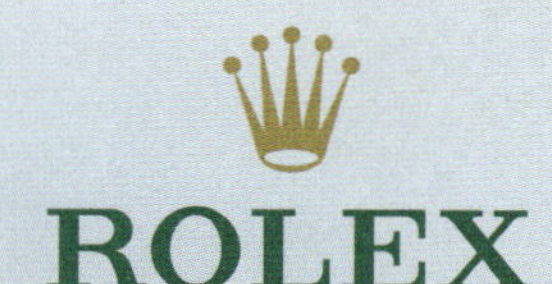

ROLEX

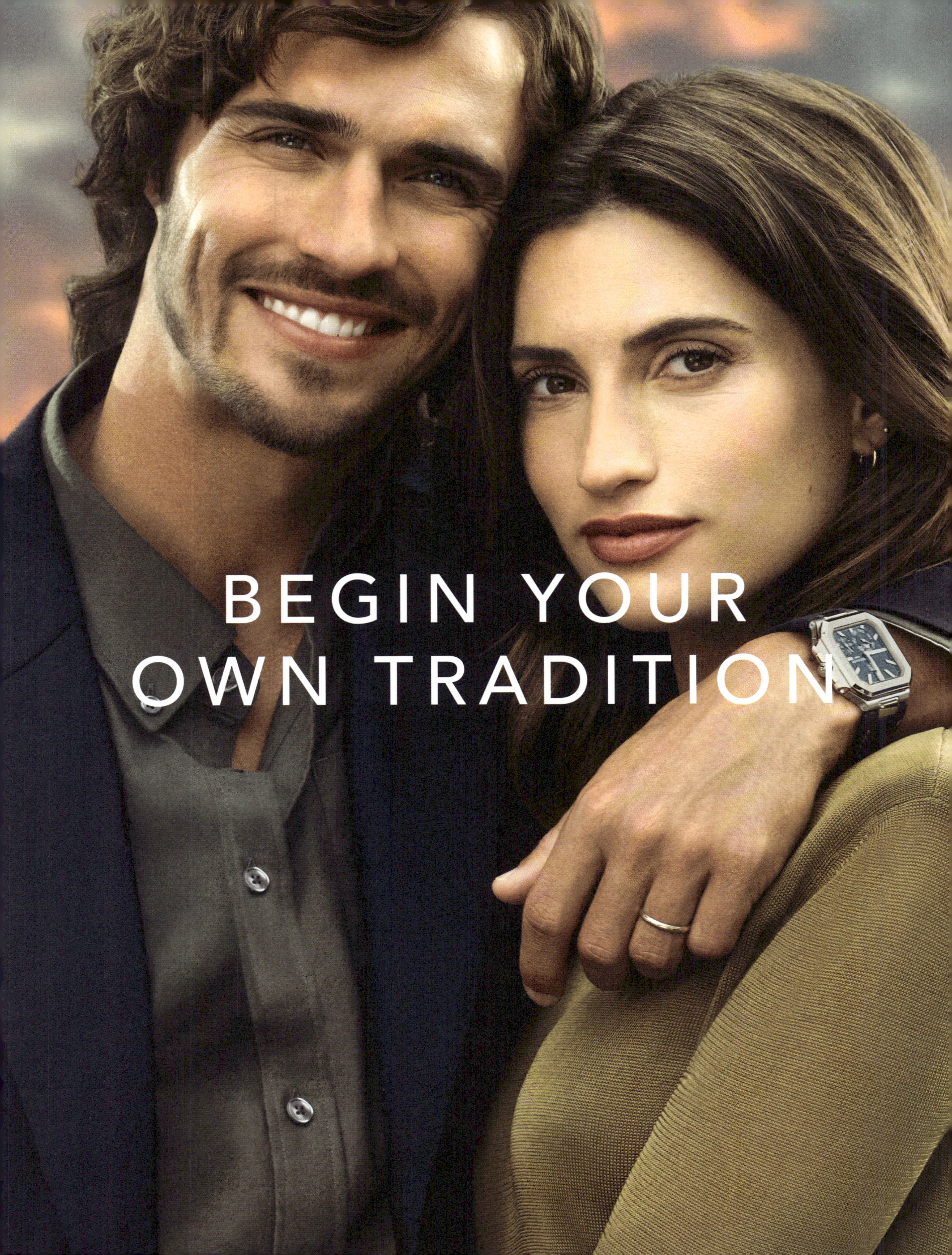

BEGIN YOUR
OWN TRADITION

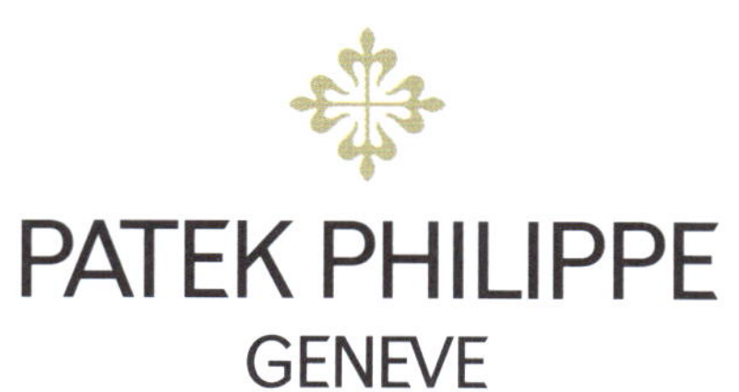

THE CUBITUS COLLECTION

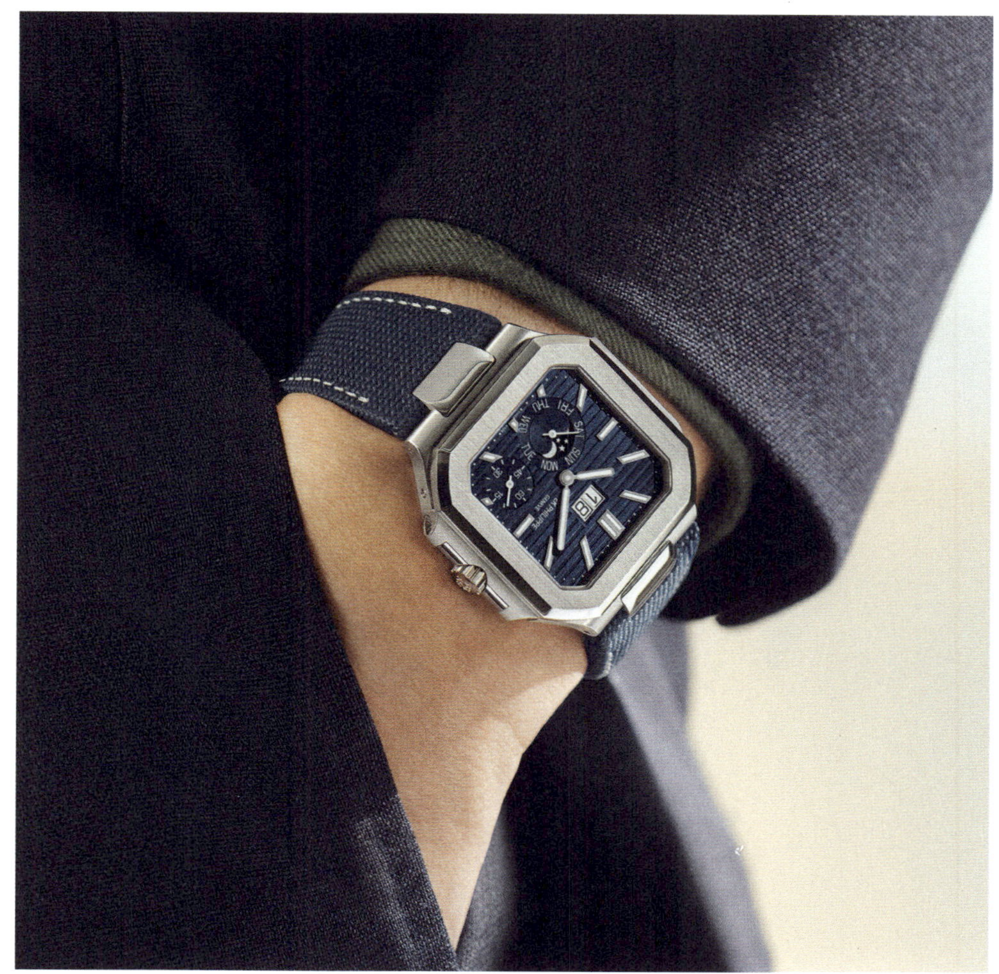

YOU NEVER ACTUALLY OWN A PATEK PHILIPPE.
YOU MERELY LOOK AFTER IT FOR THE NEXT GENERATION.

PATEK.COM

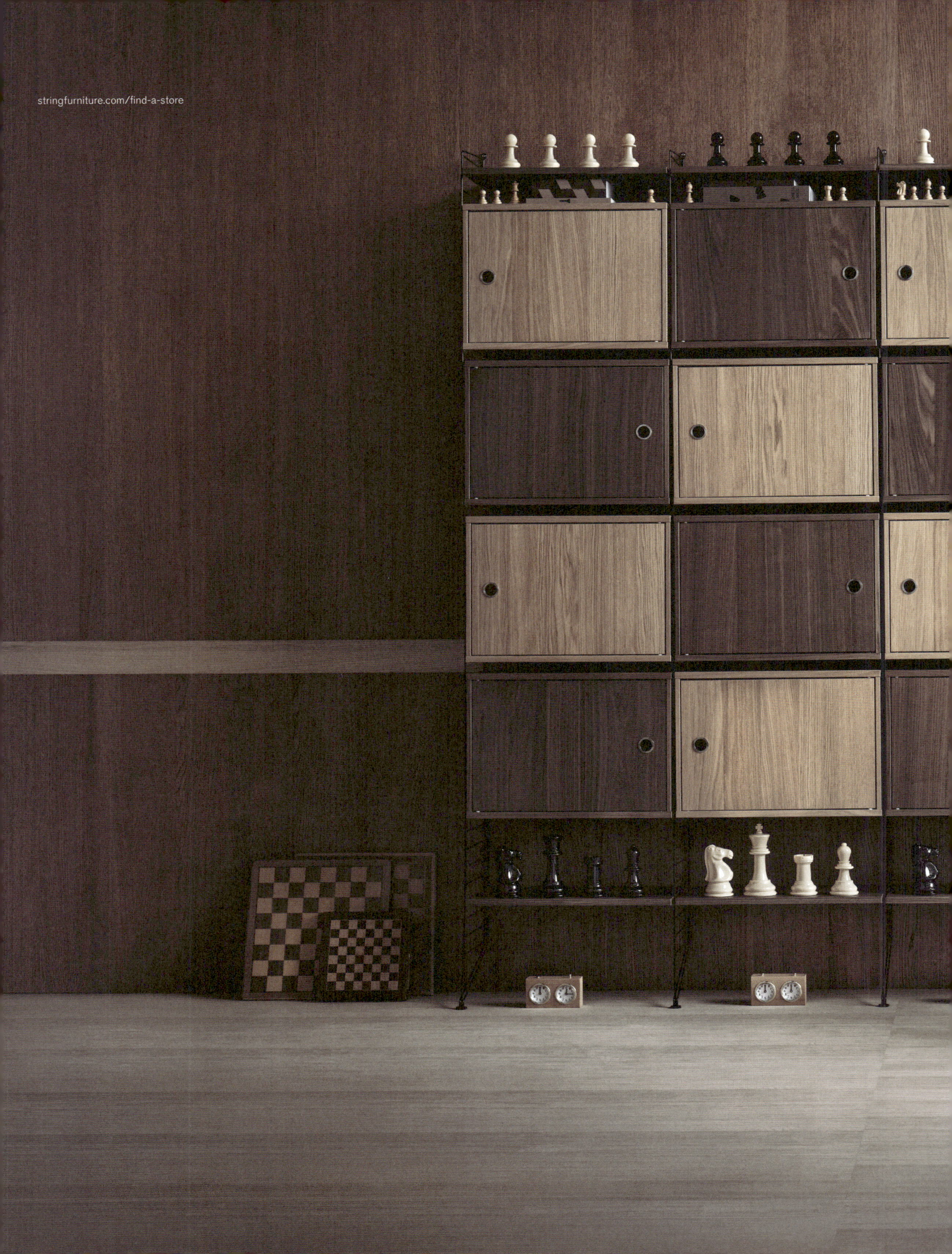
stringfurniture.com/find-a-store

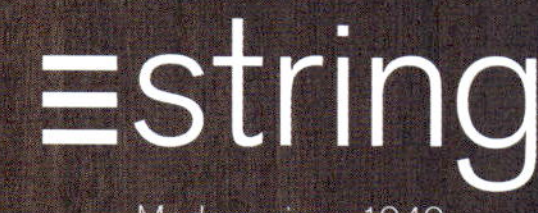

≡string®
Modern since 1949

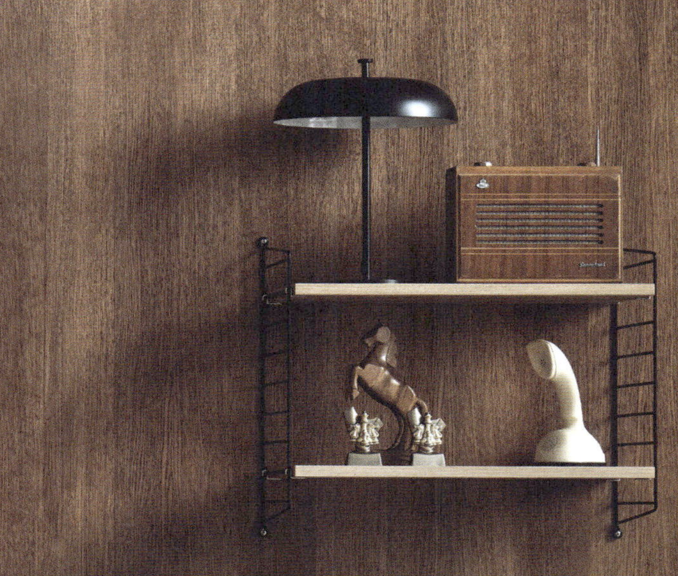

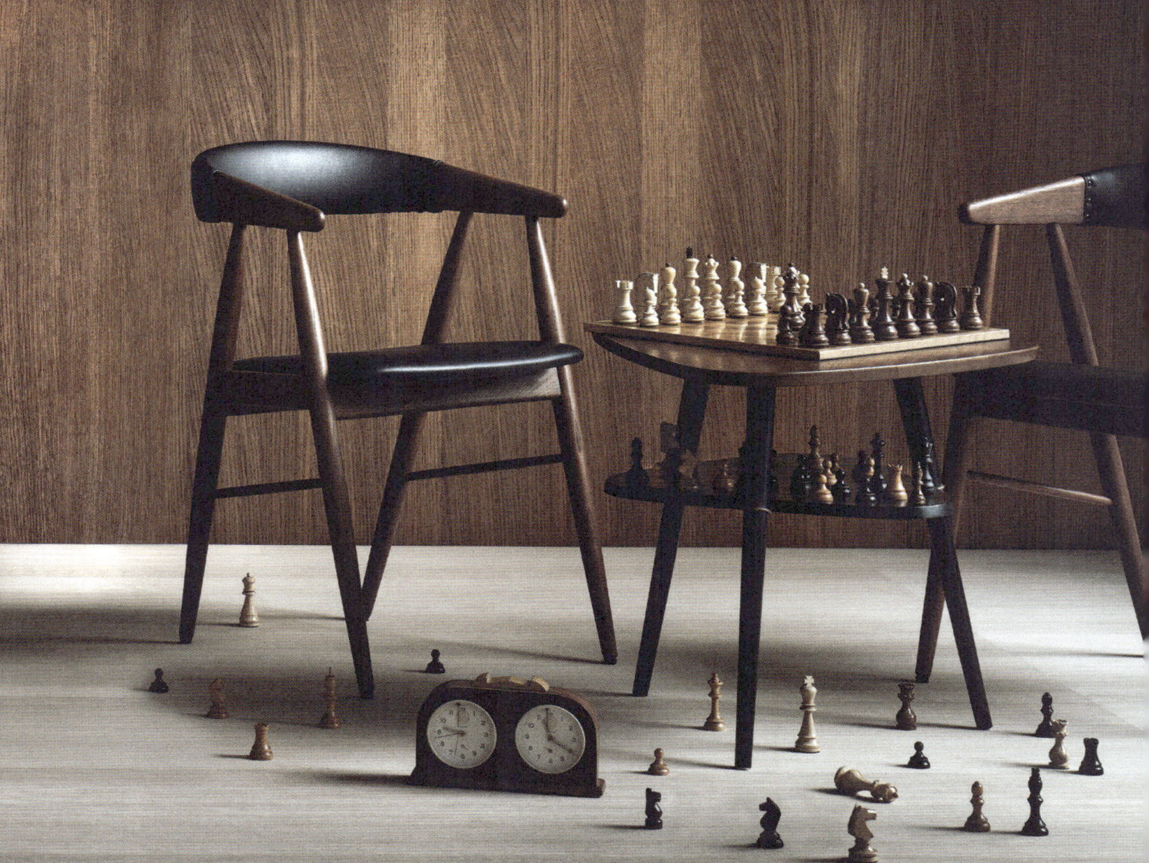

THOUSANDS OF NEW COMBINATIONS YET TO BE DISCOVERED

Swan

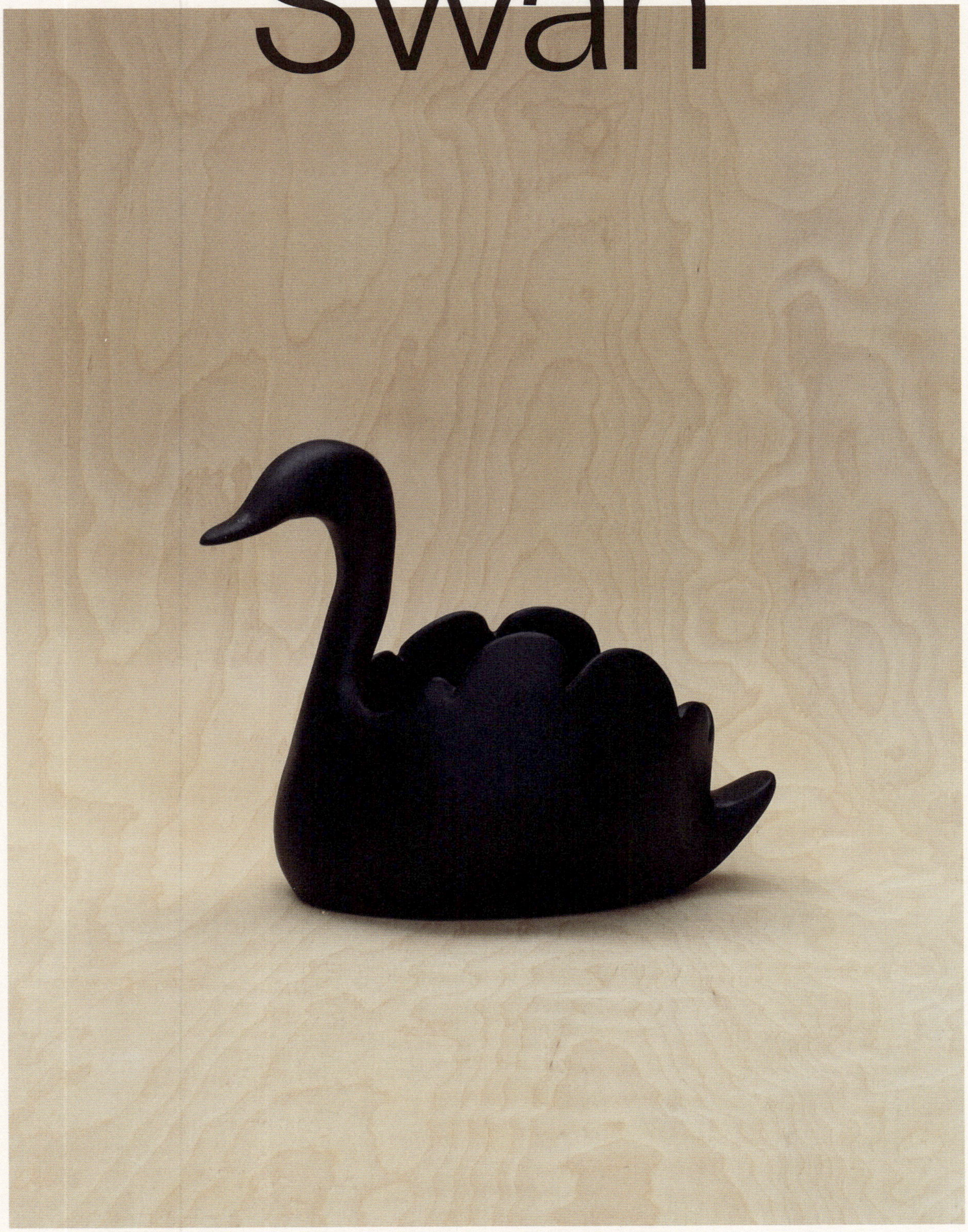

Vessels embodying the grace of swans, crafted with care, protective of their cargo, and symbolizing the bond of love between mates.

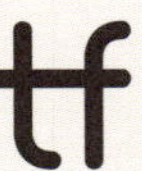

Explore the collection at
tf.design

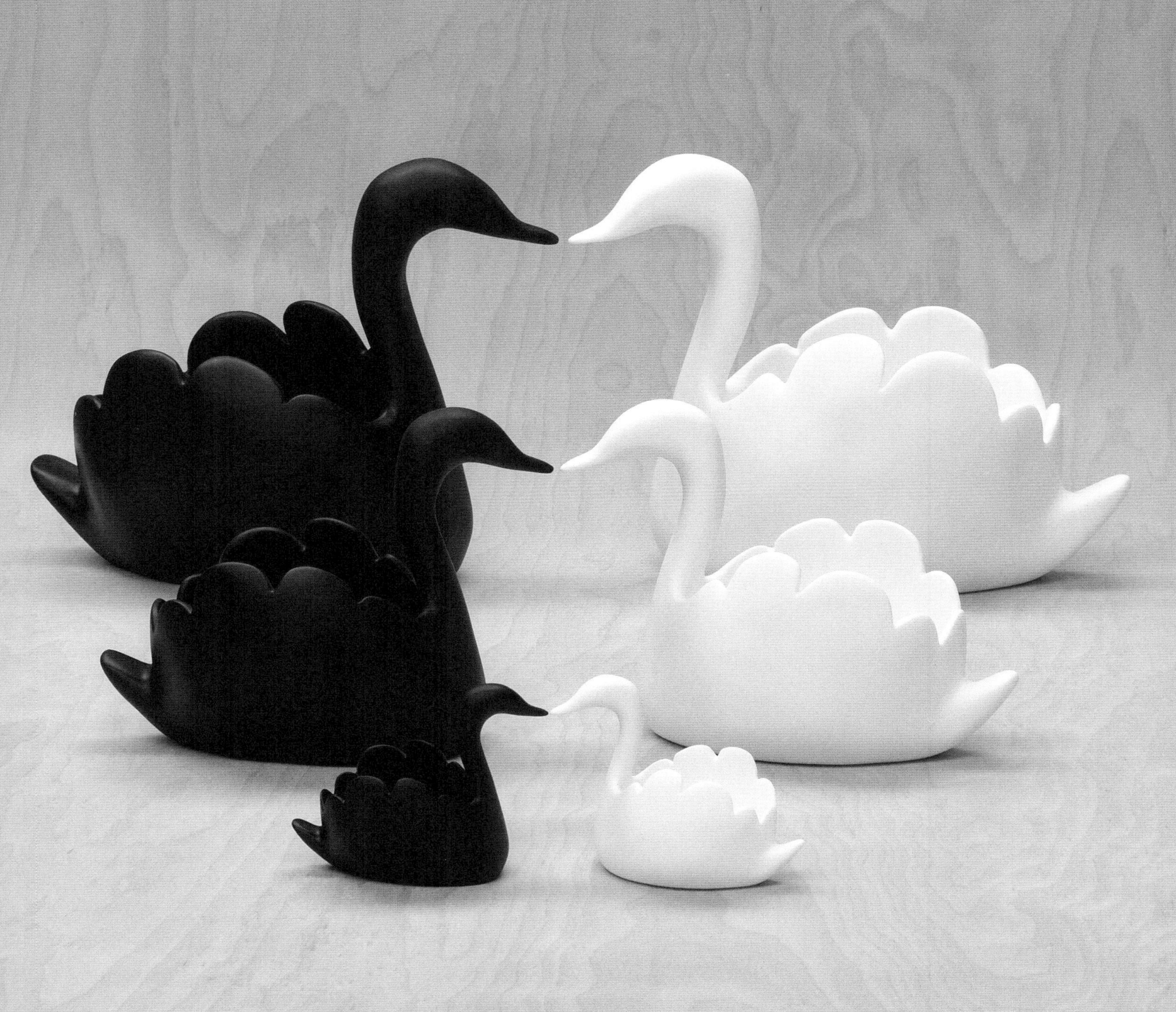

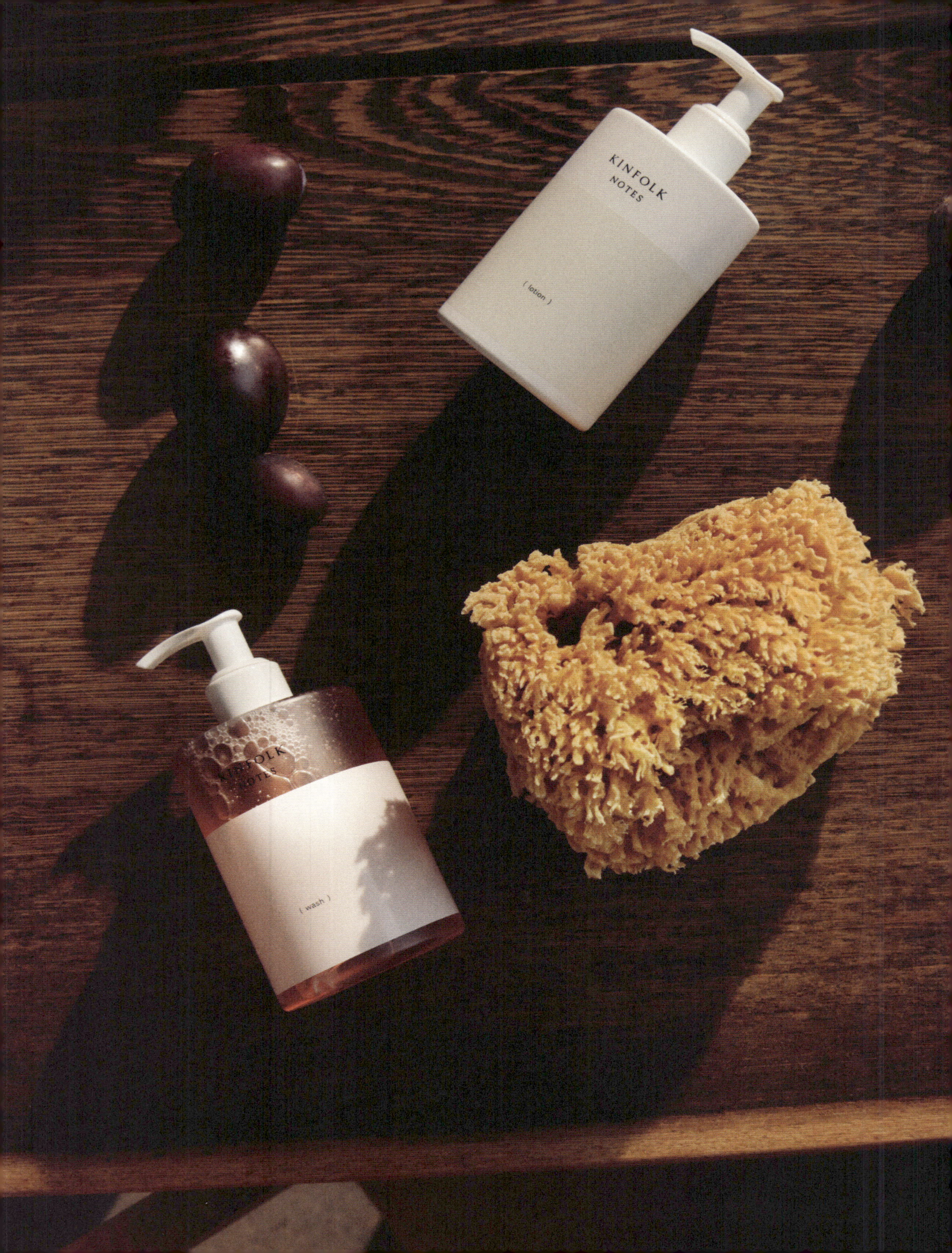
KINFOLK
NOTES
(lotion)
KINFOLK
NOTES
(wash)

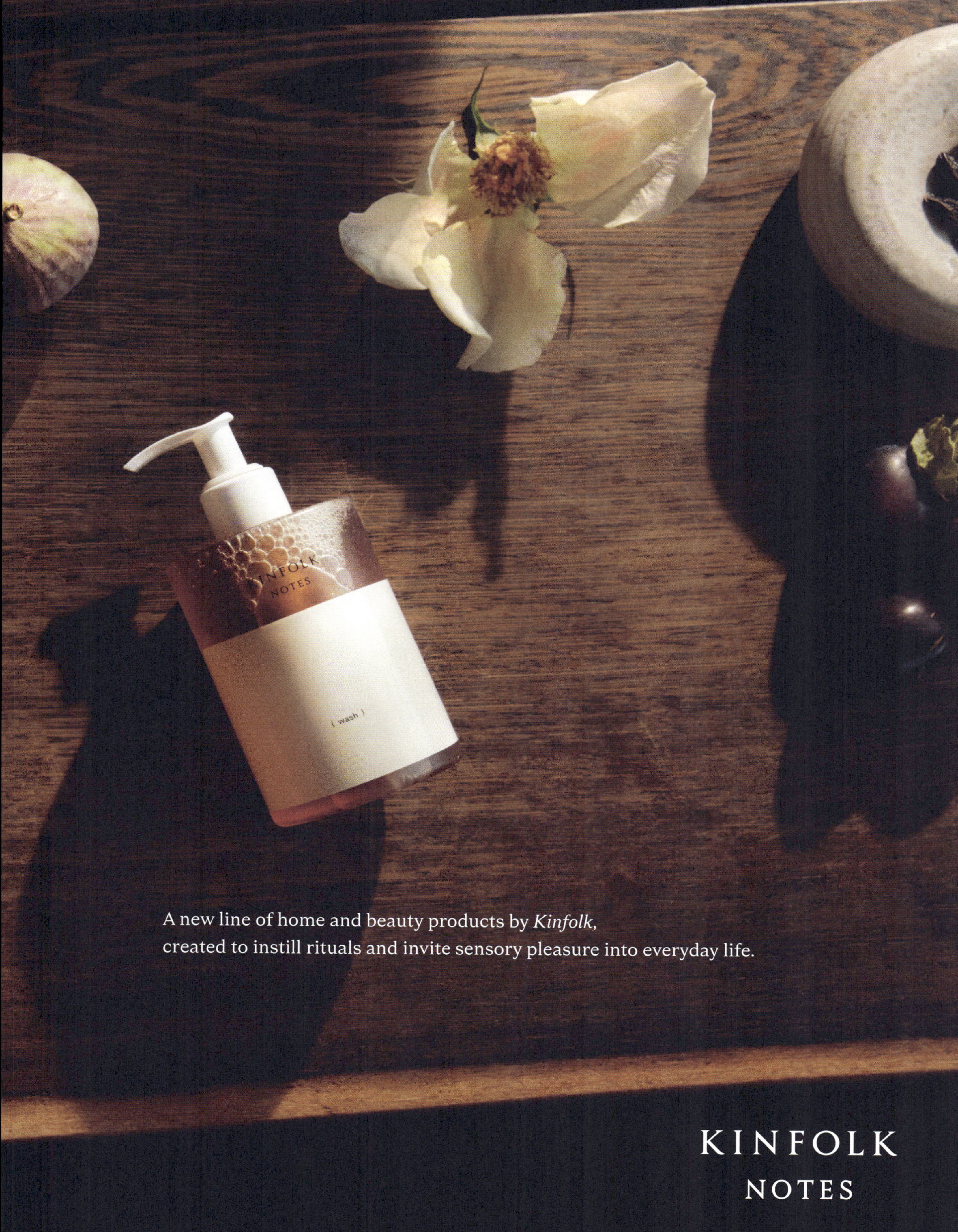
KINFOLK
NOTES
(wash)
A new line of home and beauty products by Kinfolk,
created to instill rituals and invite sensory pleasure into everyday life.
KINFOLK
NOTES

KINFOLK

TEAM

—

EDITOR IN CHIEF — John Burns
DEPUTY EDITOR — George Upton
ART DIRECTOR — Isabel Lea
DESIGN DIRECTOR — Alex Hunting
COPY EDITOR — Rachel Holzman
PUBLISHING DIRECTOR — Edward Mannering
DIGITAL MANAGER — Cecilie Jegsen
ENGAGEMENT EDITOR — Rachel Ellison

—

CROSSWORD — Mark Halpin
PUBLICATION DESIGN — Alex Hunting Studio
COVER PHOTOGRAPH — Guillaume Garat

WORDS

—

Fedora Abu
Precious Adesina
Allyssia Alleyne
Alex Anderson
Lavender Au
Julia Webster Ayuso
Melissa Baksh
Ed Cumming
Benjamin Dane
Cyrus Dunham
Elle Hunt
Robert Ito
Tara Joshi
Francis Martin
Ali Morris
Emily Nathan
Celine Nguyen
Rebecca Thandi Norman
Hettie O'Brien
George Papam
Benjamin Alva Polley
Nicole Rucker
Laura Rysman
Natasha Stallard
Sophie Wyburd

STYLING, SET DESIGN, HAIR & MAKEUP

—

Maureen Barbier
Joséphine Daru
Britta Dicke
Annie Hertikova
Damien Lacoussade
Miguel Lauper
Aartthie Mahakuperan
Romane Martini
Camille Pouyat
Hanna Ruecker
Stephanie Stamatis
Sandy Suffield
Tamara Tott
Ellen Walge
Sarah Whiteside
Chris Yuille

ARTWORK & PHOTOGRAPHY

Zaineb Abelque
Pie Aertes
Mauricio Alejo
Richard Andre
Jason Andrew
Aleksandr Babarikin
Aaron Bernstein
Oscar Calleja
Tobias Delcroix
Alicia Dubuis
Matias Galeano
Guillaume Garat
Nathan Wolf Grace
Maartje ter Horst
Cecilie Jegsen
Nils Jorgensen
Sarah Hartvigsen Juncker
Annika Kafcaloudis
Alixe Lay
Alex Li
Thea Løvstad
Meola Interiors
Sam Nicklin
Claire Rousay
Julien Sage
Felix Speller
Katherine Squier
Bill Stamatopoulos
The Voorhes
Aaron Tilley
Jan Erik Waider
Joe Whitmore

PUBLISHER

—

Chul-Joon Park

The views expressed in *Kinfolk* magazine are those of the respective contributors and are not necessarily shared by the company or its staff. *Kinfolk* (ISSN 2596-6154) is published quarterly by Ouur ApS, Amagertorv 14B, 2, 1160 Copenhagen, Denmark. Printed by Park Communications Ltd in London, United Kingdom. Color reproduction by Park Communications Ltd in London, United Kingdom. All rights reserved. No part of this publication may be reproduced, distributed or transmitted in any form or by any means, including photocopying or other electronic or mechanical methods, without prior written permission of the editor in chief, except in the case of brief quotations embodied in critical reviews and certain other noncommercial uses permitted by copyright law. The US annual subscription price is $80 USD. Airfreight and mailing in the USA by WN Shipping USA, 156-15, 146th Avenue, 2nd Floor, Jamaica, NY 11434, USA. Application to mail at periodicals postage prices is pending at Jamaica NY 11431. US Postmaster: Send address changes to *Kinfolk*, WN Shipping USA, 156-15, 146th Avenue, 2nd Floor, Jamaica, NY 11434, USA. Subscription records are maintained at Ouur ApS, Amagertorv 14B, 2, 1160 Copenhagen, Denmark. SUBSCRIBE: *Kinfolk* is published four times a year. To subscribe, visit kinfolk.com/subscribe or email us at info@kinfolk.com. CONTACT US: If you have questions or comments, please write to us at info@kinfolk.com. For advertising and partnership inquiries, get in touch at advertising@kinfolk.com.

RICHARD MILLE

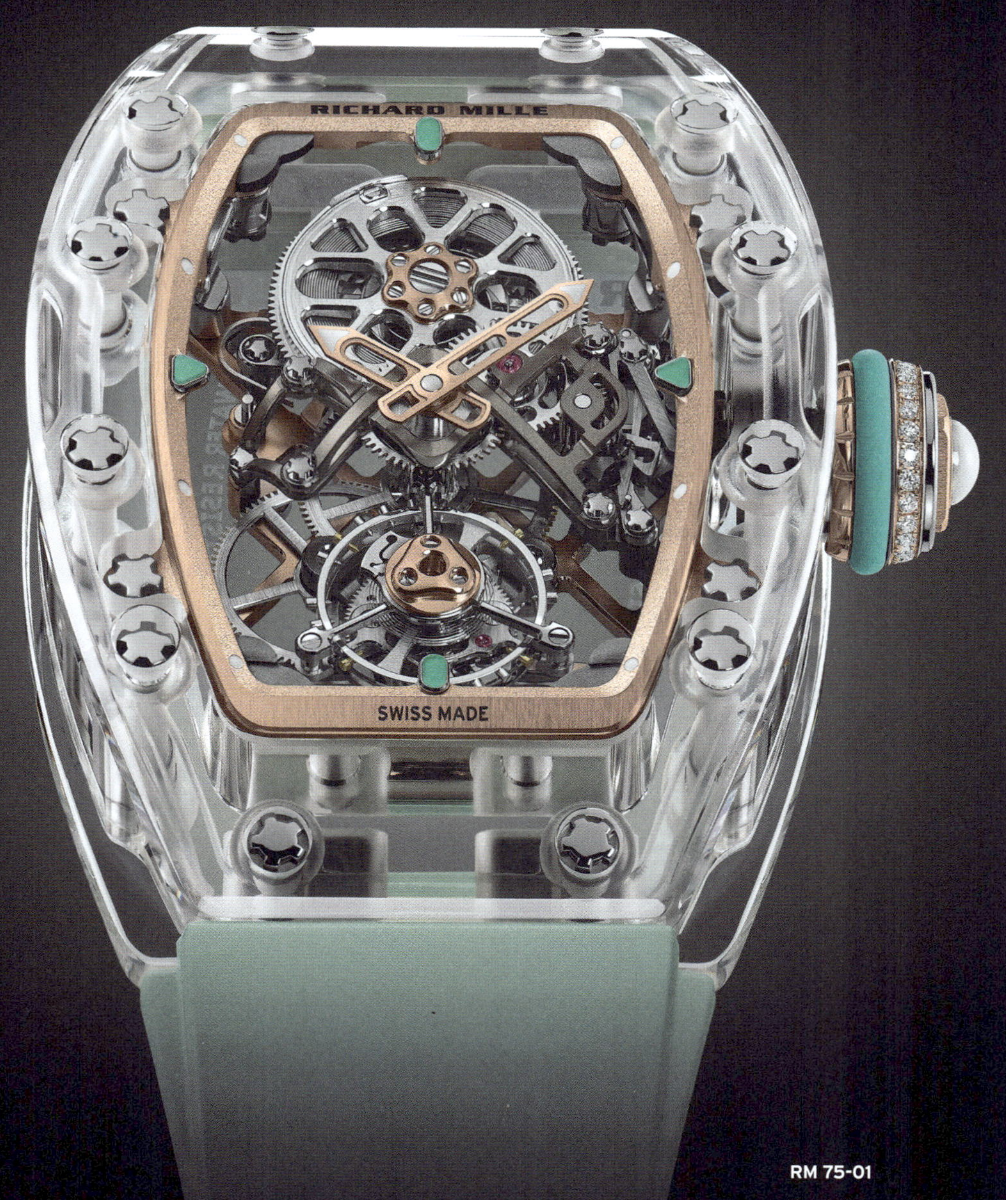

RM 75-01

Skeletonised manual winding tourbillon calibre
65-hour power reserve (± 10%)
Baseplate and bridges in titanium,
5N gold and grey PVD treated
Flying tourbillon with variable-inertia balance
Fast-rotating flying barrel
Case in clear sapphire
Limited edition of 15 pieces

A Racing Machine
On The Wrist

WELCOME
The Money Issue

Budgeting. Investing. Pensions. Debt management. Property ownership. There's a reason money is hard to talk about, not least because it's a dreary topic for a dinner party. Despite being one of the few universal human experiences, discussing money can make people feel awkward, anxious or uncomfortable, regardless of how much they have.

Issue Fifty-Eight examines our relationship with money—not as currency or an endgame, but how it exists emotionally in our lives, shaping how we live and who we become. To break the taboo, we talk to writer Otegha Uwagba, who thought deeply about the subject while writing her memoir, *We Need to Talk About Money*. As she recounts her journey toward financial independence, she points to the widening divide—insurmountable to some and yet, in this tough economy, increasingly critical to your chances in life: the gap between those who inherit money and those who do not. "Your progressive friends are probably too embarrassed to tell you that parental help, not sensible saving, is what landed them their new apartment," she tells Allyssia Alleyne on page 104.

On the other side of the coin, on page 76, writer Hettie O'Brien meets the recipients of extreme intergenerational wealth and discovers that privilege does not necessarily bring peace of mind: "I didn't understand how the world worked," admits Iris Brilliant, who grew up rich and now coaches other wealthy families to give money away. Anyone interested in donating some of their own money might first wish to consult our conversation with Elie Hassenfeld, the CEO of GiveWell, whose empirical approach to philanthropy ensures his platform is one of the few ways of knowing the amount of good your money has actually done. "If it costs one organization $100,000 to save a single life, I'd rather give that to another organization that will use it to save 20 lives," he explains on page 85. Lastly, those feeling a little more frivolous can read our profile of Jo Ellison, whose job, as the editor of *HTSI*, gives her authority on "how to spend it" on page 126 (although you might want to check whether that bag, bracelet or vacation is worth it first; we ask industry insiders to help justify the cost of luxury goods on page 154).

Elsewhere, we offer alternative routes into an abundance mindset: We meet five Scandinavian business leaders reshaping their companies around values beyond profit; our fashion editorial pays homage to the idea that the greatest wealth of all is health; and chef Sophie Wyburd proffers probably the only way to get rich quick—in the kitchen, thanks to her five indulgent recipes for winter.

WORDS
JOHN BURNS

AFTER SERIES

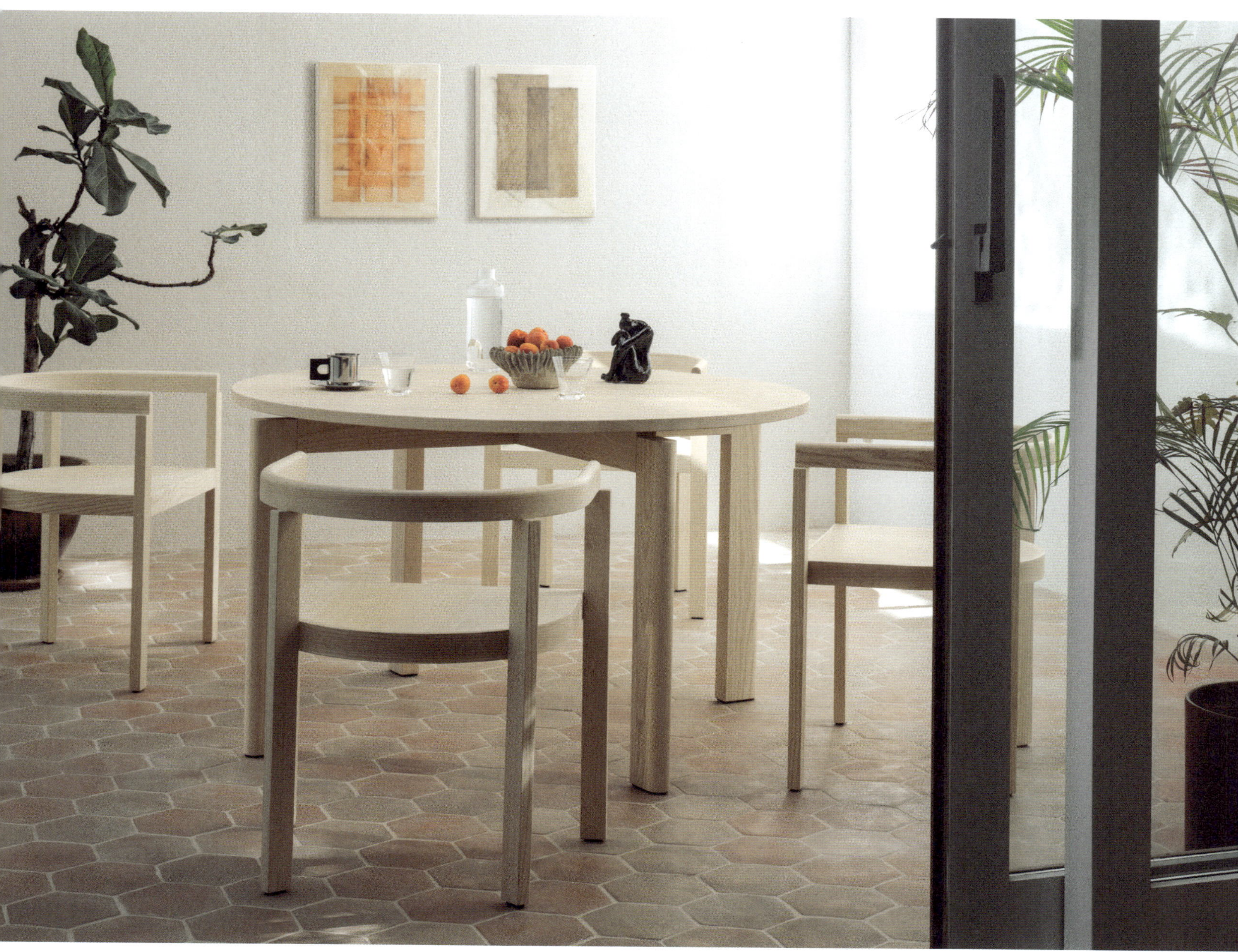

Timeless shapes, reimagined. The After Series by Michael Anastassiades is an invitation to pause, reflect, and experience design with lasting presence.

See more at **fritzhansen.com**

After Series - chair and table
Michael Anastassiades

FRITZ HANSEN

STARTERS
On cash, tipping and moral ambition.

20 — 48

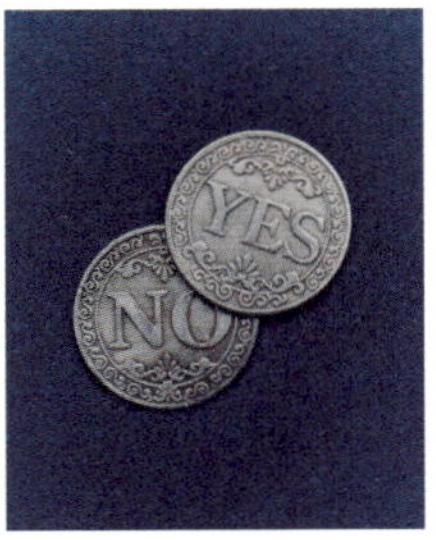

20	Tipping Point	34	The Price of Peace
22	What Are You Working On?	36	Mark William Lewis
24	Emotional Exchange	38	Word: Hypernormalization
26	Zoom Out	40	Spot the Difference
27	Just One Look	41	Earthly Desires
28	Cult Rooms	42	Rutger Bregman
30	Object Matters	46	For What It's Worth
31	Odd Jobs	48	How To: Hibernate
32	Liquid Assets	—	—

FEATURES
In Paris, Greece and California.

50 — 96

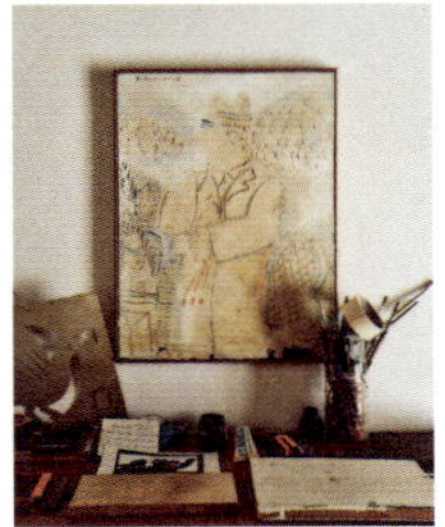

50	At Work With: Lina Gotmeh	76	The Anxieties of the Ultra-Rich
60	New Perspectives	80	Elie Hassenfeld
64	Home Tour: Alekos Fassianos	86	It Shouldn't Cost the Earth

"The greatest wealth is this: to create your world." (Alekos Fassianos – P. 73)

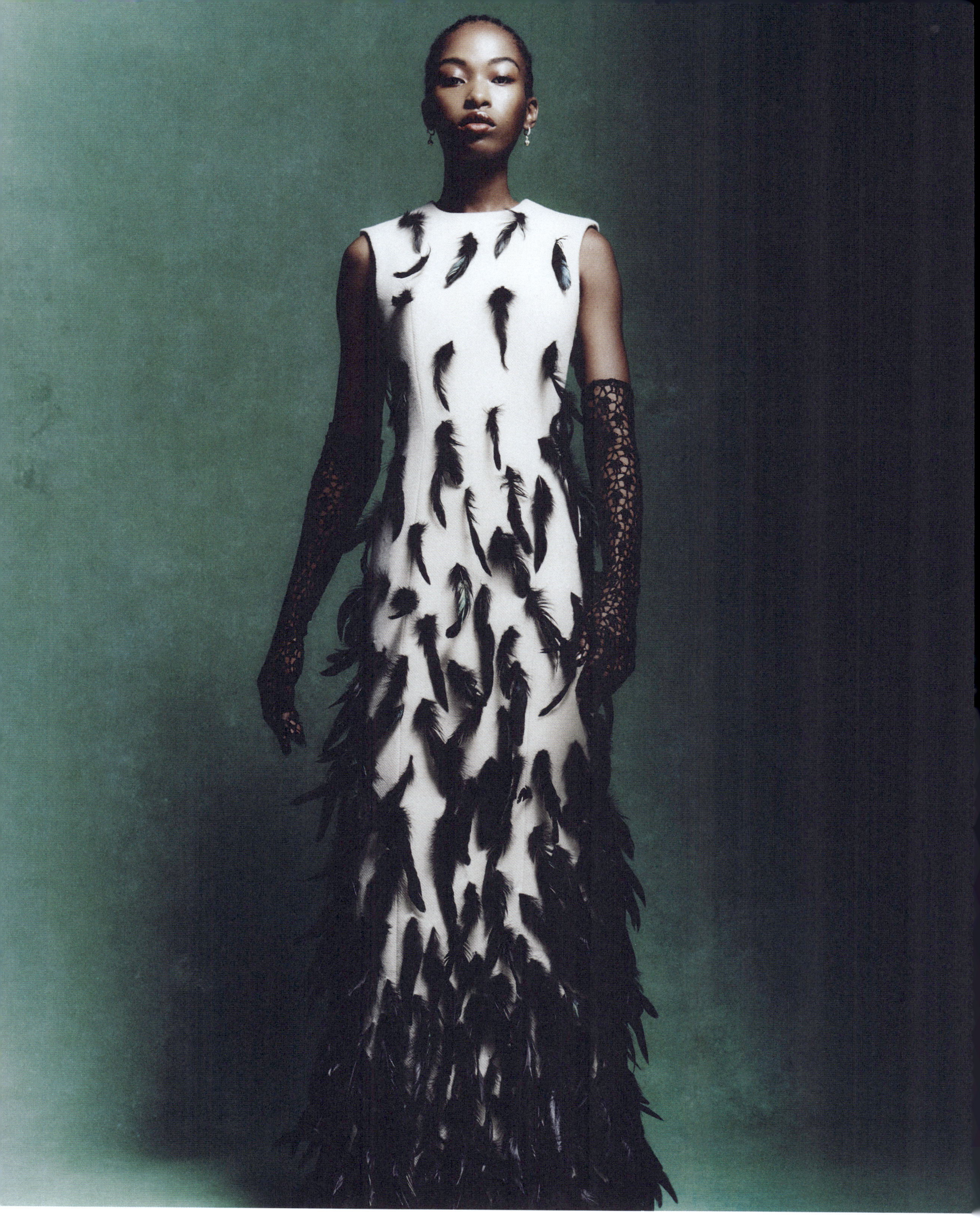

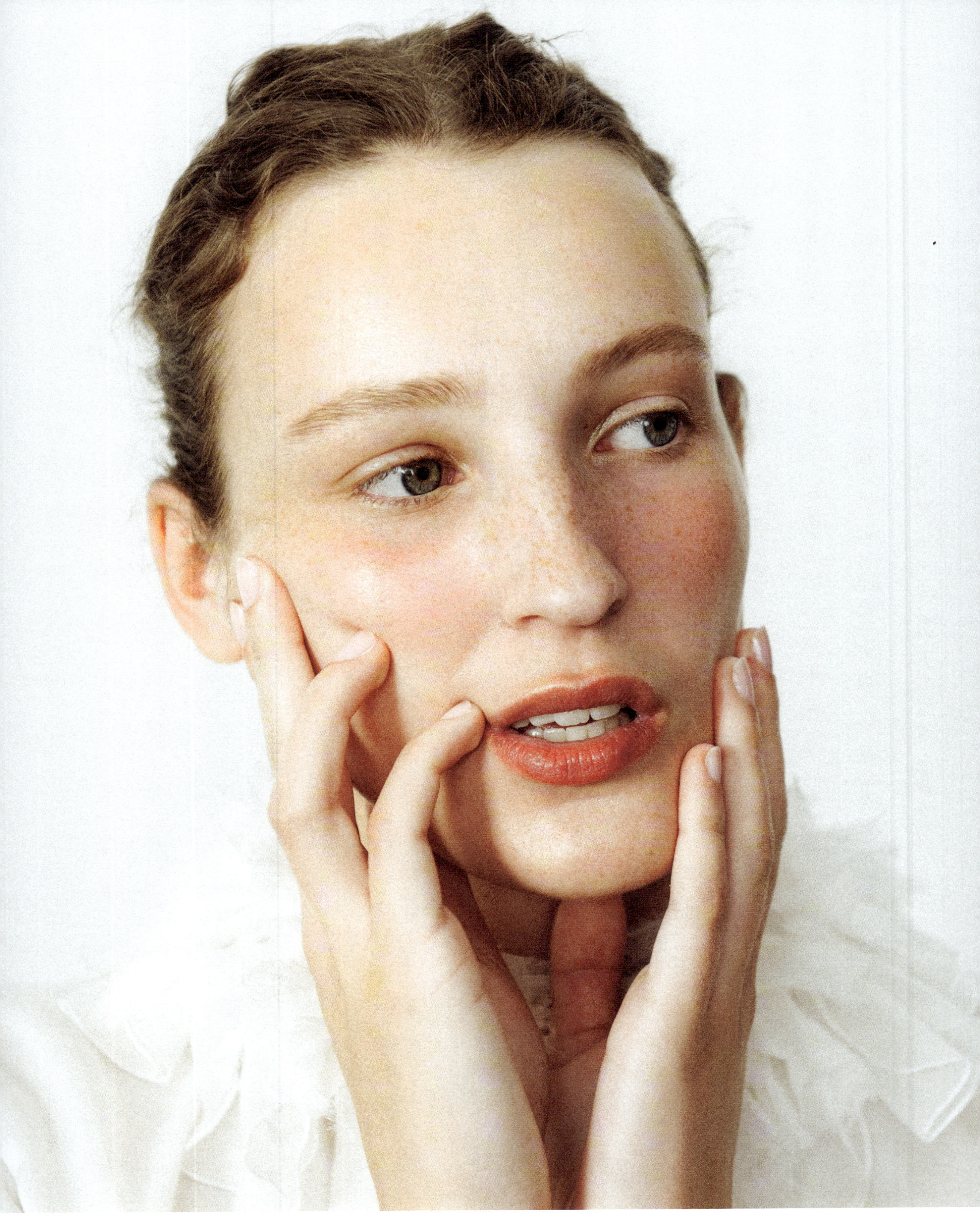

98 — 160

MONEY
What do you value?

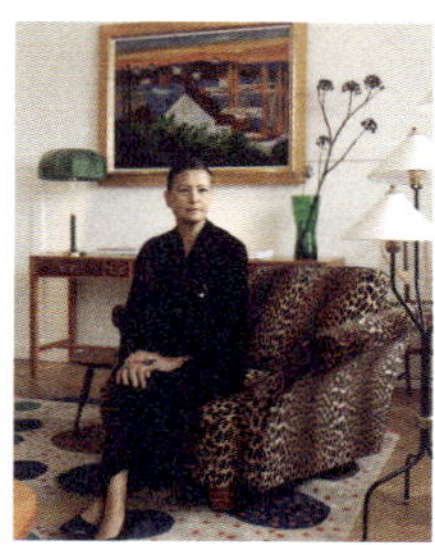

98	Otegha Uwagba	134	Rich
108	Health Is Wealth	146	Expensive Mistakes
116	For Love, Not Money	154	Accountable Aspiration
126	Jo Ellison	—	—

162 — 176

DIRECTORY
Cultural counsel and a crossword.

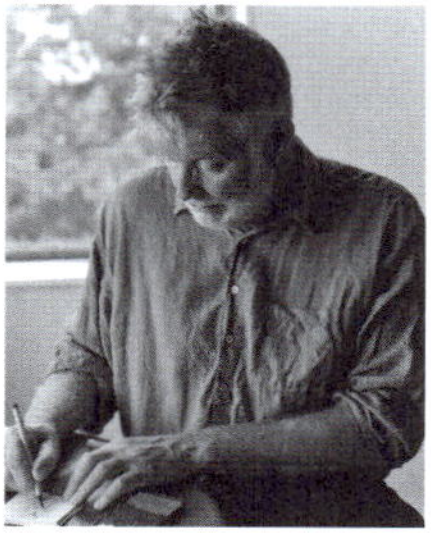

162	Field Notes	171	Top Tip
163	Recipe Card	172	Power Tool
164	On the Shelf	174	Credits
166	Behind the Scenes	175	Stockists
168	Crossword	176	Point of View
169	Received Wisdom	—	—

STARTERS:

20 Tipping Point
22 What Are You Working On?
24 Emotional Exchange
26 Zoom Out
27 Just One Look
28 Cult Rooms
30 Object Matters
31 Odd Jobs

34 The Price of Peace
36 Mark William Lewis
38 Word: Hypernormalization
40 Spot the Difference
41 Earthly Desires
42 Rutger Bregman
46 For What It's Worth
48 How To: Hibernate

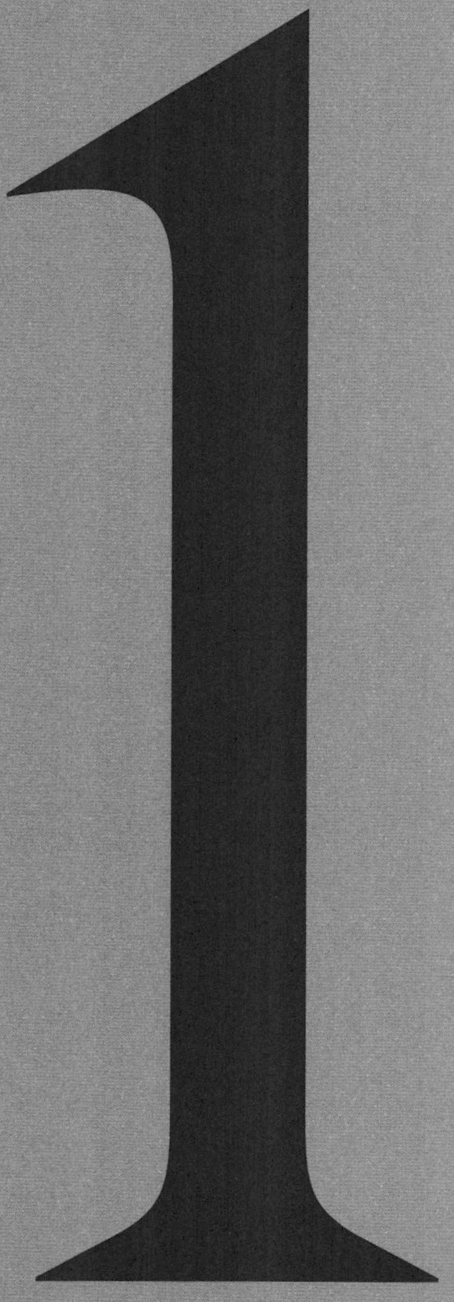

TIPPING POINT
Have gratuities become gratuitous?

WORDS
ROBERT ITO
PHOTO
SAM NICKLIN

Growing up in California, one learned to tip decent service—not doing so pegged you as a cheapskate, possibly a snob, and certainly no friend to the working class. I first received cash tips when I was 15, working as a dishwasher at a family-style steakhouse, where I got a tiny cut of the waitstaff's pooled earnings, and later as a busboy and cook. Today, I always tip when I go out for a sit-down meal, and always 20%, unless the service is truly lousy.

A recent trip to Tokyo, however, offered a pleasant jolt to the system. In Japan, as in many countries around the world, people don't tend to tip, nor are they expected to. It's on the employers to pay a decent wage, meaning that tips aren't necessary and, in some eyes, are mildly insulting, as they imply that the tipped worker is either underpaid or somehow inferior to the giver. In fact, the practice of tipping in the US has its roots in slavery: Following the Civil War, bosses would hire formerly enslaved people to work in restaurants or on trains for little to no pay, leaving tippers to make up the difference.

The system isn't really all that different today, with the federal minimum wage for tipped workers at two dollars and change an hour, far below the standard minimum wage for everyone else. No one here can live on that, so under this system, what heartless person wouldn't tip?

Tipping culture in the US went haywire during the pandemic however, with tip jars popping up in coffeehouses, taco trucks, donut shops and takeout-only burger joints. Generally speaking, people were happy to tip, given the risks servers were taking to get us our double latte. But the explosion in point-of-sale touch screens that has followed, placing the tipping process in full view of everyone in line behind you, as well as the employee you are potentially tipping, has made things worse. It doesn't help that the default on many of those machines is 20% of your bill, sometimes more, leaving one to noodle around on an unfamiliar device to leave a more reasonable amount—or to tap the shameful "no tip" option.[1]

All these tip jars and POS screens have generated a sort of tipping fatigue. A 2025 survey found that 41% of Americans believe that tipping culture has "gotten out of control," and nearly everyone has a story about the latest weird place they've seen a tip jar: for me, it was at a hot dog stand at a college baseball game.

The situation has become so onerous that it's time to rethink the whole awful system. Tipping isn't really the problem, of course: It's the exploitative business practices—and the two-tiered minimum wage system—that make so many workers overly reliant on tips in the first place. Perhaps we should start with shifting how we in the US think about restaurant workers. After all, as much of the rest of the world has already understood, these people are members of a skilled profession, and they deserve both our respect and a living wage.

(1) Studies show that digital tipping prompts can lead to a 12% to 20% boost in average gratuities—a win for employees but even more so for the companies that supply the machines, such as Square and Clover, as they charge fees on the entire transaction.

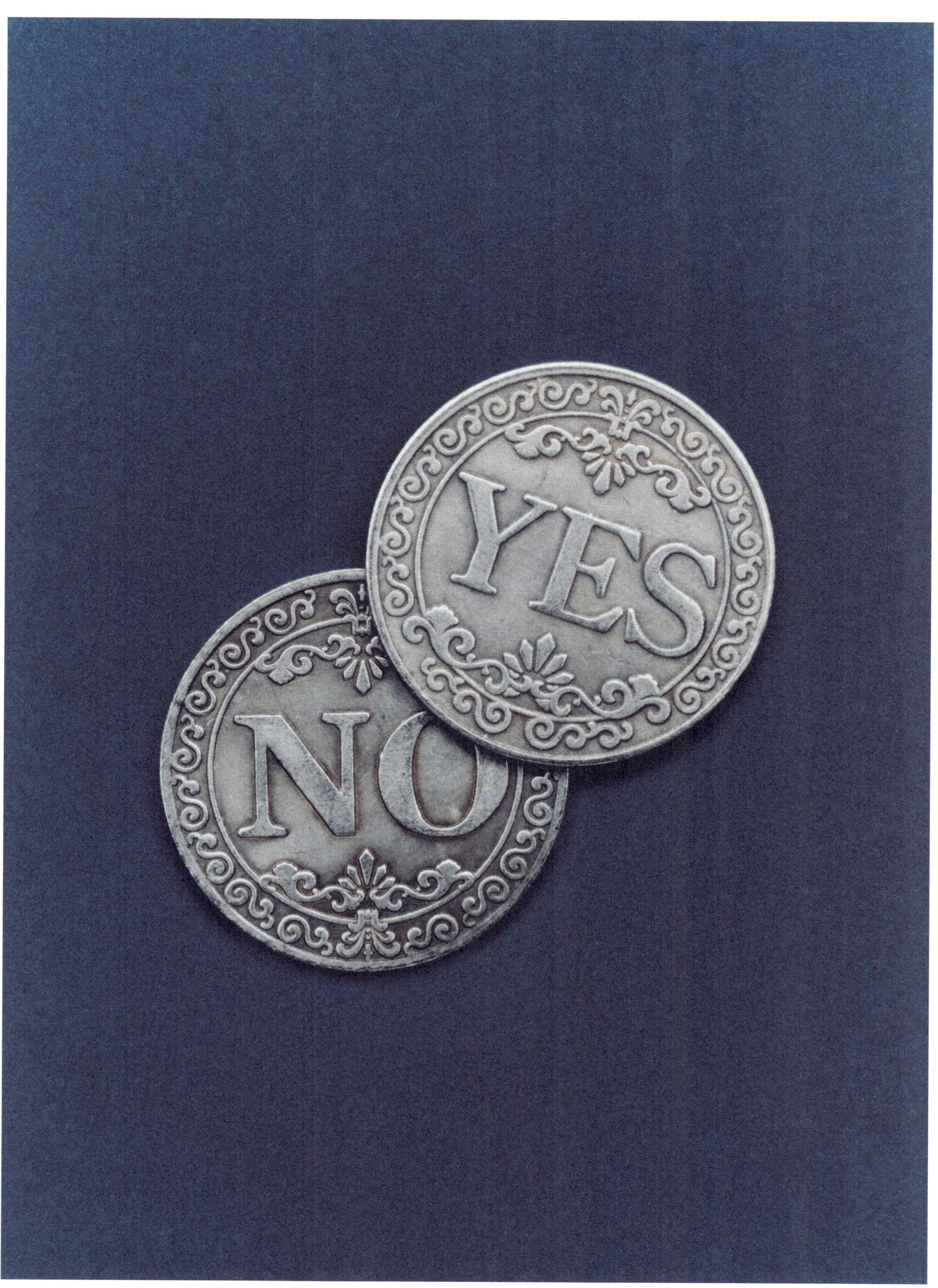
YES
NO

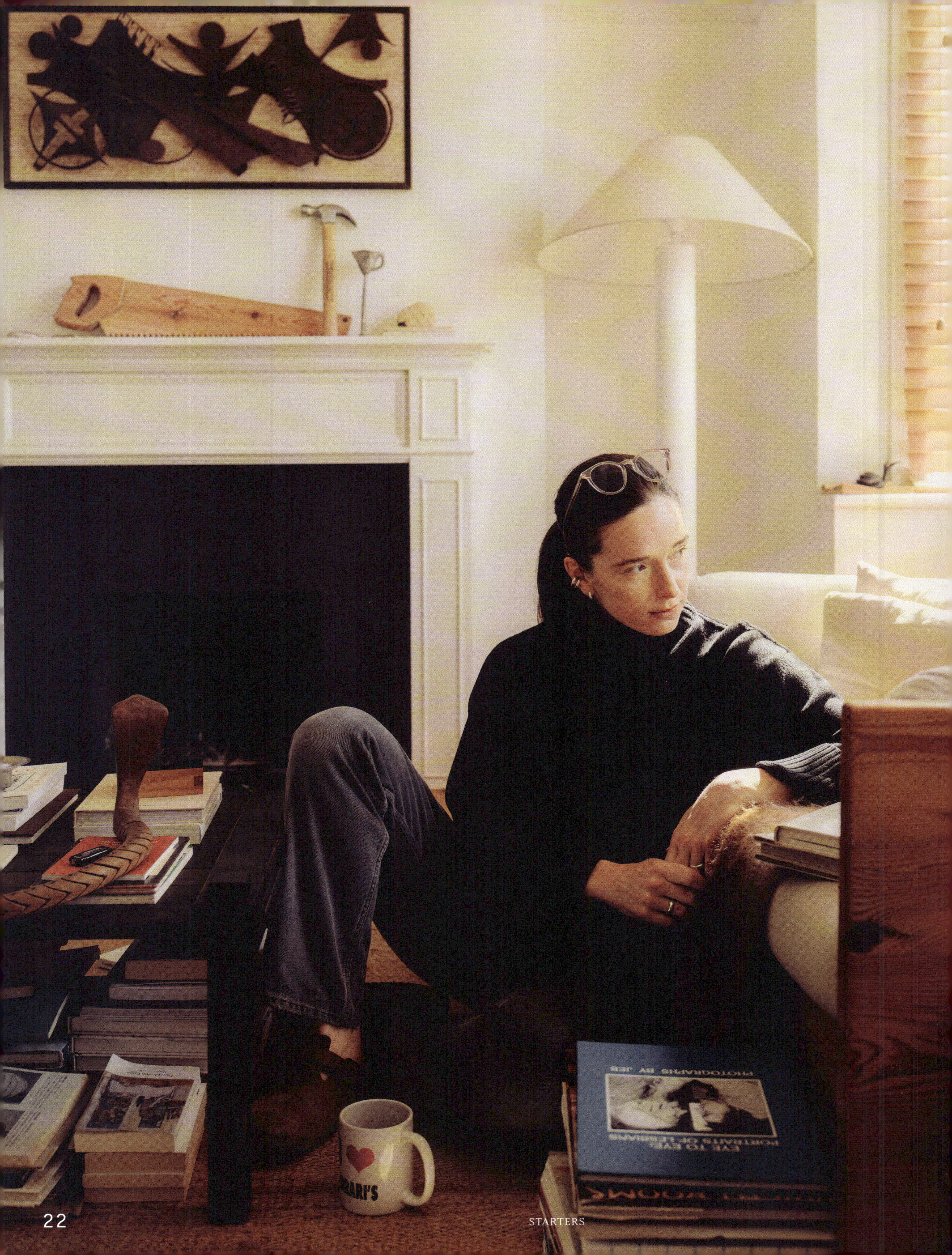

PHOTOGRAPHS BY JEB
EYE TO EYE
PORTRAITS OF LESBIANS

WHAT ARE YOU WORKING ON?

WORDS
ALI MORRIS
PHOTO
ALIXE LAY

Designer Charlotte Taylor's new direction.

Charlotte Taylor made her name sharing dreamlike, digitally rendered interiors on Instagram as Maison de Sable, amassing more than 230,000 followers in the process. In recent years, however, the designer has swapped renders for reality, expanding her practice into brick-and-mortar architecture, furniture, scenography and interior design. Her latest projects include a family home in Vienna and a series of private residences across Europe and the US, not to mention numerous upcoming furniture collections.

When we speak, she's at home in the leafy London suburb of Bromley—her childhood house, recently renovated and now serving as both sanctuary and studio base. It's a quieter setting than her former life in Hackney, in East London, but for someone who describes herself as "quite an introverted person in general," it's one that suits her.

ALI MORRIS: You started out in digital design. What sparked the shift to physical spaces?

CHARLOTTE TAYLOR: It began around three years ago, though it was always in the background. I originally applied to study architecture but realized I didn't really understand what I liked about it at the time, so I ended up studying fine art instead. The digital work happened almost by accident, while recovering from an injury. I started playing around with physical models in the workshop, which turned into illustration, then 3D renderings—and eventually, real-world commissions started coming in. I do still take on digital projects—mainly on the brand and advertising side. Everything I do feeds into each other, and I still really enjoy that side of the work. The digital is my playground.

AM: How does your approach change when working with, say, clients on their homes?

CT: I just finished a small house in Puglia, which is the first full-scale project I've seen come to life. I designed it about four years ago, in my tiny studio in Hackney. I didn't have formal plans—I just marked measurements on the wall where I imagined myself sitting, or taped outlines on the floor. It was a really intuitive, almost childlike way of designing—physically mapping things out to understand them. At the time, elevations and drawings felt very abstract to me. Now, I'm more comfortable working from plans, but I still rely on that spatial, physical sense.

AM: What's been inspiring you lately—are there particular periods, movements or themes you keep coming back to?

CT: I still draw references from all over—different eras, styles, countries, vernacular architecture. But recently, my research has been more theory-based. I've been reading a lot about spatial theory and sound, especially after working with an acoustician on a listening bar project. I've become really interested in how other senses—sound, tactility, scent—can be integrated into the experience of a space. So rather than focusing on a particular era, I'm more inspired by ideas around how we perceive and inhabit space.

AM: Is there a common thread running through your work?

CT: Definitely playfulness and also, not in a bad way, a lack of seriousness.

AM: Your interiors often feel more lived-in and atmospheric than the pristine images of new projects that we're used to seeing. Is that something you deliberately set out to challenge?

CT: I think so much interior and architectural photography—especially what's shown in magazines and online—completely erases signs of life, which just isn't how we live. With collectible design in particular, it's often put on such a pedestal that it loses any personal or bodily connection. I want to show something different: spaces that feel familiar and comfortable, where people can actually imagine themselves living.

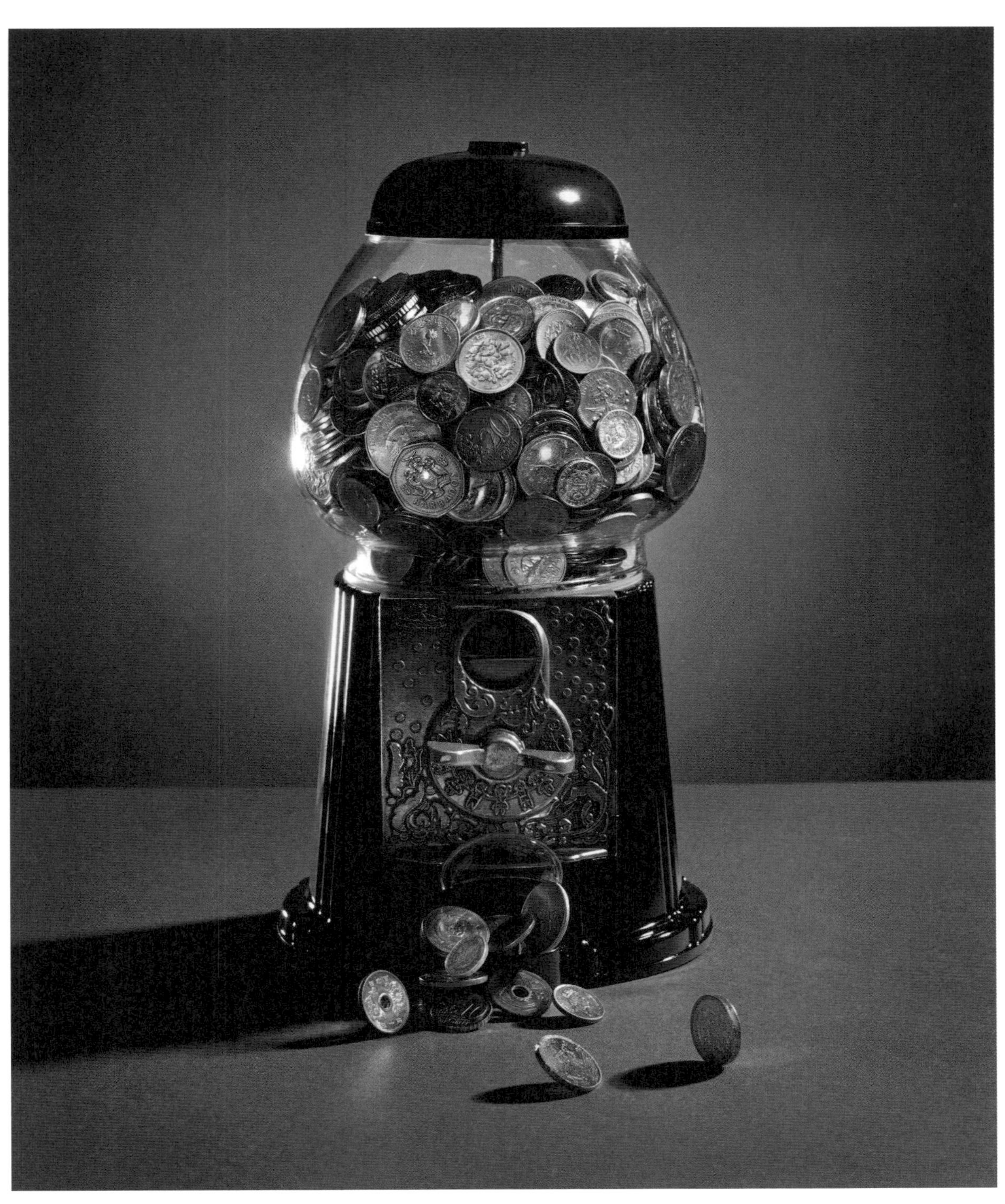

24

EMOTIONAL EXCHANGE
When does money mean something?

WORDS
CYRUS DUNHAM
PHOTO
THE VOORHES

My grandma used to give me a twenty-dollar bill on my birthday. She was a woman who lived her life in shades of beige, proudly claiming it as her favorite color: beige sweater sets, beige leather sofas, beige cars. Her curly apricot pixie cut was the lone accent color in her skin-tone story. Besides the money, she only ever gave me butterscotch candy from her pocketbook (pronounced "pock-a-book"), a deeper shade of neutral.

I pinned the bills to the corkboard above my little desk, waiting for the right thing to spend them on. It was the late '90s and many delightful things could be bought for twenty bucks, even in New York City: lip gloss, a crystal from the new age store, an Old Navy tank top, comic books, glossy magazines from the corner stand, a couple movie tickets.

With my basic needs otherwise provided for, the paper money offered the possibility of indulgence, an opportunity to enact something about my young self through the act of purchasing. In other words, I was supposed to participate in that consummate form of self-creation in a world shaped by and out of money. But nothing seemed to hold as much value as the paper bill itself, which carried with it a very particular meaning: "money from Grandma Dottie." And so each year a new bill was added to the board, forming a grid of Dottie's twenties.

I did not, in adulthood, retain this propensity for saving my bills. Or, rather, the income of a writer and a PhD student did not leave much space for saving. Plus, numbers in a checking account did not have the same significance as gifts from Grandma. This, at least, is the story I tell myself to justify my lack of a 401(k), a mutual fund or even a flush checking account. There have been numerous attempts in my adult life to become a saver, through tracking my spending, making budgets, auditing every expense and trying to cut excess. Yet, whenever I get close to that coveted prudential reserve, the administrative, bureaucratic, car-owning, dog-owning, renting world delivers an unexpected, nonnegotiable cost. I never account for them and yet they always come.

In certain spiritual traditions in the Buddhist world, paper money and coins are given as offerings to ancestors, spirits and insatiable demons that haunt the human world.[1] The offering of money is a way of both honoring and placating the formerly human, nonhuman, and otherwise difficult to perceive beings who linger amongst us. When I have no choice but to spend money (I imagine this is an almost universal experience in our culture, save for those with near infinite sums), I picture a transfer from my hands to the hands of some entity with unfinished business, or unresolved exchanges, in the human world. I prefer this to handing my money over to municipal, federal and medical conglomerates.

I realized in writing this that Grandma Dottie passed away, in her mid-90s, before I'd ever spent those twenties. I was a young adult, and they remained pinned to my childhood corkboard. They stayed there for a few more years, until my parents moved, my childhood bedroom was disassembled, and the twenties were returned to the ocean of money from which they came, to be spent on some temporary good, by someone, and then another someone, and then another someone. Perhaps each transaction is a little offering back to Dottie.

---

(1) The practice often involves burning joss paper, or "spirit money"—a symbolic offering, since burning actual currency is considered both unlucky and, in many countries, illegal.

In September 2020, six months into the pandemic, *The Economist* asked: "Is the office finished?" Working from home had rapidly become the new normal, and with conference calls replacing conference rooms, the future of work seemed to be remote-first, forever.

Five years later, it's clear that although the death of the office has been greatly exaggerated, the technologies we have come to rely on more than ever before—email, Slack and Zoom—are actually making us more aware of the value of in-person communication.

"Humanity is carried on the voice," the behavioral scientist Nicholas Epley has observed. Pure text, he discovered, lacks the subtle cues that "reveal the presence of a thoughtful and intelligent human being." In a 2019 study, he found that merely reading an account of someone's political views—instead of listening to or watching that person speak—made it easier to judge them as "less refined, cultured, rational, logical and sophisticated."

Videoconferencing software is an improvement, but it's not perfect. In a study published in 2020, Melanie S. Brucks and Jonathan Levav—professors at Columbia and Stanford's business schools, respectively—found that people who brainstormed together on Zoom came up with fewer, less creative ideas than those who brainstormed in person. To appear engaged and present, we typically focus on our screens during videoconferencing calls, and this narrow visual focus leads to a narrow cognitive focus, suppressing creativity. "Virtual interaction," Brucks and Levav concluded, "uniquely hinders idea generation."

Being physically present matters. In *The Last Human Job*, the sociologist Allison Pugh writes that the best conversations can offer "emotional resonance" and "deep connectedness" with others. For teachers, therapists and doctors, this resonance is an obvious part of the job. But Pugh's research led her to conclude that this "connective labor" is "the secret ingredient of economic activity of all kinds, from journalism to management."

Working well together involves more than just showing up to meetings and completing deliverables on time. A brief, unplanned chat in the office kitchenette might help a young intern acclimate to their industry. A free-ranging conversation over lunch can make it easier to collaborate on a high-stakes, high-stress project. A candid discussion after work might be how someone learns that they're underpaid compared to their peers. The office can be a place of camaraderie and creativity, and that happens best when you're in a room with other people—not separated by a screen.

ZOOM OUT
Why we should work in person.

WORDS
CELINE NGUYEN
PHOTO
MAURICIO ALEJO

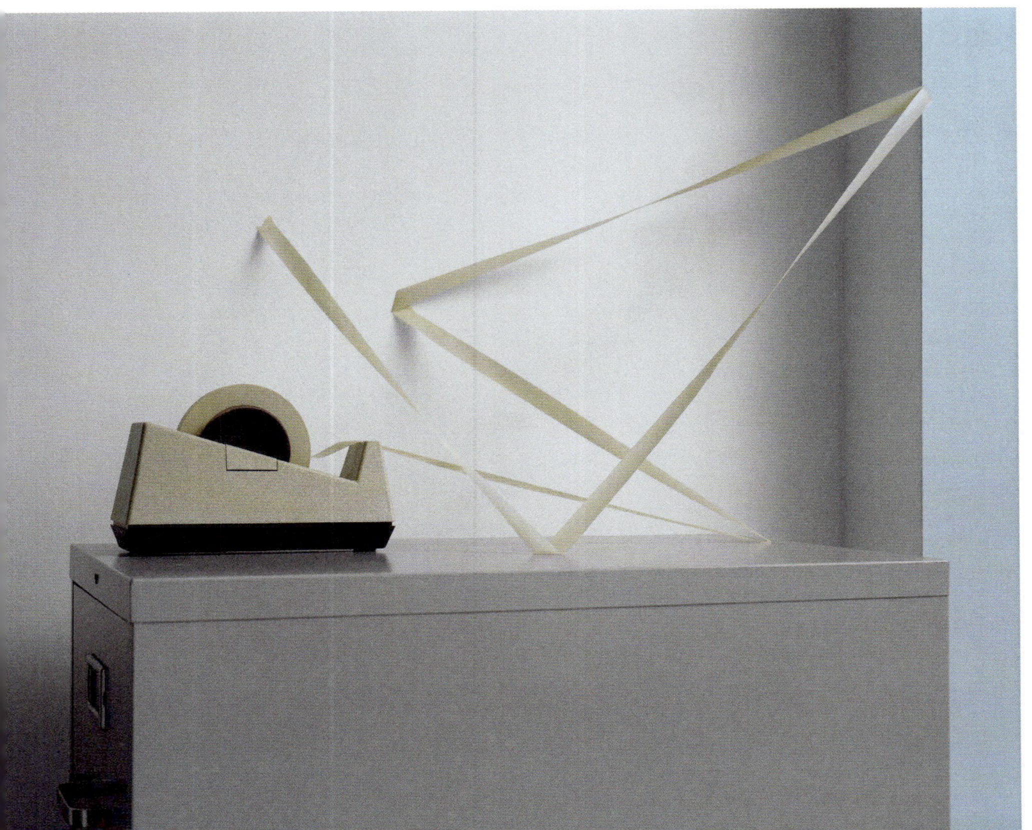

It's funny that both the coolest, best-dressed people in history and some of the least fashion-conscious share a penchant for wearing the same thing over and over again. Consider fashion designer Dapper Dan's three-piece suits and the cult New York writer Fran Lebowitz's Anderson & Sheppard blazers and boots, against the identical nondescript T-shirts worn 24/7 by mega-rich tech types.

What separates them, of course, is intention and flair. For the Silicon Valley billionaire crowd, repeating the same outfit ad nauseam is a productivity hack, albeit one that manages to suck all the pleasure out of getting dressed (and having money, for that matter). On the other hand, for those who understand the power of clothes, a signature look can be a means of affirming one's identity, melding into and enhancing their personality—the late *Vogue* journalist André Leon Talley's appropriately regal capes being just one example of many.

To some, the prospect of a go-to look might seem dull, much like it would be to eat the same thing every day. But while a head-to-toe rinse-and-repeat look is tricky to execute without becoming a cartoonish parody of oneself—or someone who doesn't know how to dress for the social context—the best signature looks allow a degree of play. This could be a silhouette—in the case of Talley, his voluminous capes became a canvas for custom creations by the great designers. Accessories, too, offer a way of asserting one's style without stifling expression in other areas. Jackie O.'s oversized sunglasses not only acted as a shield from the paparazzi but also heightened her mystique, and she wore them with everything from shift dresses to sandals. Prolific hat wearers such as David Hockney and André 3000 also come to mind.

In an era in which we're flooded with choice, and each passing week brings with it a new "aesthetic" or "core," there's something quietly rebellious about embracing a signature look—communicating, as it does, an increasingly rare self-awareness and conviction in one's taste. And if you've learned what works for you and makes you feel most confident, then congratulations: You've stumbled upon the secret of dressing well.

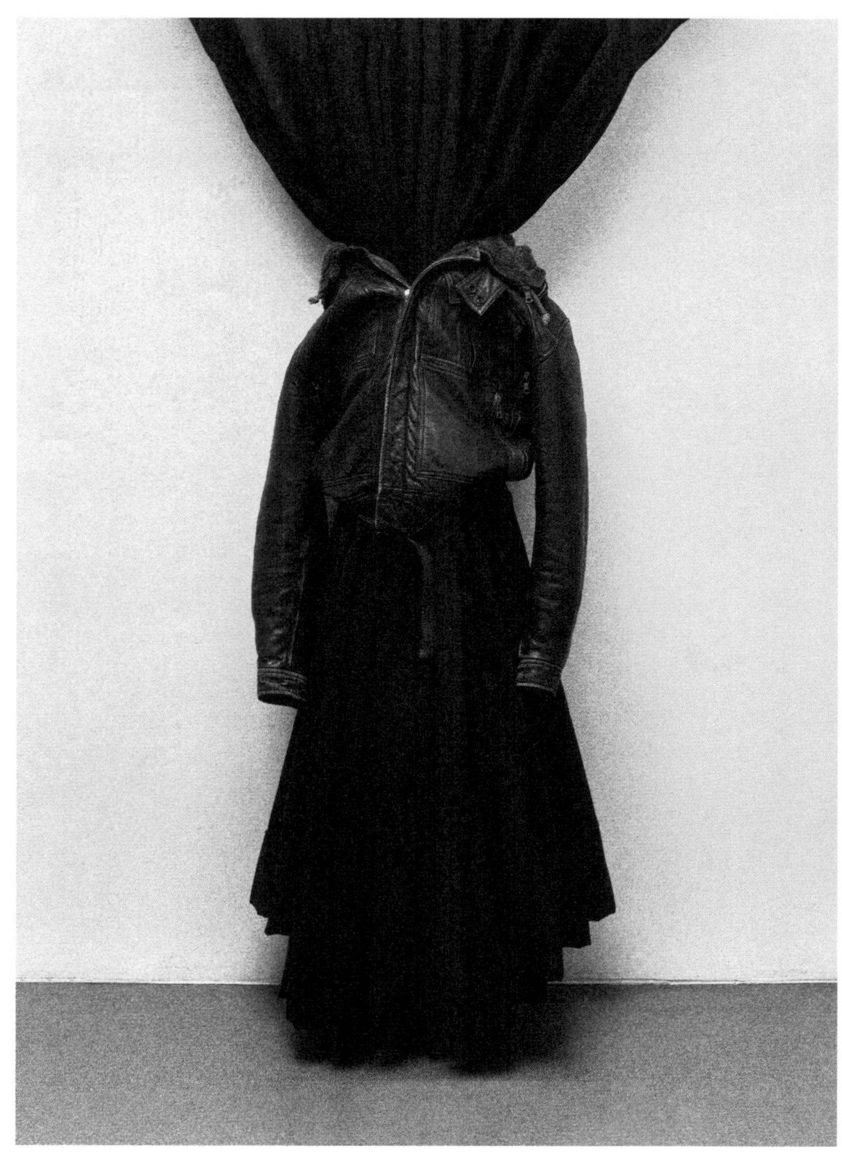

WORDS
FEDORA ABU
PHOTO
RICHARD ANDRE

JUST ONE LOOK
The fantasy of less fashion.

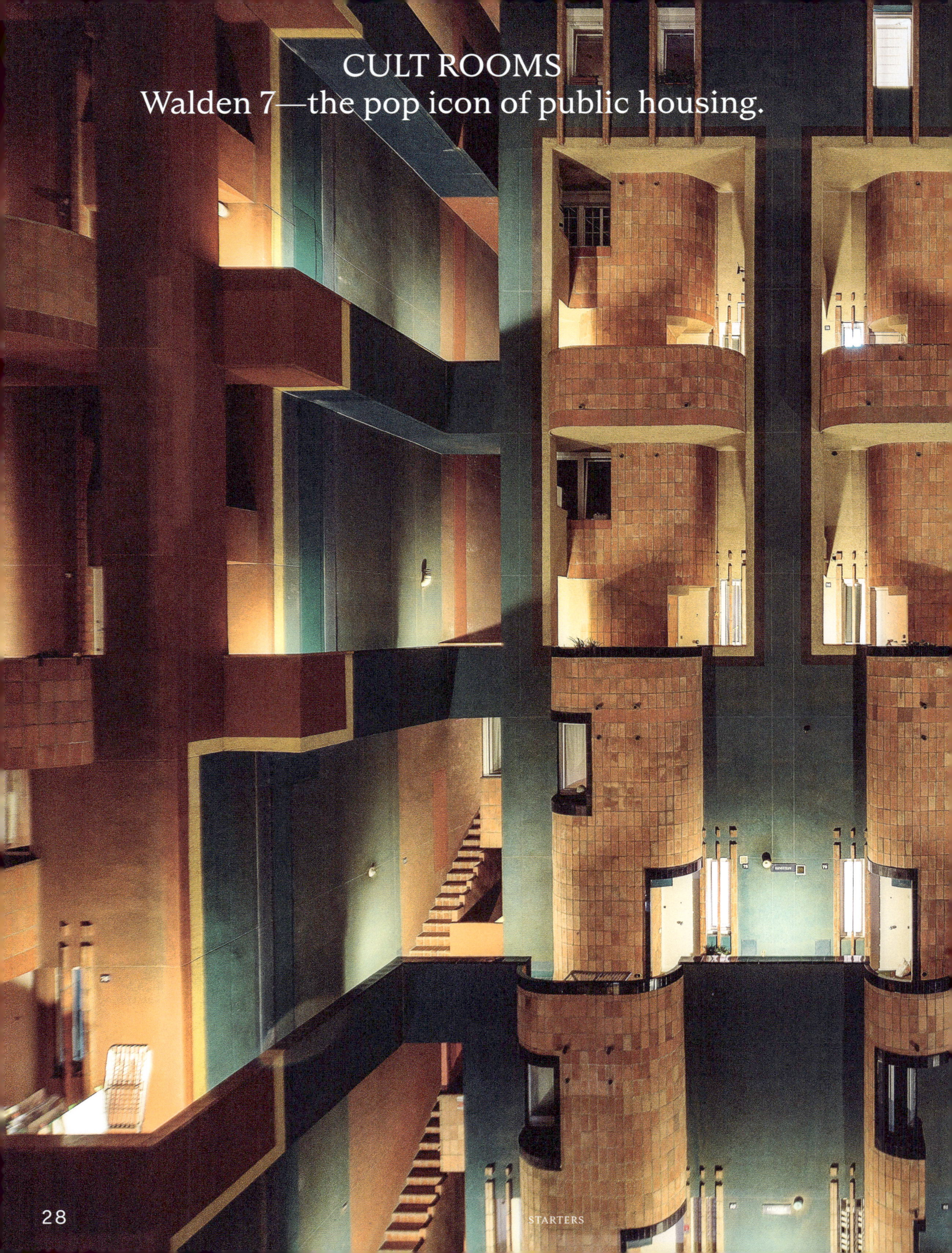

CULT ROOMS
Walden 7—the pop icon of public housing.

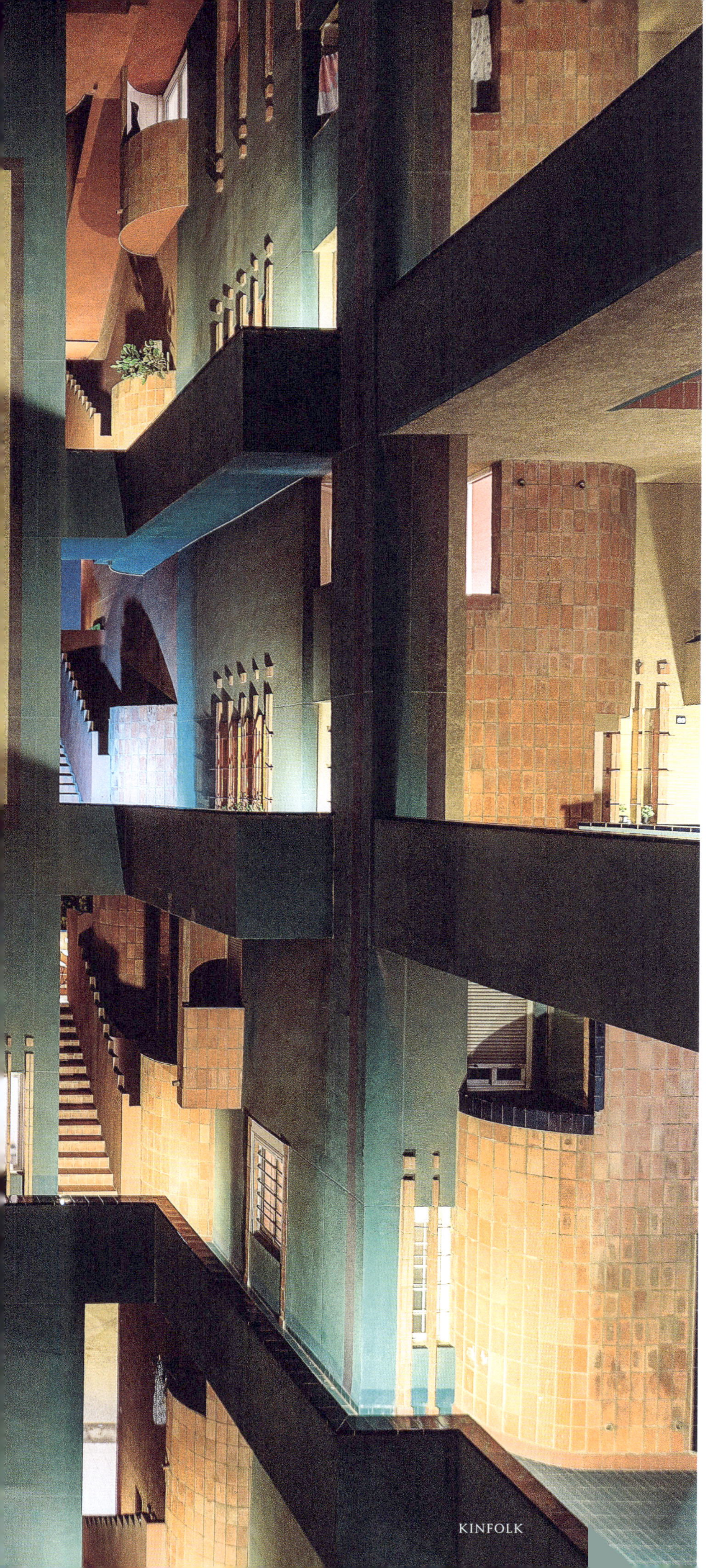

Ricardo Bofill's Walden 7 rises Tetris-like from the gray urban sprawl of Sant Just Desvern, on the outskirts of Barcelona. Built in 1975, and named for Henry David Thoreau's treatise on intentional living, the idiosyncratic housing complex of 446 subsidized apartments was an attempt to prove that imaginative architecture could exist outside of luxury commissions. Its labyrinthine structure is formed of 18 interlinked buildings, each 14 stories high. Five courtyards painted in ultramarine and celadon, connected by bridges, staircases, balconies and walkways, thread through the development, creating a journey that alternates between intimate, plant-dotted corners and vertiginous open spaces.

Bofill's firm, Bofill Taller de Arquitectura, envisioned Walden as a "city within a city," providing residents with everything they might need, including amenities like bars and shops on the ground floor and two rooftop pools. The interiors, designed around modular units of 320 square feet, could be reconfigured to suit residents' needs and were equally radical, with freestanding bathtubs set boldly in the center of the unit (a feature most residents removed after moving in).

Walden 7 has a slightly tarnished legacy owing to technical flaws. The original ceramic tiles on the facade began detaching due to faulty adhesive, prompting an expensive recladding, and the building's complexity has made maintenance challenging. But over time, perceptions have shifted: The dramatic forms and generous communal spaces came to outweigh its faults, and the building gained cult status among a new generation of architecture and design enthusiasts. Rent is no longer subsidized, but the relatively affordable prices have attracted a mix of artists, designers and young professionals, drawn to both the architecture and the strong sense of community it has successfully cultivated.

Walden 7 endures as a striking experiment: proof that ambitious, characterful housing can be realized on a modest budget, but also a cautionary tale of how visionary design can falter in practice. Its improbability has only added to its allure, cementing its status as both the fulfillment of a utopian dream, and a testament to why so many utopias remain on paper.

WORDS
ALI MORRIS
PHOTO
MATIAS GALEANO

In recent years, designers have been embracing imperfection. Where once, pale, uniform timbers epitomized good taste; now, it's woods marked by an idiosyncratic swirl of colors, knots and grain. Burl wood sits at the forefront of this shift. Technically a deformity—an irregular growth on a tree caused by stress, injury or fungus—it produces rich, almost psychedelic patterns when cut and polished.

Designers have long recognized burl wood's allure: It was prized in 17th- and 18th-century Europe for ornate cabinets and desks, revived in the art deco era with sleek, lacquered veneers and embraced mid-century for bold, sculptural forms.[1] Noticing its resurgence in the 2010s, family-run Italian brand Meola Interiors shifted from sourcing antiques to working with artisans to produce statement furniture in the material.

"Burl delivers that sense of style, depth and rarity, while also reflecting a heritage of craftsmanship," notes the company's creative leads, Vincenzo Meola and Joel Gibson. Most recently, the brand has begun exploring the use of olive burl—a timber with an extraordinary swirling grain deeply rooted in Italian tradition. "Ecologically, it's a great option. Cutting the burl doesn't kill the tree; in fact, it can help the tree redirect energy back into producing olives."

Other designers, it seems, can't get enough: Rose Uniacke has created side tables in burl, and Studio Ashby and Tatjana von Stein have embraced it in their interiors too—a reflection of a growing appetite for design that is tactile, storied and, by definition, unique.

WORDS
ALI MORRIS
PHOTO
MEOLA INTERIORS

(1) The prominent art deco designer Émile-Jacques Ruhlmann reserved amboyna burl—the rarest and most expensive of burls—for his most prestigious commissions. At the height of his fame, a single bed made from the wood was said to cost more than a large house.

OBJECT MATTERS
On the beauty of burl wood.

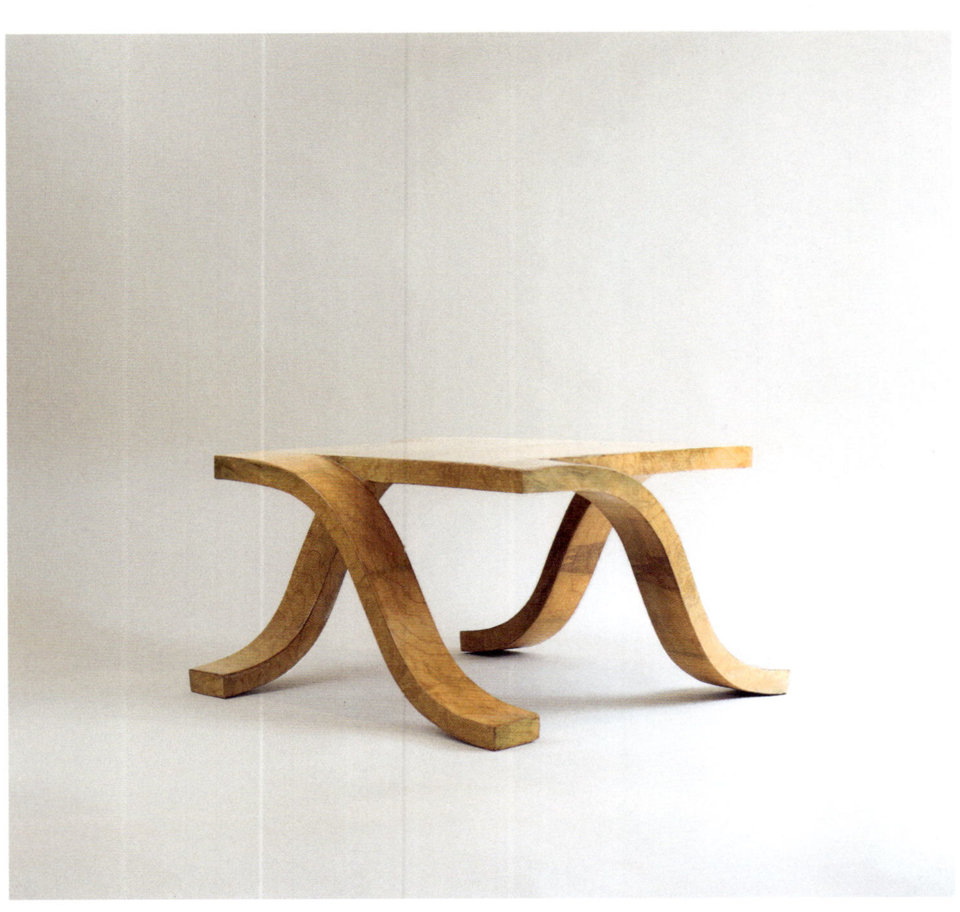

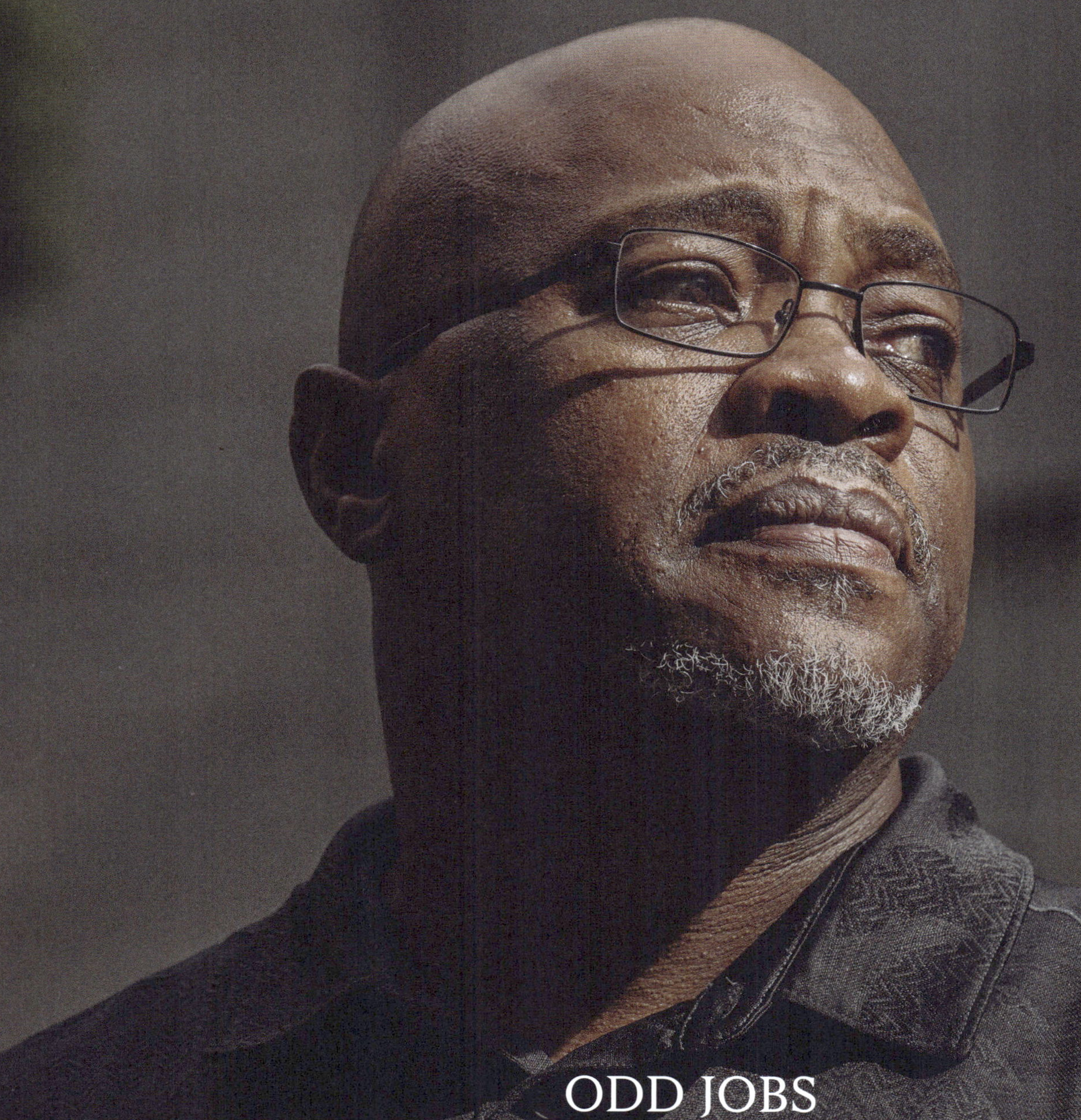

ODD JOBS
Brian Thompson, banknote designer.

You might not know Brian Thompson's name, but you'll know his work. Until recently, Thompson was one of only three journeyman banknote designers in the United States. Having joined the Bureau of Engraving and Printing in 1989, Thompson worked his way up—by way of a seven-year-long apprenticeship—to redesign $50 and $100 bills in 2013. When they were released, he became the first Black person to design an American banknote.

ELLE HUNT: How is a banknote different from other design briefs?

BRIAN THOMPSON: I always say designing currency is the most difficult puzzle you will ever do. There are certain things that a banknote has to have, like security features, but you've got to be careful that the design works and is pleasing to the eye. It's a subtle dance between authentication and aesthetics.

EH: Why do we have beautiful notes at all?

BT: It would be boring if they were just pieces of paper with numbers, for one, but you also want a banknote to be almost like a passport to your country. The US dollar is a world currency. When we were designing, we were constantly being reminded of the symbolism of our banknotes. If something's on there that's hard to explain, it won't fly, and you can't have something depicting war. What if your money goes to Vietnam?

EH: How did you get started?

BT: My father worked at the Bureau of Engraving and Printing, making the cylinders that rotated the printing plates. When I was in my senior year of high school, my dad told me of an "art job" coming up. I took my portfolio in and was shocked to learn that the job was "banknote designer for the United States government." I had no idea banknotes were even designed.

EH: You recently retired after 36 years in the job. How did the profession evolve in that time?

BT: Early on, the time constraints were how long it takes to do a drawing or an illustration. When you look at US notes, you see the portrait, the overall border designs, the corner elements—that all takes time to lay out. Over the years, the timelines got shorter and it became tougher to meet them, but you can't rush that process.

EH: Is banknote design a dying craft?

BT: Today there are only a handful of big companies designing currency. It's pretty sad, because you're going to end up with a world where banknotes look the same. I've gotten to the point where I can tell which company designed it.

EH: You are the sole designer of the $100 bill that was released in 2013. How does it feel to be behind such an iconic design?

BT: I didn't realize its impact until after I retired. While I was working there, it was just another job, but I designed it as an artwork. It was never just for commerce, something to go in and out of a machine. I achieved the best result by making it look like art.

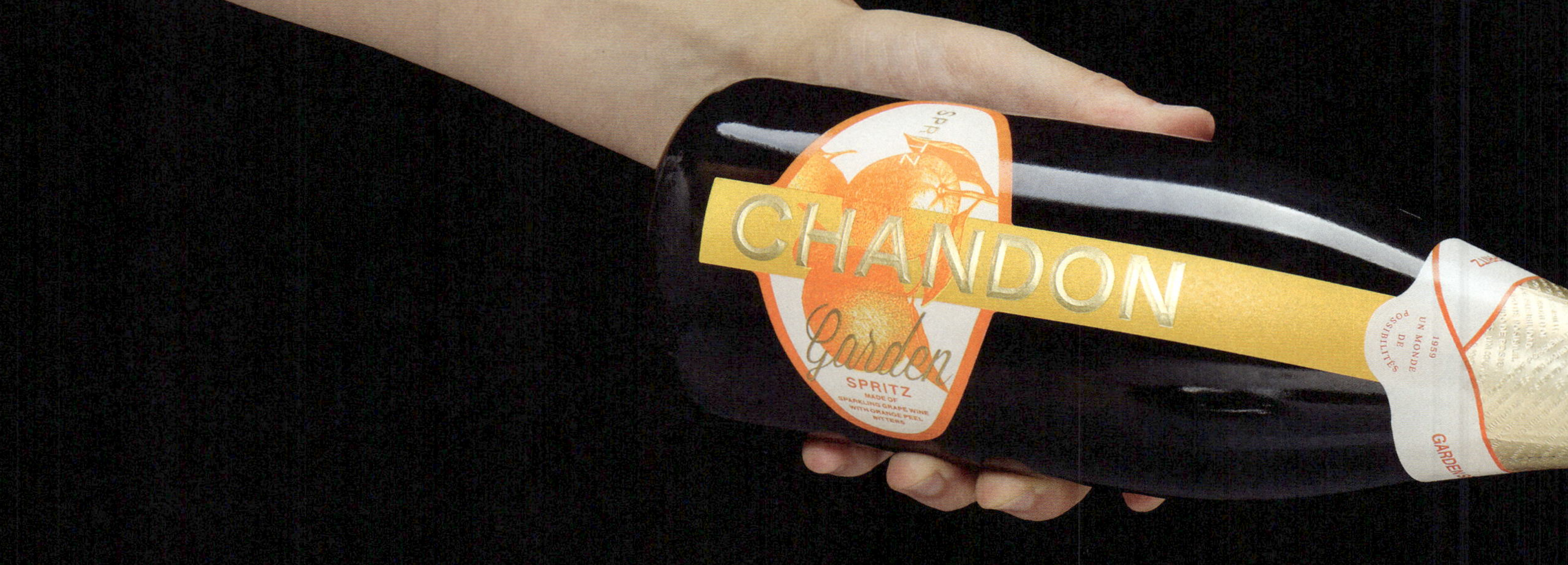

LIQUID ASSETS
An effortless way to brighten winter toasts.

When the days grow shorter and the air turns crisp, the drinks we reach for often follow a familiar profile: spiced, heavy, mulled. They warm the hands and feel cozy, but they can also be a little predictable, and there's a certain appeal to a lighter and brighter counterpoint to the darkness of the season.

Sparkling, citrus-forward and delicately spiced, CHANDON Spritz makes a convincing case for a more vibrant take on the festive tipple. Recasting the spritz as a winter staple, it is celebratory without being sentimental, refreshing without losing its wintry warmth.

The drink's signature garnish, for example—a dried orange slice—anchors it firmly in winter tradition. Prized as a rare luxury, oranges were often gifted during the holidays, slipped into stockings or strung on garlands to scent the home; here they complement CHANDON Spritz's blend of premium sparkling wine and bitters crafted from orange peel.

Serving a winter spritz requires little effort: Pour over ice in a large glass and add a slice of dried or fresh orange, along with a cinnamon stick or a sprig of rosemary for an aromatic lift. The result is visually striking—a glass that glows like an ember in the cold—and versatile enough to suit any occasion, from a holiday aperitif to an intimate toast by the fire.

In a season where indulgence can often feel heavy, keeping a bottle on hand offers balance—at once festive and refreshing, easy yet sophisticated. Whether you're hosting friends, searching for a thoughtful gift or simply raising a glass, CHANDON Spritz reinvigorates time-honored seasonal rituals.

This story was produced in partnership with CHANDON.

WORDS
BENJAMIN DANE
PHOTO
AARON BERNSTEIN

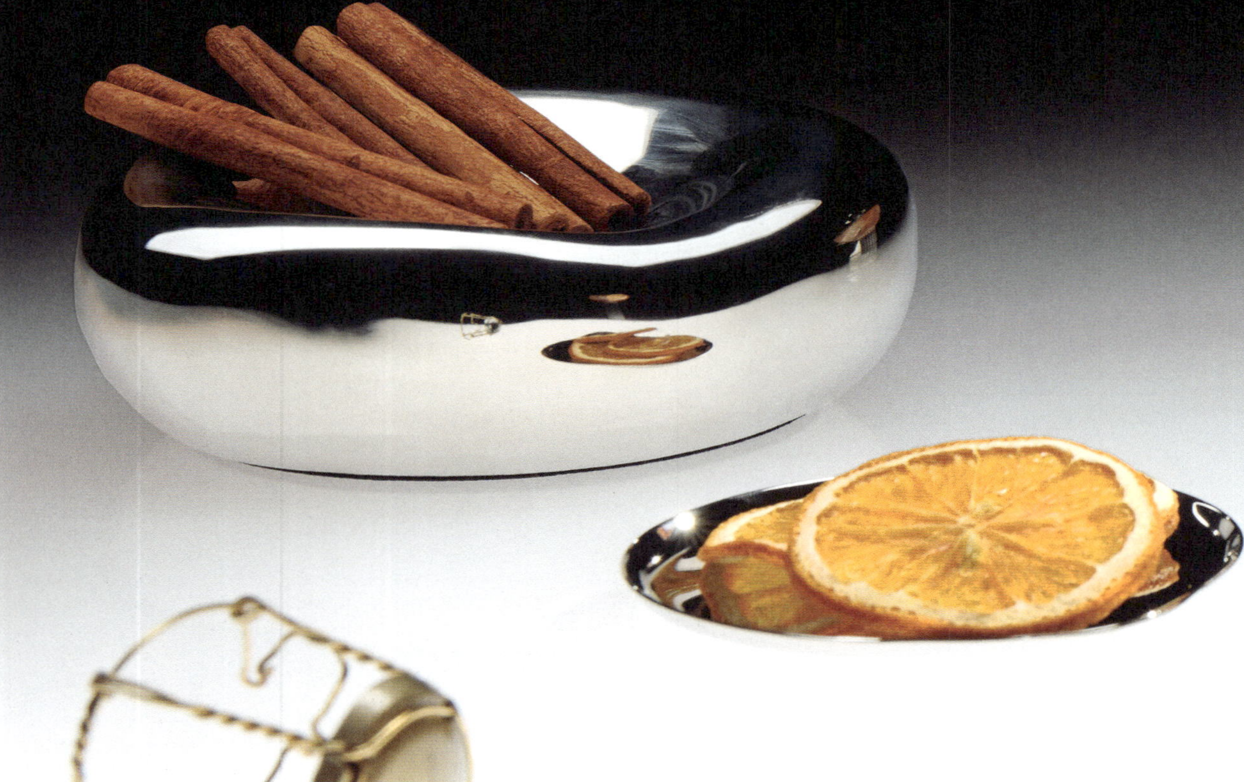

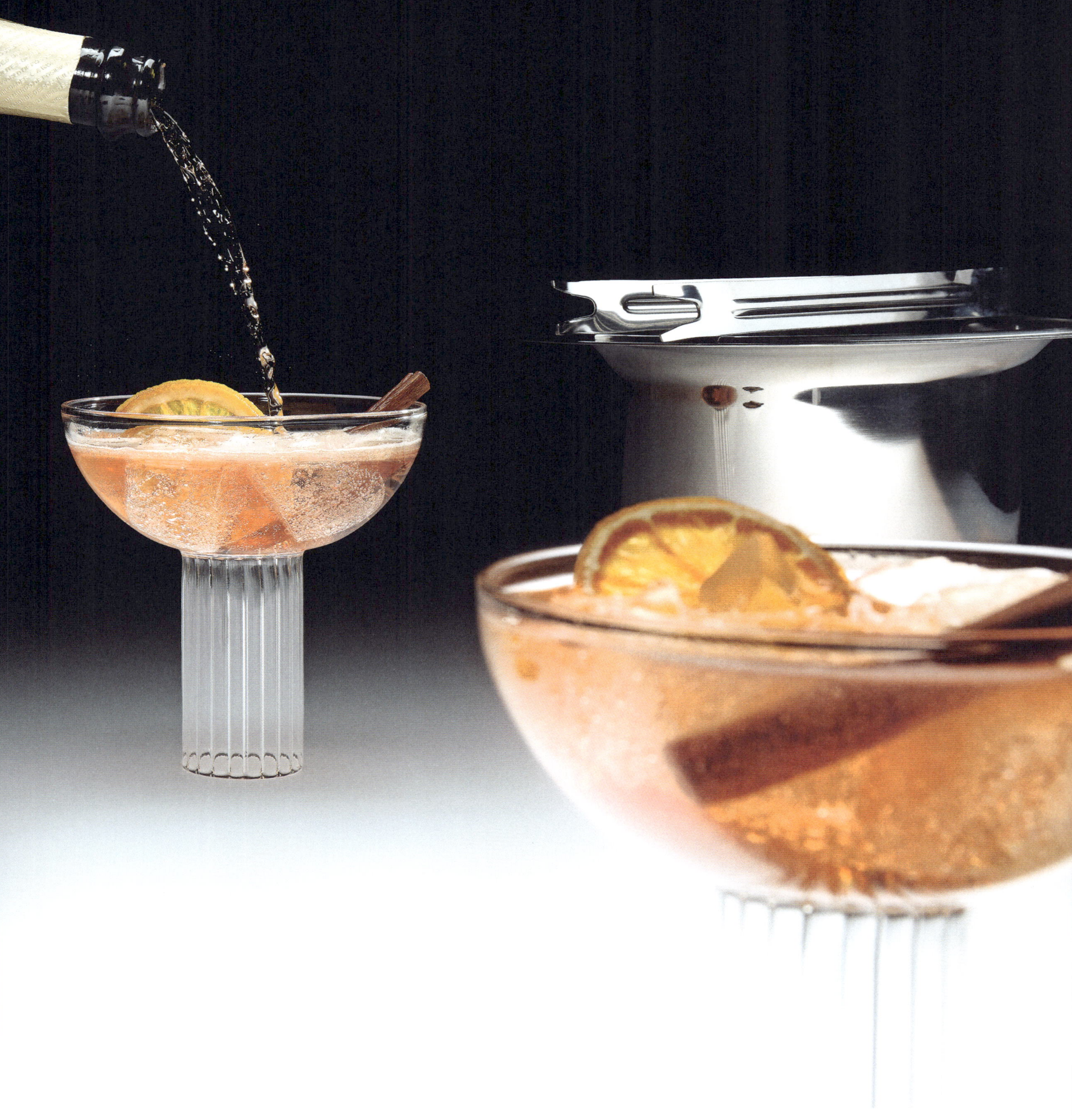

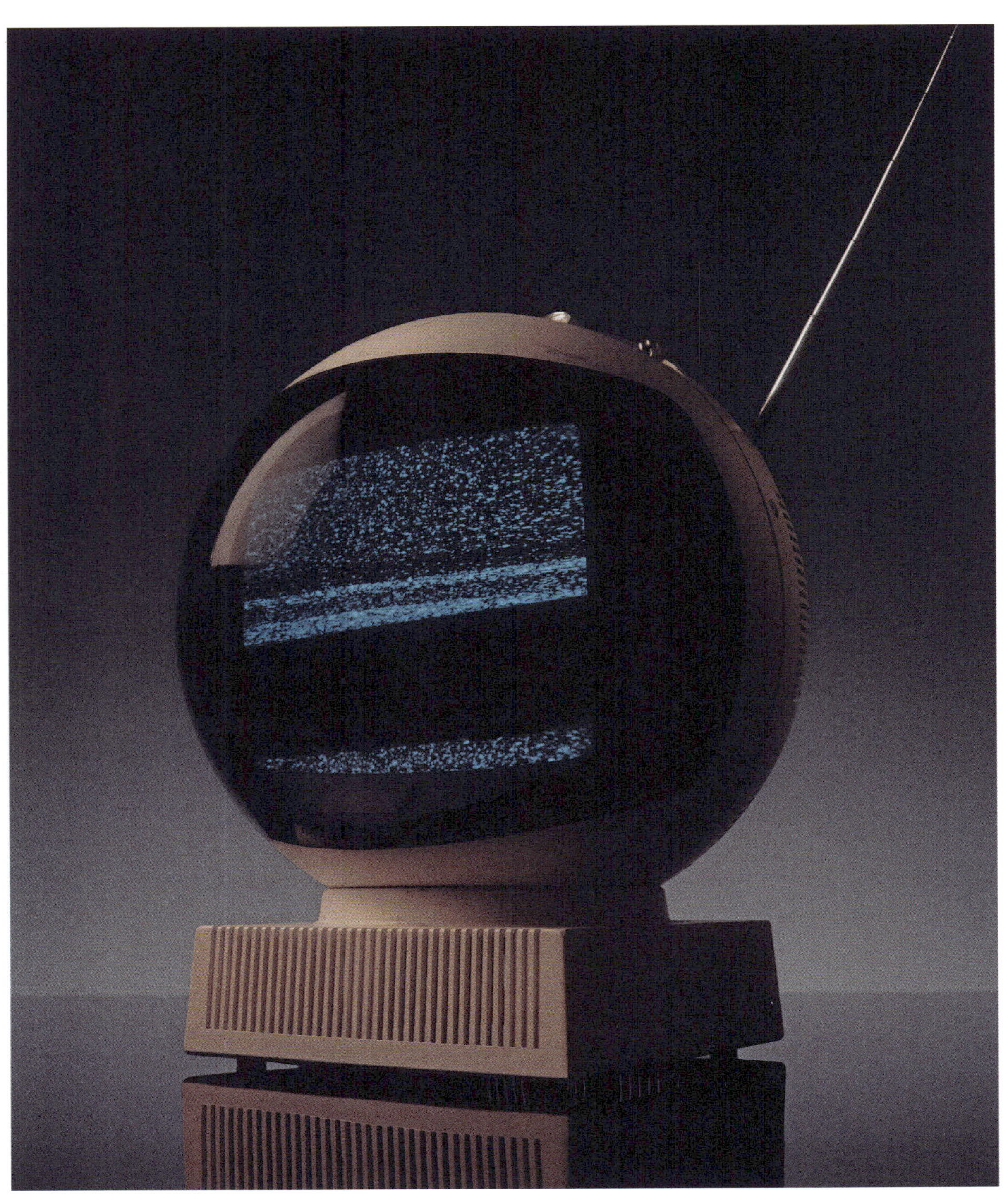

34

THE PRICE OF PEACE
On the rise of the annoyance economy.

WORDS
PRECIOUS ADESINA
PHOTO
OSCAR CALLEJA

There once was a time when commercials were prized for their artistic merit, and meant to be enjoyed. Yet the recent rise of streaming services and social media platforms has given way to another approach, where companies see ads less as an expression of brand identity, and more as a way to encourage users to sign up for new subscription tiers.

Netflix launched its less expensive, ad-supported tier in 2022; Instagram added ads to its search results a year later, and soon after, YouTube began introducing 30 seconds of unskippable ads to accompany certain videos. As a result, streamers and services are being incentivized to show more ads, for longer, with many users complaining that they have become dull, disruptive and repetitive. In other words, what was once an art form is now engineered as an annoyance.

This new relationship to ads has come a long way since the internet's first banner—a simple, small rectangle promoting AT&T on the former online magazine *Hot-Wired* in 1994. In part, this is down to digital platforms reducing their ad prices, allowing companies with smaller budgets a chance at the prime spots. Today's digital come-ons are often cheaply made or AI-generated, jarring or misleading, and strategically placed to interrupt the video or article you are trying to enjoy.[1]

Regardless of quality, a 2018 study by music streaming service Pandora, authored by the California-based company alongside scientists from Netflix and Uber, found that when users are faced with countless ads, they are more likely to convert to an ad-free subscription. The success of such tactics—creating a diminished experience that customers can pay to fix—has seen many other services follow suit. Some of the biggest dating apps, such as Hinge, Bumble and Tinder, now limit the number of people you can express interest in, how visible you are to others, or even the type of matches you receive until you opt into a premium service. Users of Duolingo are now also required to pay to remove the presence of timed ads after every lesson in the language learning app.

It's not a surefire approach. The Pandora study also found that, when ads are unbearably frequent, more customers will leave a service than subscribe, and a recent study by the media platform Picnic and the market research company YouGov discovered that more than two-thirds of people now find online advertising unpleasant. Taken together, these two studies suggest that ad-supported tiers could lead a service to hemorrhage users.

For now, most companies are doubling down, and the practice has rapidly become the norm. The New York–based market research firm Antenna estimated that, at the end of the first quarter of 2025, there were nearly 100 million ad-supported subscribers to subscription-based streaming services like Netflix and Hulu in the US. This figure is expected to double by 2027. And in any case, as cultural critic Ted Gioia notes, platforms like TikTok are so deliberately addictive that, even when ads come up, we're much less likely to move on to something else. "They pace the videos to give the kids a jolt of dopamine every few seconds," he writes, "and the users keep scrolling." These days, at least online, anything that seems free comes with a price: advertising.

(1) The Coalition for Better Ads was founded in 2016. Though presented as an effort to improve the online experience, its formation was largely driven by industry fears that the rise of ad-blockers threatened the digital advertising ecosystem.

MARK WILLIAM LEWIS

WORDS
TARA JOSHI
PHOTO
NATHAN WOLF GRACE

Meet A24's only musician.

Mark William Lewis is a kind of 21st-century troubadour. The South London–based artist writes songs that evoke dusk in the city, all smudged guitar lines, sighing harmonicas, a soft voice full of yearning and lyrics that weave together the mundane and the beautiful—a sonic magical realism. With his arresting self-titled album recently released, Lewis discusses his process, avoiding prescriptiveness and becoming the first artist signed to A24's record label.

TARA JOSHI: What first drew you to music?

MARK WILLIAM LEWIS: I grew up around poetry and novels more than music; my dad was a writer, and we had a lot of books in the house. I started writing short stories and poems from a really young age. But we also had instruments—my brother played guitar and I played drums. I guess our parents wanted us to play music because they didn't. So it's been this lifelong project of letting those two interests become one.

TJ: Are you prescriptive about what you want your music to mean?

MWL: I like not quite knowing what you want it to mean, or what it's going to mean for other people. I went to art school and I remember talking about that a lot; as soon as the "meaning" of an artwork becomes prescribed, for me, that's the minute it becomes uninteresting. I have always tried to avoid that. I'm really into the John Lennon idea where he prioritizes how the word feels in your mouth rather than what it means—didacticism is not for art.

My songs do often relate to specific things for me, but I always want them to be open for people to project their own experiences onto.

TJ: Is there an element of your work that feels diary-like then?

MWL: I actually have a page-a-day diary in my bag. If I'm feeling anxious about something, I'll write it down because it helps make it feel more manageable. Or if I've got a shopping list, I'll write that in there. If I'm writing a song, I'll write lyrics in there. I like the oneness of that, like: Why can't the anxieties or the shopping list become a song? This is the third year I've done it. I like the idea that anything that goes in there could become part of what I put out in the world, honoring where I was at in specific moments.

TJ: You're the first artist to sign to A24's record label. Did something about their approach to filmmaking resonate with your sensibilities as an artist?

MWL: What drew me to do it was the people that I was talking to, not the reputation or identity of A24—that was important, but an afterthought. The people were competent, passionate, intelligent, driven to make it big. I'd had conversations with other labels who I didn't feel had the same clarity of vision. I didn't think about it in the sense of, *Oh my god, I'm the first*, but, because I'm the only artist on the label at the moment, there's lots of energy and time being put into it. That feels exciting. Then it feels like a really good fit in terms of the niche that they've carved out in film—how they present certain genres in a new and fresh way.

TJ: Is there anything else you'd like people to know about your work?

MWL: There's always this challenge: I've made it, and now I have to figure out how to talk about it in a way that doesn't ruin it. Ultimately, I just want people to experience it.

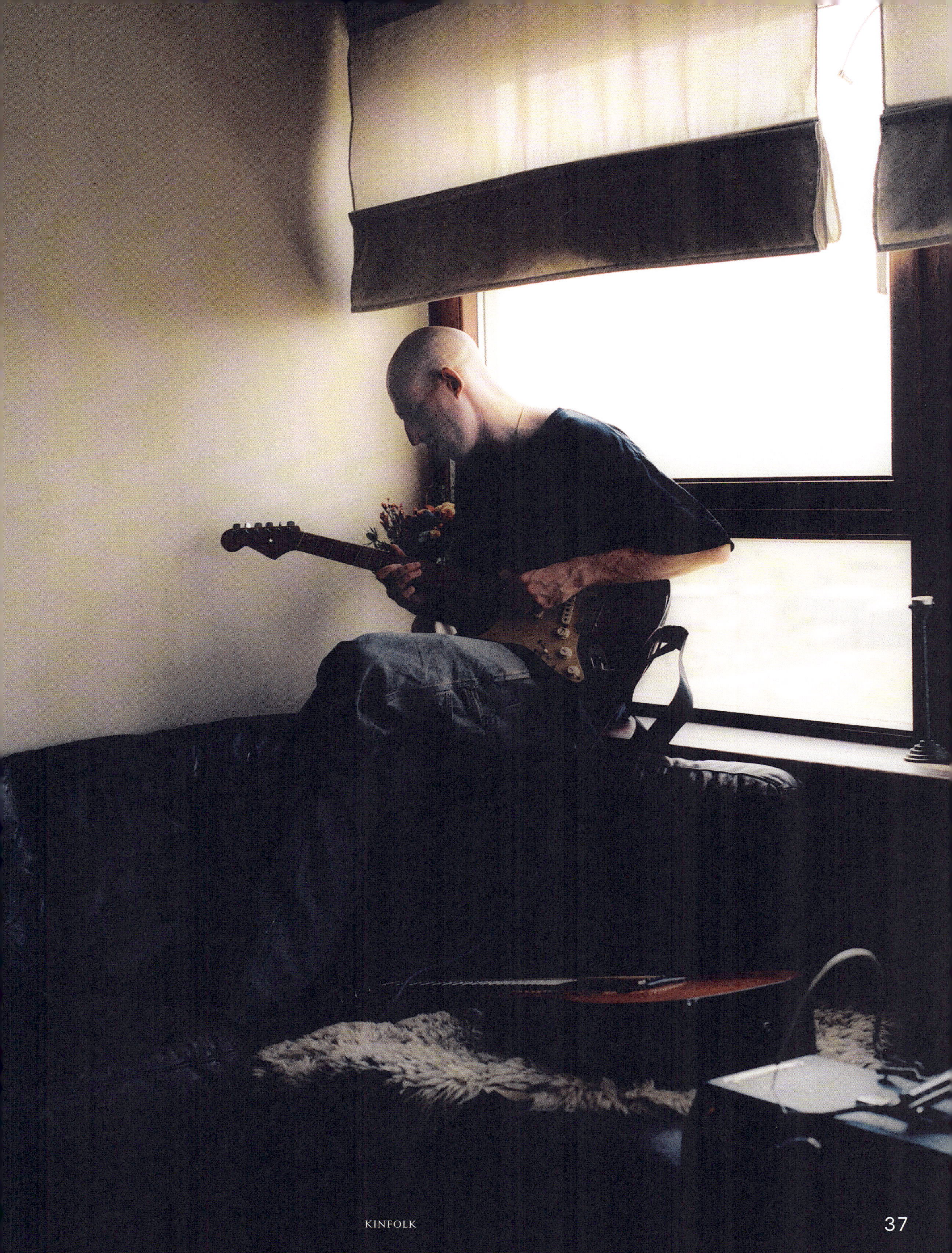

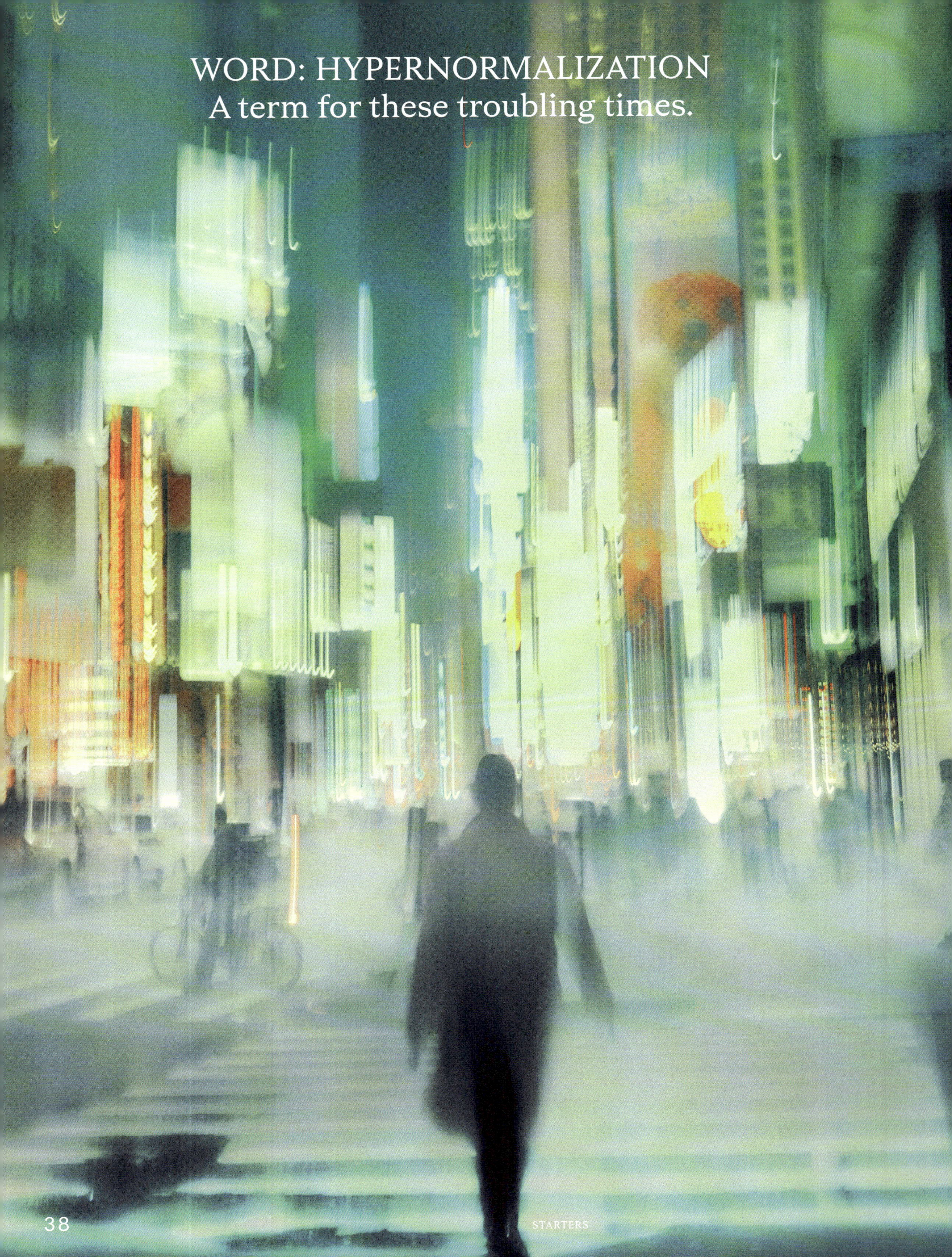
WORD: HYPERNORMALIZATION
A term for these troubling times.

STARTERS

WORDS
FRANCIS MARTIN
PHOTO
ALEKSANDR BABARIKIN

Etymology: The term "hypernormalization" was coined by the anthropologist Alexei Yurchak in 2005 to describe a linguistic peculiarity in late-Soviet society: Following years of ideologically driven usage, words had been hollowed out of their meanings and, as a result, could no longer be interpreted outside of the definitions given to them by the state.[1]

The term was later popularized, and anglicized, by the British filmmaker Adam Curtis in his 2016 documentary, *HyperNormalisation*. Curtis employed it more broadly to describe the propensity of governments and corporations to promote simplified narratives as an anesthetic to the more complex, and more frightening, reality.

The compound term "hypernormalization" can thus be divided in two ways to give connected but slightly different interpretations: "Hyper-normalization" is the intensified process of normalization, while "hypernormal-ization" is the takeover of a new normal. Yurchak is using it in the latter sense; Curtis in the former.

Meaning: What are the chances, do you think, that this article was written by AI? Two years ago, you'd have laughed at the idea. Now, you might well be scanning the prose for a telltale sign—an em dash, perhaps. And if you experience a sense of disquiet about the pace at which AI is learning to mimic human creativity, but would rather not think about it too much and instead continue to use ChatGPT to make your life easier, you might be a (willing) victim of hypernormalization, as Yurchak understands it.

Curtis extracts a dizzying array of examples for his notion of hypernormalization, including the dramatic spike in the number of suicide bombings in the past 30 years, the recasting of Colonel Muammar al-Qaddafi by Western politicians from enemy to ally to enemy again, and the rise of digital realities. His documentary of the same name ends with the emergence of Donald Trump as a political force, but was released before his first election victory. Viewed with hindsight, the phenomenon Curtis describes has only intensified in the ensuing decade, as the mundane routines of daily life become more frequently juxtaposed with news of once-in-a-lifetime climate disasters, starving children and the increasing instability of the US's democratic norms.

In both cases, "hypernormalization" works because cognitive dissonance is preferable to existential crisis. Take the fable of two frogs, one in a boiling pot and the other in water that is being slowly heated: The first scrambles out as soon as it touches the boiling water, the other will sit there quite happily, unaware of the danger until it is too late—a nonchalance that recalls, literally, human inaction over climate change. As T.S. Eliot once wrote: "Humankind cannot bear very much reality."

(1) In *Everything Was Forever, Until It Was No More: The Last Soviet Generation,* Yurchak explains how this linguistic peculiarity reflected the way Soviet citizens perpetuated official ideology and continued to act as if the state was functioning while privately acknowledging that their lived reality was diverging increasingly from official narratives.

39

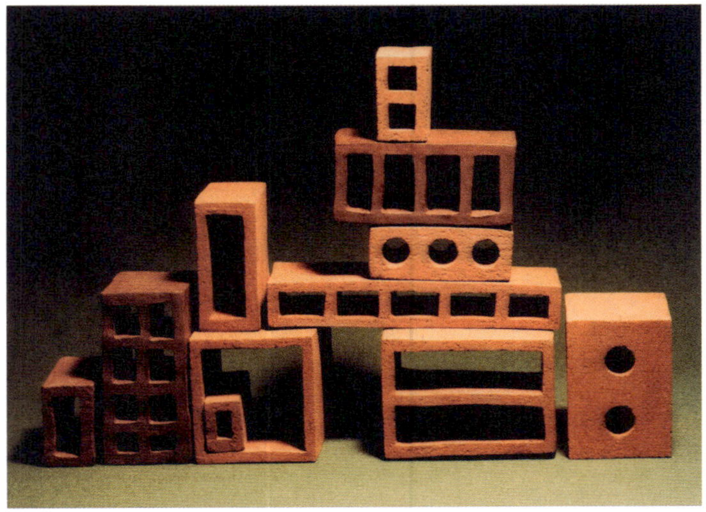 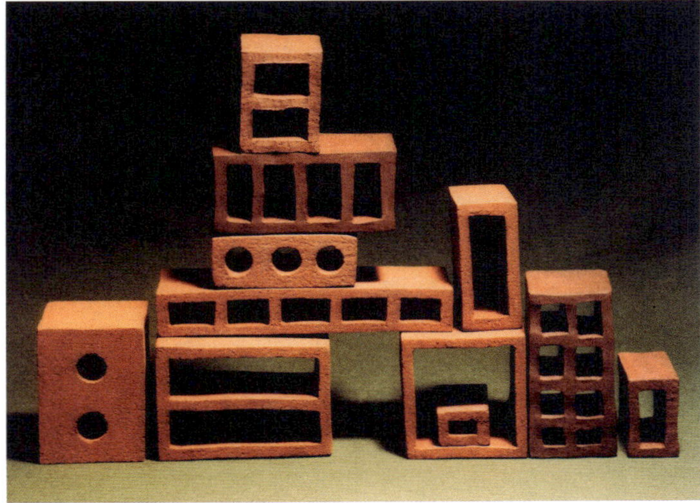

SPOT THE DIFFERENCE
On architectural mimicry.

In the shimmering heat, massive columns encircle a piazza in front of a high-domed basilica, its form instantly recognizable as one of the most important—and largest—churches in the world, a place of pilgrimage for the world's 1.3 billion Catholics. A breeze carries sounds of cows across the plaza…. Cows?

This basilica, as it happens, is not Bernini and Michelangelo's masterpiece presiding over St. Peter's Square at the Vatican but an ever-so-slightly larger replica looming over the fields outside Yamoussoukro, the capital of Ivory Coast. Inching out the original in terms of size and height (contrary to the wishes of the pope at the time), the Basilica of Our Lady of Peace of Yamoussoukro seems as much a monument to Félix Houphouët-Boigny, the first and longest-serving president of Ivory Coast, who commissioned the church in the 1980s, as it is an expression of Christian devotion.[1]

Here imitation is not flattery, but one-upmanship. The National Theater of Nigeria conveys a similar message. Its overtly technological concrete masts and suspended roof almost exactly duplicate Bulgaria's Palace of Culture and Sports—but at four times the size. Commissioned under General Yakubu Gowon's military government and completed in 1973, during an oil boom and after two decades of postcolonial independence, the building announced Nigeria's new wealth and cultural ambition. If Europe had pioneered such monumental forms, Nigeria now demonstrated that it could match—and even surpass—them in scale.

Architectural duplication has become a crucial political tool throughout much of the world. While Western critics may disdain copying creative works because it "withers… the aura of the work of art," to quote German philosopher Walter Benjamin, elsewhere, replicating important buildings bestows their symbolic power on the imitator. Municipalities throughout China have recreated famous Western buildings—London's Tower Bridge, the Leaning Tower of Pisa, the Kremlin, the Colosseum, an entire Austrian village—not merely as architectural curiosities, but as assertions of strength. In *Original Copies: Architectural Mimicry in Contemporary China*, Bianca Bosker emphasizes that copying architecture is meant to project the nation's global reach. "While it once considered itself the center of the world," she explains, "China is remaking itself into the center that actually contains the world."

Perhaps it's time to reconsider the old adage about imitation and flattery (did we ever really believe it anyway?). Copying isn't adulation; it's a sure bet, an easy return on investment. While only a few people claim most of the profit, maybe we all benefit a little from duplicates of great buildings like the Parthenon and St. Peter's proliferating out there.

(1) During its construction, Pope John Paul II asked that the dome be built slightly lower than that of St. Peter's Basilica in the Vatican. The architect Pierre Fakhoury lowered the dome accordingly but added a giant cross, making the church 72 feet taller than St. Peter's and, as a result, the tallest Catholic church in the world.

WORDS
ALEX ANDERSON
PHOTO
ALICIA DUBUIS

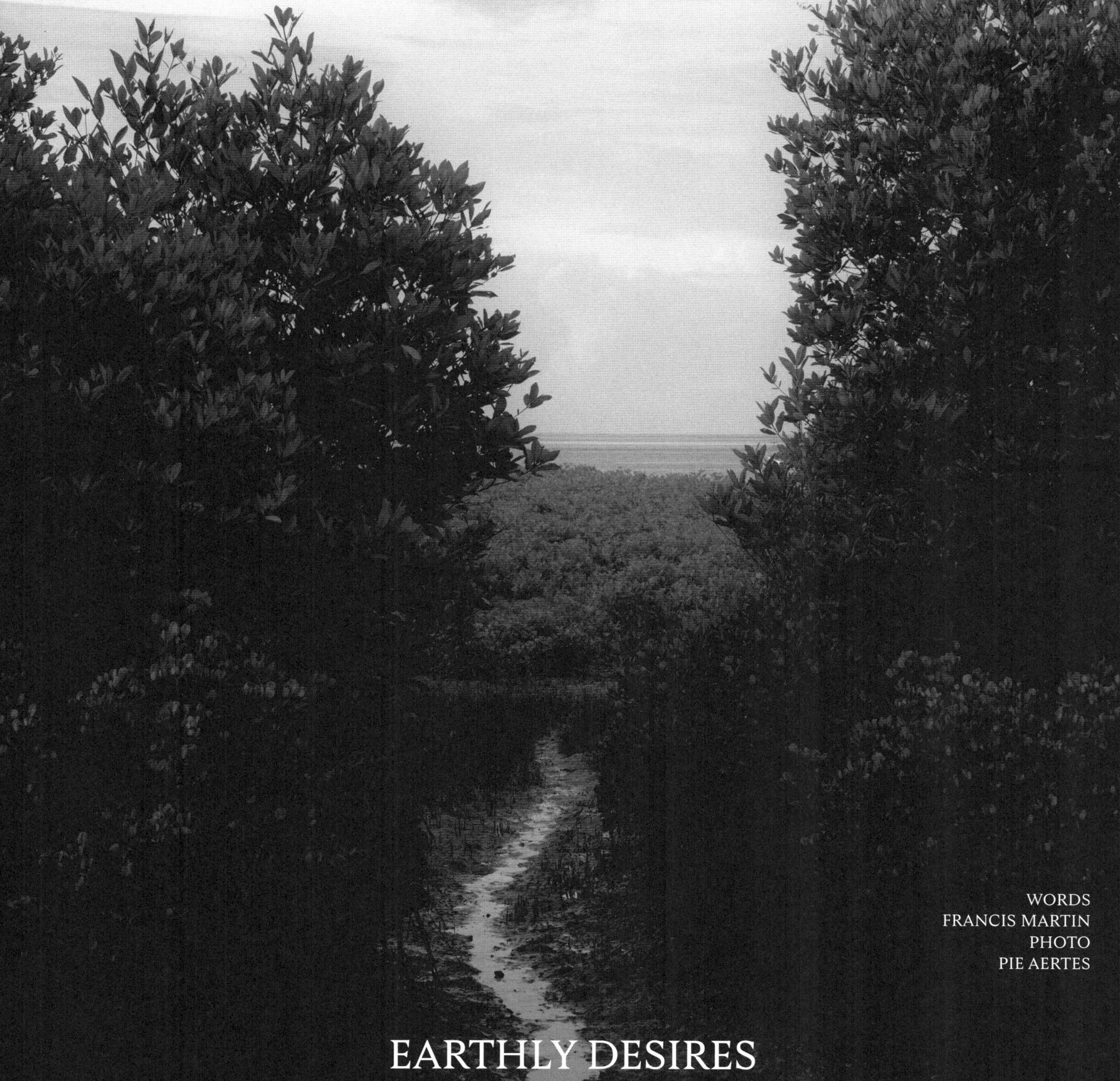

WORDS
FRANCIS MARTIN
PHOTO
PIE AERTES

EARTHLY DESIRES
The paths we tread together.

Which way would an elephant go? The Dutch term *olifantenpad*—elephant path—describes the informal paths that emerge due to the human (and apparently elephantine) tendency to take the most direct route rather than the path laid out by planners. In English, these routes are called desire paths, and you can find them in both rural and urban settings: a path beaten through the forest to reach a beauty spot; a line worn in the grass, bypassing the sidewalk from the parking lot to the building entrance.

Contrary to the name, desire paths are normally formed by necessity and convenience—they don't even need to lead anywhere. Often they will run alongside a paved path in a park, formed by joggers who prefer the softer ground.

While designing new campuses, several US universities opted to let students vote with their feet and built paths along those that emerged organically. The result, viewed from the air, looks like a web spun by a spider who stayed too late at a frat party: The paths form an asymmetrical maze that no landscape architect would be able to anticipate, but they work for those who use the space, rather than against them.

It's a philosophy far removed from the pristine lawns of Oxford and Cambridge, which are protected by signs warning time-strapped students to "keep off the grass." But efforts to thwart the will of pedestrians rarely succeed in the long term. A subreddit on desire paths charts a pattern, some examples of which are evidenced in a series of Google Street View screenshots. The first shows the emergence of the desire path; then an obstruction is put in its way, such as shrubs or a bench; the path mutates to avoid the obstacle; and eventually whoever owns the land bows to the wisdom of the masses and puts down paving stones along the desired route.

In Munich, there's a desire path formed by a more profound form of resistance. A line of bronze cobblestones snakes down Viscardigasse, an otherwise nondescript street, tracing the path taken by people avoiding a Nazi monument and the obligatory Hitler salute they had to perform as they passed it. Taking a diversion down Viscardigasse became a form of quiet disobedience during the Nazi regime, and the cobblestone artwork was installed in 1995 to commemorate those who took the route. In a dictatorship, as in a poorly designed urban landscape, sometimes the only option is to vote with your feet.

RUTGER BREGMAN

WORDS
HETTIE O'BRIEN
PHOTO
MAARTJE TER HORST

On moral ambition.

A banal but terrifying fact of human existence is that we will never get our time back. Despite this, many of the world's most intelligent and well-educated people waste their lives in soul-sapping jobs that are pointless or even harmful. For the Dutch historian and writer Rutger Bregman, they represent a huge opportunity.

Bregman shot to fame in 2014 with the publication of his first book, *Utopia for Realists*, which updated long-standing left-wing causes, such as universal basic income and affordable housing, with bite-size history lessons and polemical flair. He followed this with *Humankind: A Hopeful History*, in which he argued that "most people, deep down, are pretty decent." Both books were seductively optimistic, suggesting that individuals have the power to change the world through imagination and resolve.

Why, then, does it feel as though things are getting worse? Bregman's latest book, *Moral Ambition*, takes aim at the privileged and apathetic, those who waste their talents doing what the anthropologist David Graeber called "bullshit jobs." He wants to convince these high-flyers to forego the allure of wealth and status and instead work toward making the world a better place. To that end, in 2024 Bregman launched an NGO, the School for Moral Ambition, which attempts to translate these ideas into tangible action by recruiting people with impressive CVs to work on programs that aim to eliminate harmful industries, such as big tobacco and intensive farming.

HETTIE O'BRIEN: Your new book is in many ways positive. But before we get to this, I wanted to ask you about the negative. There is a growing awareness that political leaders are totally unconstrained by international laws or moral norms. A lot of people feel understandably powerless about their capacity to change anything.

RUTGER BREGMAN: Well, I won't beat around the bush. We're living through an incredibly dangerous, scary and disturbing moment in world history. In the case of the US, I'm often reminded of the fall of the Roman Empire, which was accelerated by profound decadence and the failure of the elites. But I've also wondered what it must have felt like to live in Europe just before the First World War or in Germany in the 1930s. People back then didn't know how their story would end. Their future was fundamentally open. In 2025, we also don't know what our story is. The script has not been written yet. But it will be written by small groups of really committed, determined people. And what I worry about the most right now is apathy. People are tuning out. They're doomscrolling. They're putting in their noise-canceling headphones. Meanwhile, the ideologues are waiting in the wings.

HOB: So what would you say to someone who has already been on a protest, and now they want to go further? But they also have two kids, a mortgage to pay and they've become restrained by the golden handcuffs of their corporate job.

RB: I'm trying to convince people that they don't have to be bystanders. They don't have to be political hobbyists who consume the news on a daily basis and then think, "I've done my job as a citizen because I know how terrible everything is." We can do so much better than that. I'm trying to convince people that they're agents. There's this quote that I keep coming back to from the anthropologist Margaret Mead: "It's small groups of thoughtful, committed citizens who change the world. In fact, it's the only thing that ever has." Most people don't change the world, because they just follow the script of what they're

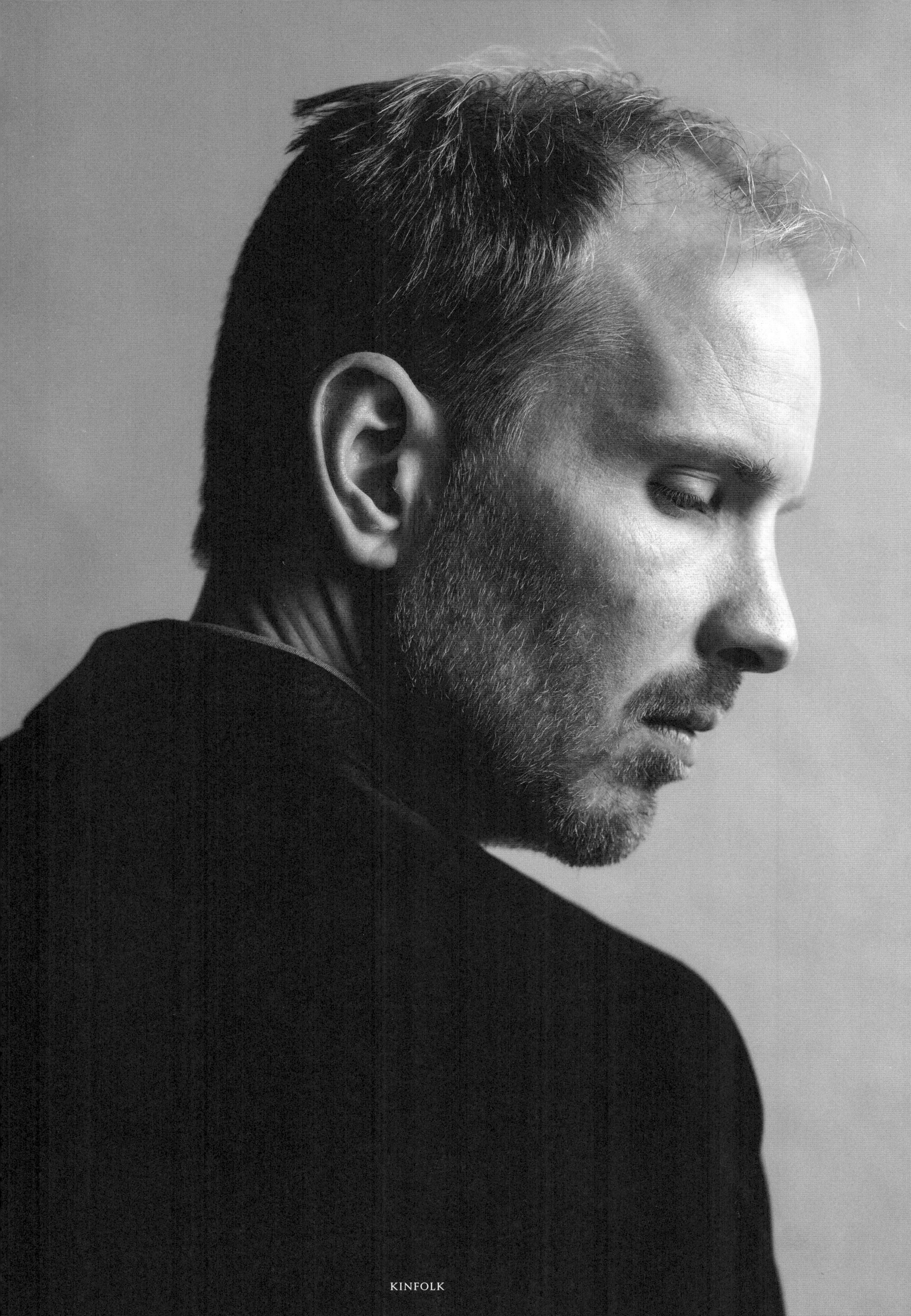

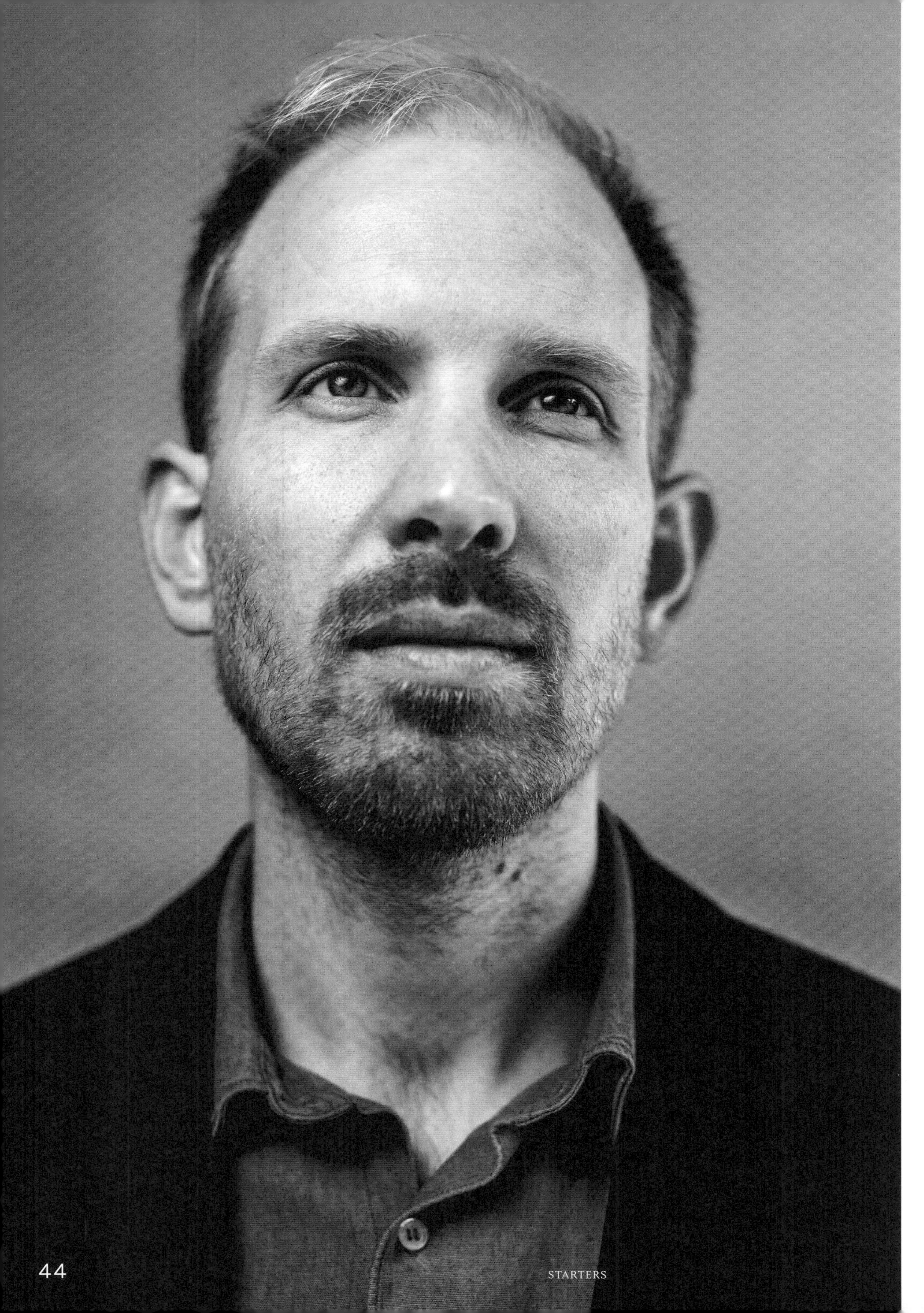

supposed to do. They study at a good university and they go into the Bermuda Triangle of talent—consultancy, corporate law and finance. But you don't have to do that. You can go down a much more challenging but also much more interesting and fulfilling path. And yes, I'm quite explicitly talking about people who have privilege and human or financial or cultural capital, and who are utterly wasting that capital. But I also believe that anyone can be morally ambitious. In the book, I've got quite a few case studies of people who weren't born into wealth or great privilege, but still massively changed the world.

HOB: It seems recently like the right has been much more morally ambitious than the left. Conservative Catholics who believe abortion should be criminalized have been effective at enforcing this politically. It's the same with philanthropists who have funded right-wing think tanks that lobby for particular policies. What do you think progressives can learn from this?

RB: I've never hidden the fact that I'm an old-school European social democratic. But I can think of a few lessons the right can offer. One is the importance of coalition building, of working together with people and organizations and groups that you don't always agree with. When I studied the women's rights movement of the 19th and early 20th century, it struck me how disciplined these people were. Often, they had to bite their tongue. They had to work with people who they agreed with for perhaps only 80% of the time. The second thing is long-term planning. What I see in the world of philanthropy among progressive do-gooders is an emphasis on having results in the next two or three years. Whereas when you study how the right built the conservative movement in the US, a number of people threw a shitload of money at funding think tanks and organizations, whether it was the Federalist Society or the Heritage Foundation, and it took them 30 or 40 years to see results.[1] Ultimately, though, they managed to take over the country. A more positive example of this long-term thinking is the abolitionist movement. Of the 12 founders of the British Society for the Abolition of the Slave Trade, which I write about in the book, only one was still alive when slavery was finally abolished half a century later. Often, the most successful forms of moral ambition are those where people realize they're part of something that is much, much bigger than themselves. That's the kind of thinking that builds cathedrals; it's planting a tree when you'll never sit in the shade, or starting to build the Sagrada Família when it won't be finished in your lifetime.[2] And currently I see that far more among conservatives than among liberals.

HOB: You've spent most of your life writing books and talking about ideas. I get the sense that your desire to do something more practical is partly rooted in frustration.

RB: I have a much more challenging life nowadays, since founding the School for Moral Ambition. But it is also so much more rewarding. I started my career with this belief that ideas change the world. And maybe after a decade in what I like to call the "awareness business," the realization dawned on me that awareness is vastly overrated. Take something like animal suffering: The vast majority of people know that we are torturing billions of animals on an industrial scale, and that this is probably one of the greatest crimes we've ever committed as a species. And most people will hear about it and are not even inclined to push back. As a society, we've more or less decided to ignore it. What matters is how you translate your awareness into real action. I think very often people underestimate their own agency. When we're kids, we assume there will be a moment when we're adults and we'll be serious people who know stuff. But the moment you're really an adult is when you realize, Holy shit, no one has a clue; everyone's just trying or pretending. That's liberating. You start to realize, Hey, wait a minute, I can just start doing stuff. I don't need to wait for anyone's permission. The key is to find yourself some like-minded, committed idealists, and just get going already.

"What matters is how you translate your awareness into real action."

[1] The Federalist Society was founded in 1982 by law students at Harvard, Yale and the University of Chicago to promote a literal interpretation of the US Constitution—one that emphasizes limited central government and individual freedoms. Five of the nine current US Supreme Court justices are, or have been, affiliated with the organization.

[2] Delayed by war, economic crises, politics—and the sheer ambition of its architect, Antoni Gaudí—the Sagrada Família in Barcelona has been under construction for more than 140 years. When asked about the church's glacial pace, Gaudí is said to have replied, "My client is not in a hurry." The basilica is now on track to open in 2026, marking the centenary of his death.

FOR WHAT IT'S WORTH
On the arbitrary value of art.

In 1917, a young French artist named Marcel Duchamp bought a urinal from a local plumbing-supply store, signed it with a pseudonym and submitted it to the inaugural exhibition of the Society of Independent Artists in New York. Appalled, the board members refused to display it, despite their lofty claims of an "open-door" policy.

Fountain would nonetheless come to acquire mythical status in the annals of art history. Documented in a carefully staged photograph taken by Alfred Stieglitz, it is now seen as the archetypal "readymade"—an "everyday object raised to the dignity of a work of art by the artist's act of choice," as Duchamp later wrote. For many critics, it was the moment conceptual art was born.

Though clearly provocative, Duchamp's prank was also a critical commentary on the art-world apparatus. The essential questions it raised—what makes something valuable and who decides—haven't lost their relevance more than a century later. A vessel for waste transformed into an object of near-sacred veneration, solely through its selection by the artist? The irony is priceless: or, more accurately, it's worth millions.

Many artists have gleefully picked up the gauntlet. In the 1960s, Piero Manzoni pushed Duchamp's provocation to its visceral extreme. For his notorious *Artist's Shit*, he canned what he claimed were 90 tins of his own feces, labeled them in four languages, and priced them by weight at the going rate for gold. Collectors couldn't resist. Decades later, one of these tins fetched over €275,000, making it 100 times more valuable than the metal it was priced against.[1]

Fast-forward to Maurizio Cattelan, the Italian master of the brazen artistic one-liner. In 1991, invited to contribute to an exhibition but feeling uninspired, he went to the nearest police station and filed a report for the theft of his nonexistent artwork. The official document, framed and displayed, transformed bureaucratic bluster into smug institutional critique, a cheeky jab at an art world that was so eager to celebrate him that it happily applauded a joke at its own expense.

And then, of course, there's Danish artist Jens Haaning, who staged perhaps the cleanest distillation of this long-running punchline. In 2021, the Kunsten Museum in Aalborg offered him €72,000, a sum equivalent to his annual salary, to create a contemporary version of his own earlier works, which visualized average national incomes through banknotes affixed to canvases. He delivered the two canvases completely blank, with a new title—*Take the Money and Run*—and, accordingly, kept the cash. The museum exhibited the empty works anyway, and the ensuing lawsuit only amplified the piece's sly message about trust, labor and the ambiguous contracts we accept in the name of art.

It all serves as a reminder that in this post-*Fountain* era, the worth we ascribe to art is rarely about craftsmanship, or even concept. More often, it's about the moment artistic prestige finds a way to harness spectacle. A successful artwork today might not require skill or substance, only the right blend of provocation and timing. Whether it's Damien Hirst's tiger shark suspended in formaldehyde or a shredded Banksy, what matters is less what the work says than how much publicity it receives—and how willing we are to conflate visibility with value.

WORDS
EMILY NATHAN
PHOTOS
ALICIA DUBUIS

---

(1) Despite being held in the collections of major institutions, none of Manzoni's cans have been opened to confirm whether they contain what's claimed on the label. As a result, some speculate they may hold nothing more than plaster.

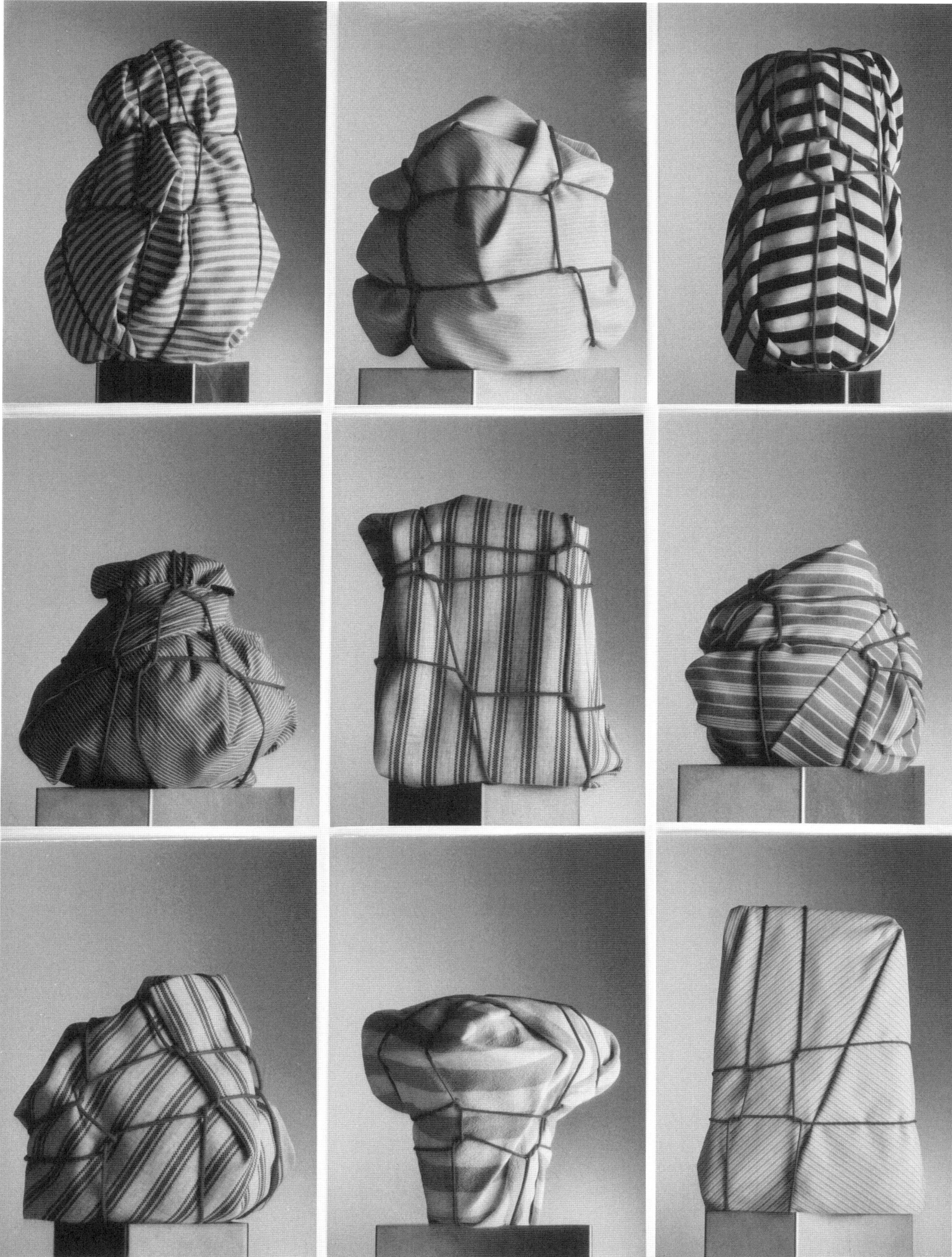

"Getting through the winter" has been one of the essential driving forces of civilization. Any fool can stay alive in a tropical environment, where mangoes drop into your lap and fish swim into your hands. Lasting from November to March in Helsinki or Anchorage, on the other hand, requires grit, cunning and a ready supply of cozy drinks.

This is one reason why so many good ideas have come from cold climates. Freezing, smoking, fermenting, drying and other tasty preservation tricks have been elevated to an art in northern locales. Double glazing, hot water bottles, *Grand Theft Auto*: all dreamed up by people trapped indoors, bored, staring into the drizzle.

The oft-touted idea that we should "touch grass" or "go for a walk," suggests we tend to see staying in as a moral failing. But as winter arrives, let's remember that it is a great privilege to be living during the golden age of home comfort. It would be the height of churlishness not to take advantage of such remarkable circumstances—after all, you can summon a single burrito or warm cookies to be delivered in less than half an hour, or order diapers in the morning and have them on your children by the evening. And besides, going out to restaurants and movies demands human interaction, and pants.

There are risks to staying at home. Unlike bears, humans do not live off their fat reserves during hibernation, but increase them, often surprisingly quickly. It is important therefore to stay active and limber, but luckily this can also be done at home, perhaps on one of the many and varied exercise machines developed to facilitate this.

Of course, staying at home can go hand in hand with too much screen time, but it needn't. A few hours of real-world engagement with, say, a book, is an easy salve. Let others brave the sleet. We lucky ones will hibernate, as nature and capitalism intended.

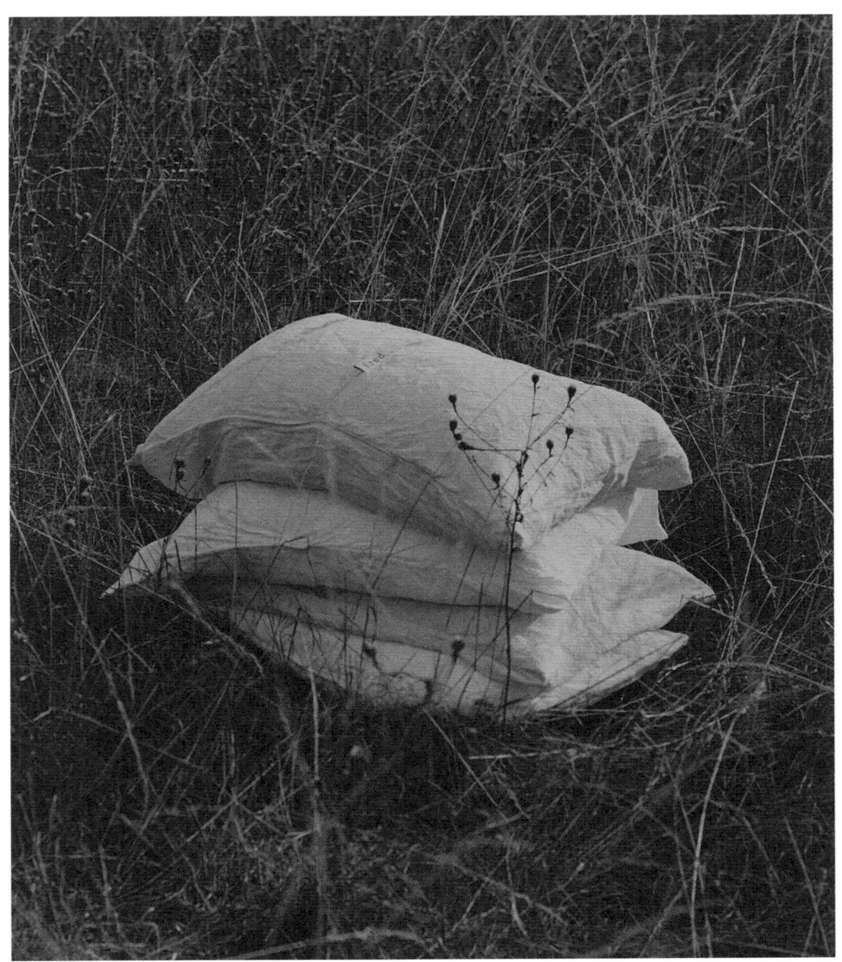

WORDS
ED CUMMING
PHOTO
THEA LØVSTAD

HOW TO: HIBERNATE
A survival guide to winter.

FEATURES:

50	At Work With: Lina Gotmeh
60	New Perspectives
64	Home Tour: Alekos Fassianos
76	The Anxieties of the Ultra-Rich
80	Elie Hassenfeld
86	It Shouldn't Cost the Earth

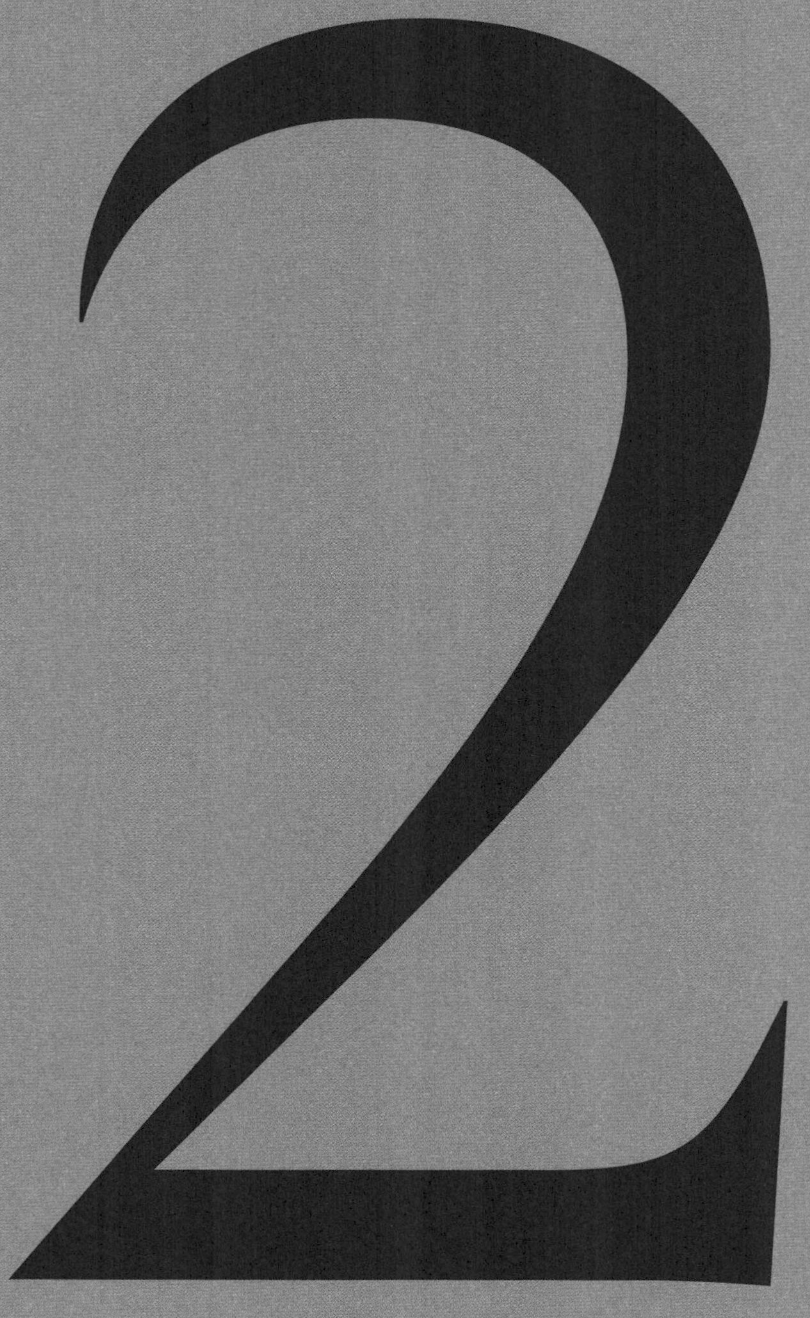

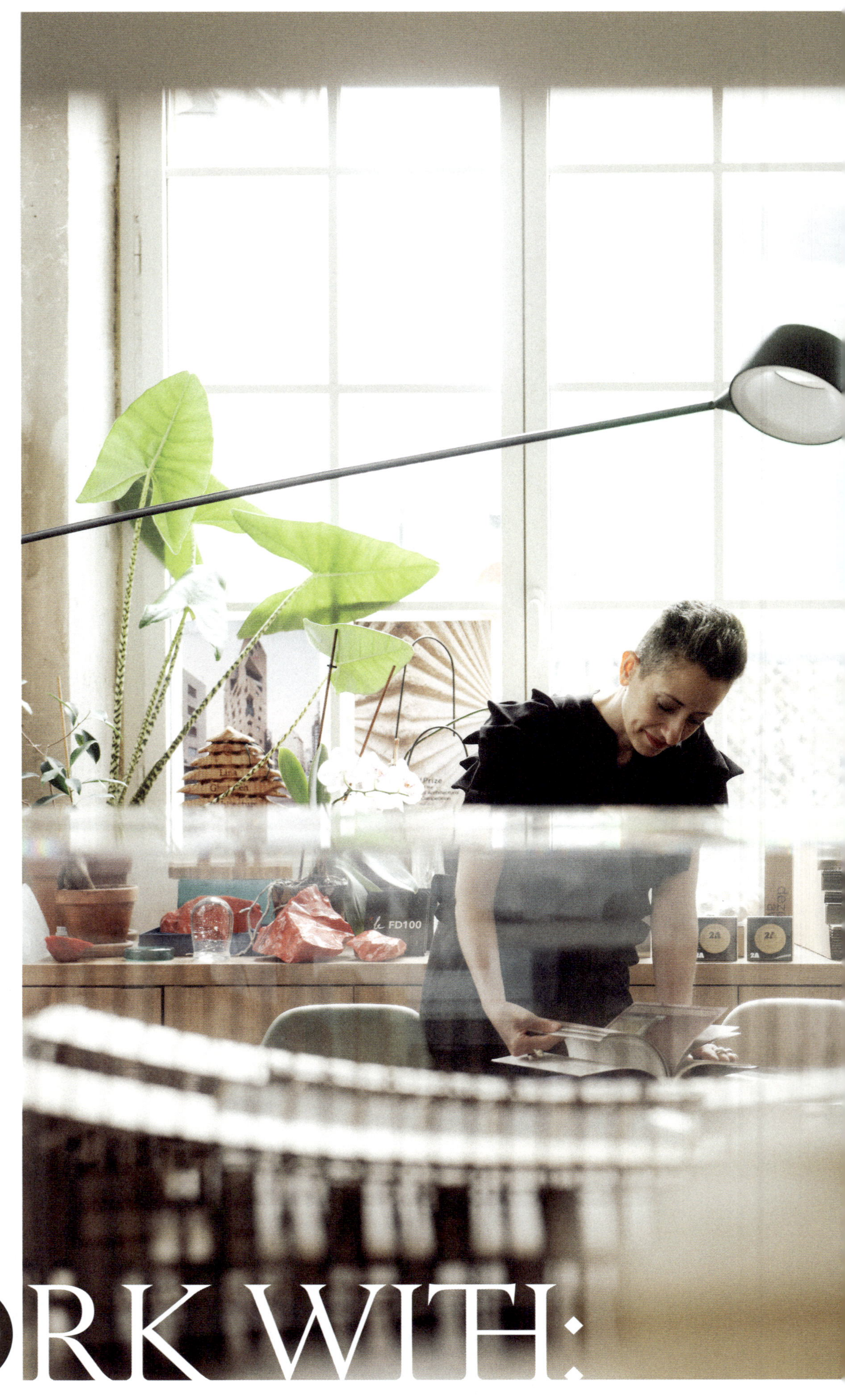

AT WORK WITH:

Words
Julia Webster Ayuso

Photos
Felix Speller

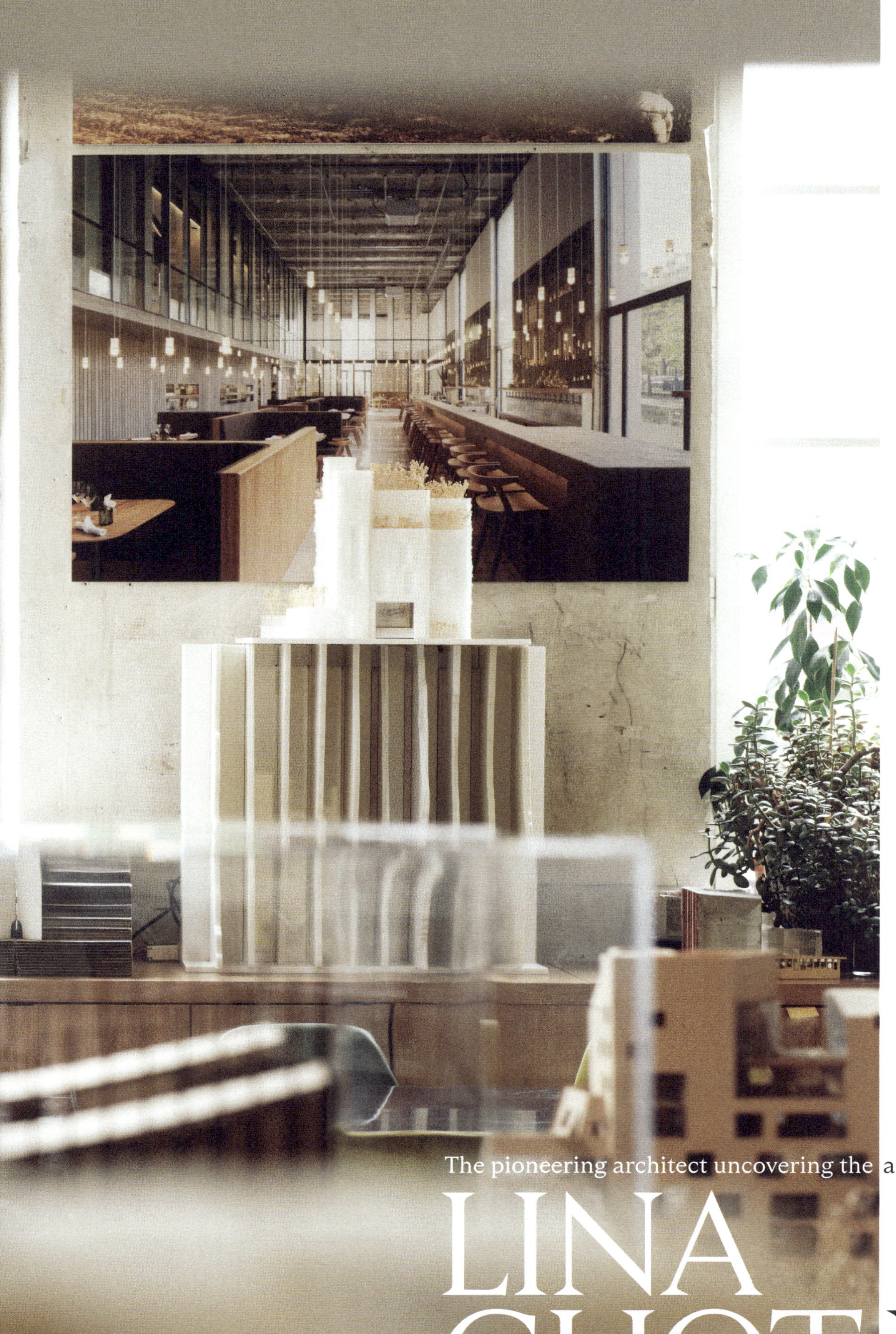

The pioneering architect uncovering the archaeology of the future.

LINA GHOTMEH

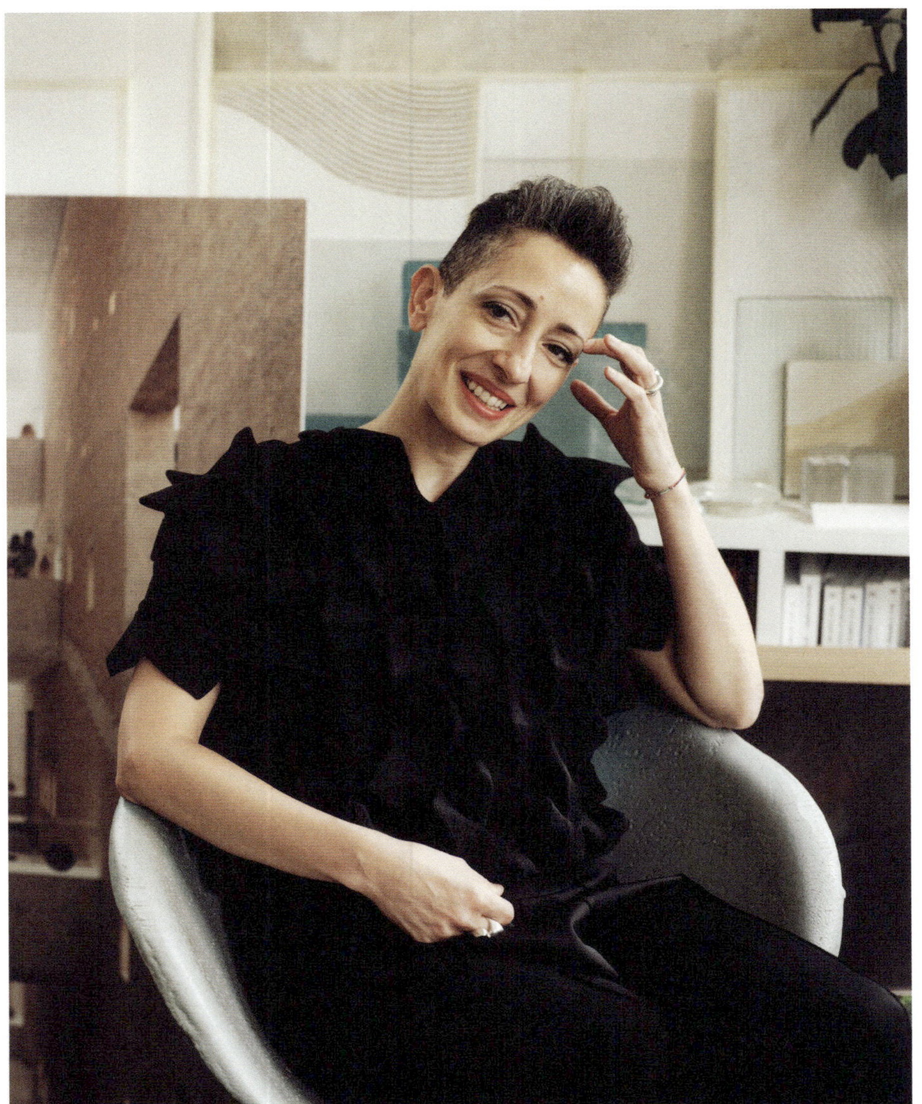

arrondissement, architectural models and sketches crowd tables and shelves. Neatly stacked handmade bricks sit beside wood and stone samples, and the occasional potted plant. On the unfinished walls, mood boards overflow with photographs and drawings.

"The atelier is a source of inspiration for me. It's a place of constant making," says the French Lebanese architect, as she takes a seat at the long lacquered table where she holds meetings each morning. Behind her, a series of tall arches lead to an open-plan office, where her team are quietly at work. The atmosphere is one of calm creativity. "I didn't want a pristine environment. I wanted it to feel like an unfinished space, which opens up the imagination," she says.

Ghotmeh moved to this space, a short walk from her apartment, when she established her eponymous practice in 2016. Since then her projects have included a residential complex in Beirut, the Qatari pavilion at the Venice Biennale and housing for the Olympic Village in Paris: work characterized by a humanist approach (which she defines as "building a relationship with the living") and by a deep respect for heritage and history. An interest in archaeology that began in childhood continues to shape her practice, informing an approach that always begins with a meticulous study of the site for any new project. "The first step is understanding the history, the geography, the climate and the materials you can find locally. It's a very sensorial, multifaceted, and even multimedia process," she explains.

Aside from site visits, a normal workday in the studio involves reviewing each project with her team, gathering materials, models, drawings and references on the

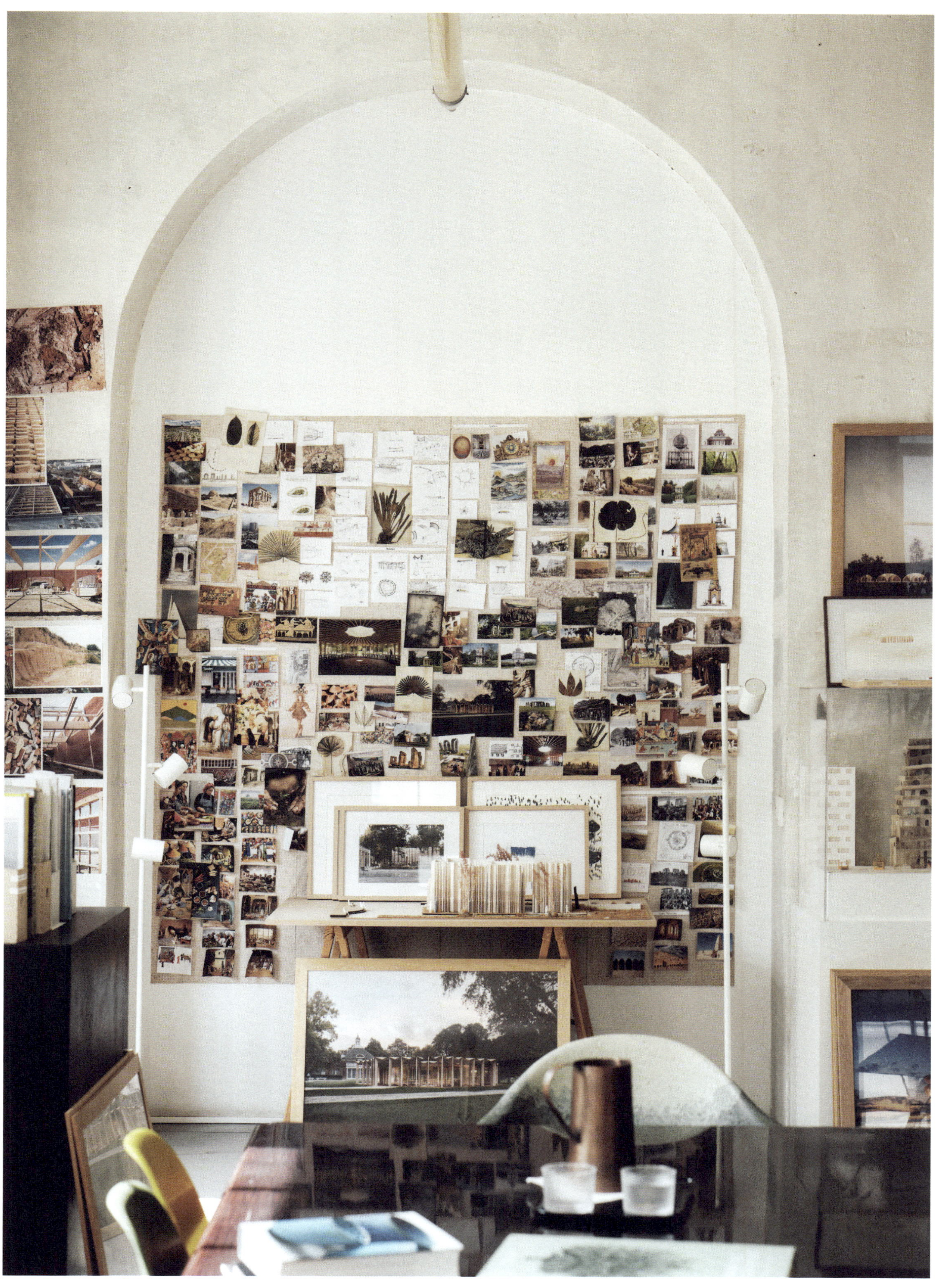

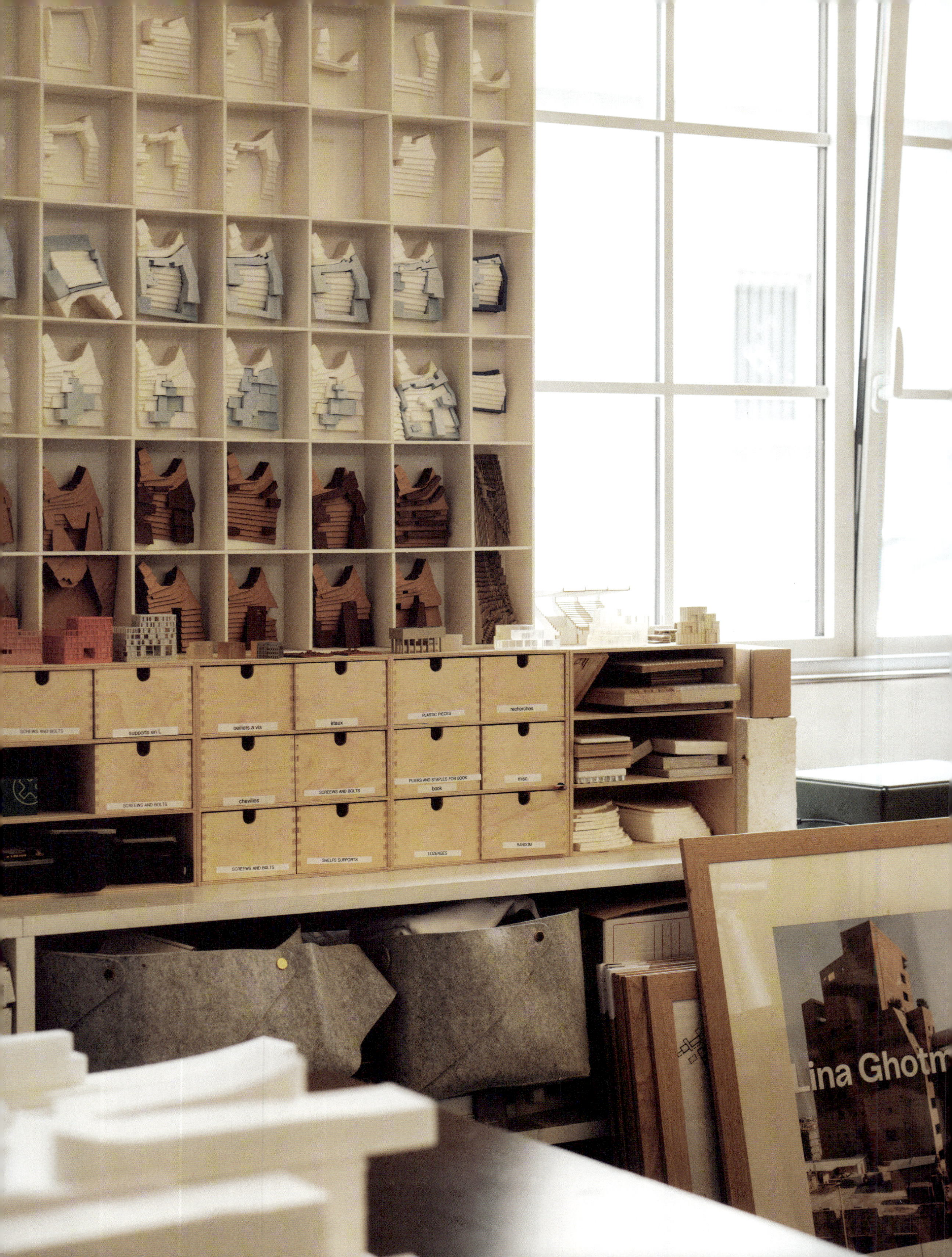

SCREWS AND BOLTS
supports en L
oeillets a vis
étaux
PLASTIC PIECES
recherches
SCREEWS AND BOLTS
chevilles
SCREEWS AND BOLTS
PLIERS AND STAPLES FOR BOOK
book
misc
SCREEWS AND BOLTS
SHELFS SUPPORTS
LOZENGES
RANDOM
Lina Ghotm

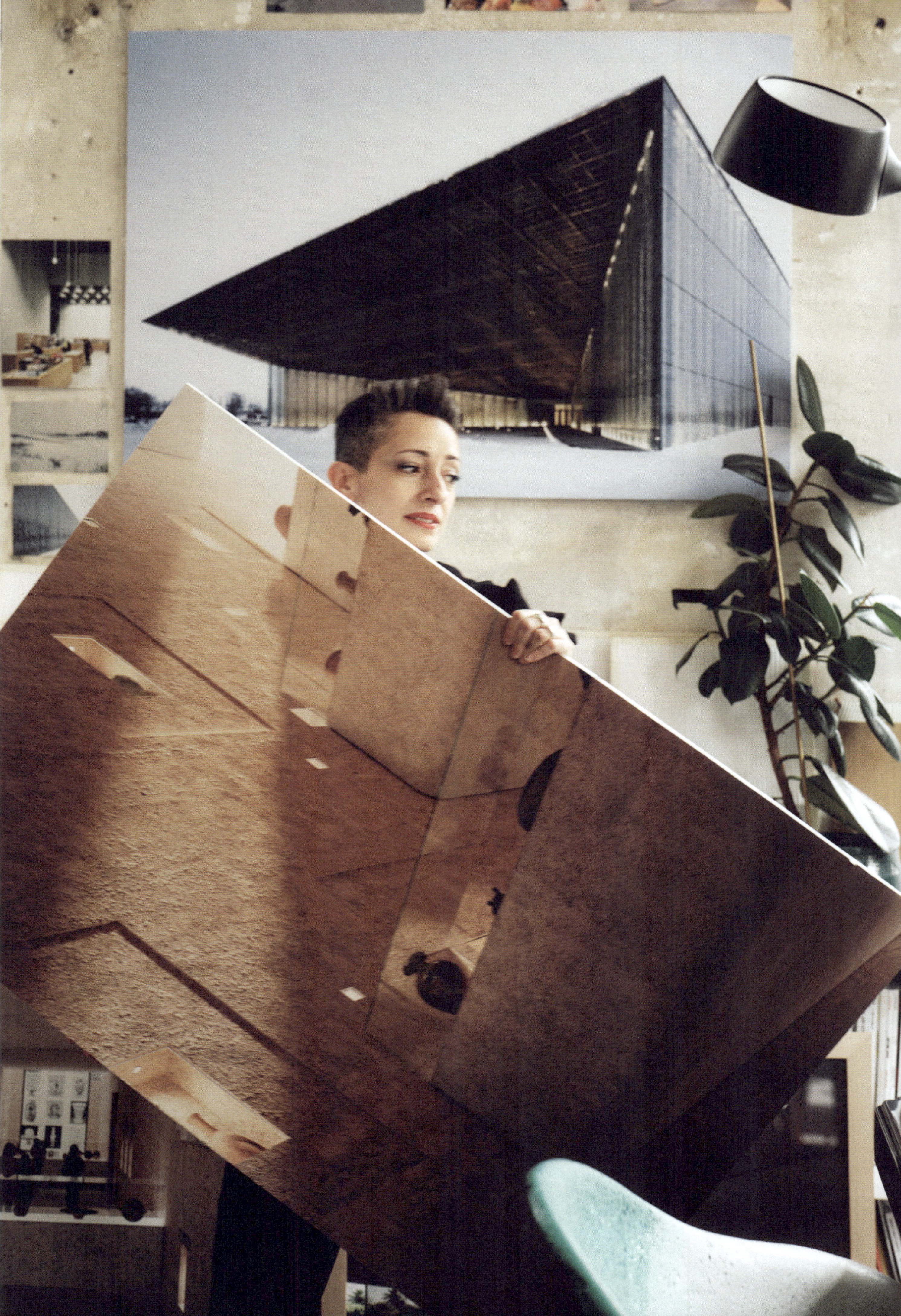

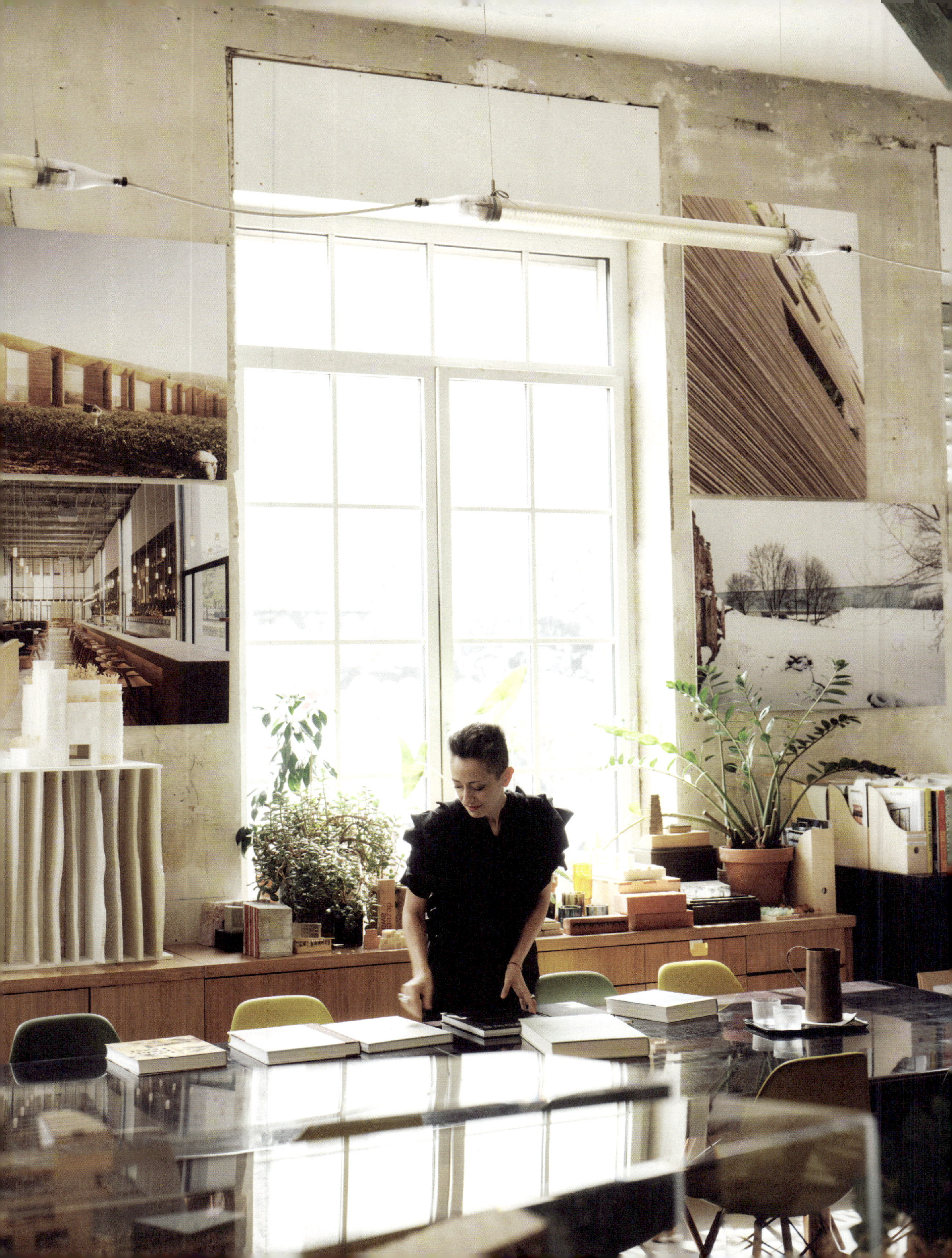

meeting table. Sketching is a tool she uses from start to finish, whether it's by hand or on an iPad. "It starts with intuition, and then sketching, and then with all the research, the idea slowly becomes more evident, more anchored," she says.

Ghotmeh's relationship with architecture began long before she trained as an architect. Born in Beirut in 1980, she grew up during the Lebanese civil war; her mother—an architect who taught at a university—instilled in her a love of drawing. Spending her formative years among the ruins of bombed-out buildings made her sensitive to the traces people leave on the built environment. "A lot of the projects necessitate questioning why we're doing what we're doing," she says. "A building has to emerge from a place, but it also has to reference its time. It has to understand the challenges of the time and try to respond."

This approach was apparent in her first major commission, her career breakthrough, which came when she was just 25. While working with Ateliers Jean Nouvel and Foster + Partners, she won a competition to build the Estonian National Museum in Tartu. The project was a way for the Baltic nation to assert its national identity and unique cultural history, and Ghotmeh's design—conceived with her former partners Dan Dorell and Tsuyoshi Tane—challenged the brief by embracing a former Soviet military airfield at the site. Completed in 2016, the vast glass structure blurs the boundary between landscape and architecture; its gently sloping roof emerges from the end of the runway to symbolize, as Ghotmeh said at the time, the "past taking off into the bright future."

"The challenge is creating a memory for a building," she says. It's a methodology she first described as the "archaeology of the future" when studying at the American University of Beirut, an approach that sees each new building as a continuation of the site's history. In practice, this philosophy usually takes the form of extensive research and detailed surveys, but it took on a literal meaning in Normandy during the construction of Hermès' leather workshop, France's first passive, energy-positive and low-carbon industrial building.

Ghotmeh designed the workshop as a single-story brick building with "galloping" arches of varying sizes, a nod to Hermès' saddle-making tradition. When construction began, however, workers uncovered a Magdalenian hearth thought to date back 12,000 years. "It was fantastic to think of this relationship between us humans today and who we were before," Ghotmeh says, still excited by the discovery of flint tools and stone pieces used to make needles, consistent with leatherworking. "It anchored the history of the project, and the whole thing made sense, in a way."

Earlier this year, Ghotmeh beat a list of top candidates—including Sir David Chipperfield—to redesign the British Museum's Western Range galleries, home to some of the institution's most famous objects, such as the Rosetta Stone, the Parthenon Sculptures and Lion Hunt of Ashurbanipal. Ghotmeh's proposal included two halls that extend up to the roof and down into the vaults, with the walls clad with waste material from Portland stone quarries.

Her vision of architecture as something akin to an "archaeological dig" appealed to the British Museum at a time when its collection and management have come under scrutiny. According to its website, the project aims to "rethink" the entire museum, a challenge Ghotmeh feels prepared to take on. "In my work, I'm always dealing with complexity and dealing with multiple subjects," she says, coming back to the idea of museums as, above all, places for the exchange of ideas. "Architecture can play a role in allowing interaction and dialogue to happen."

Ghotmeh also sees architecture as a "a tool to revive craft, to revive knowledge," and tries to incorporate local artisans where possible. "It's about being proud of what you make, and proving that architecture can have a positive impact," she says. On the floor of the office is a piece of concrete, a test for the facade of Stone Garden, a 13-story apartment building she designed in the center of Beirut. Using specially designed "brushes," local craftspeople shaped the rugged facade of cement and earth, creating striations that recall the process by which rocks form over time.

By evoking the geology beneath the building, Ghotmeh sought to pay homage to her hometown's history and resilience—something that came, in turn, to be embodied by the building itself. The devastating explosion in Beirut's port in 2020 shattered the building's windows and damaged interiors, but the structure stood strong. "For me architecture is a way to bring people together and to build peace," she says. "So it was a surreal moment, as if what had led to the design of the project manifested itself in real time."

Ghotmeh's work stands firmly in the tradition that architecture should be rooted in its environment, learning from what came before it—a slower but more deliberate approach that she argues is essential. "Architecture is a field that reaches out to people. Our life is composed of so many different aspects, so it's about incorporating that complexity into a physical, intelligible form," she explains. "It should also have novelty in it," she adds. "And the power to bring poetry and beauty to the world."

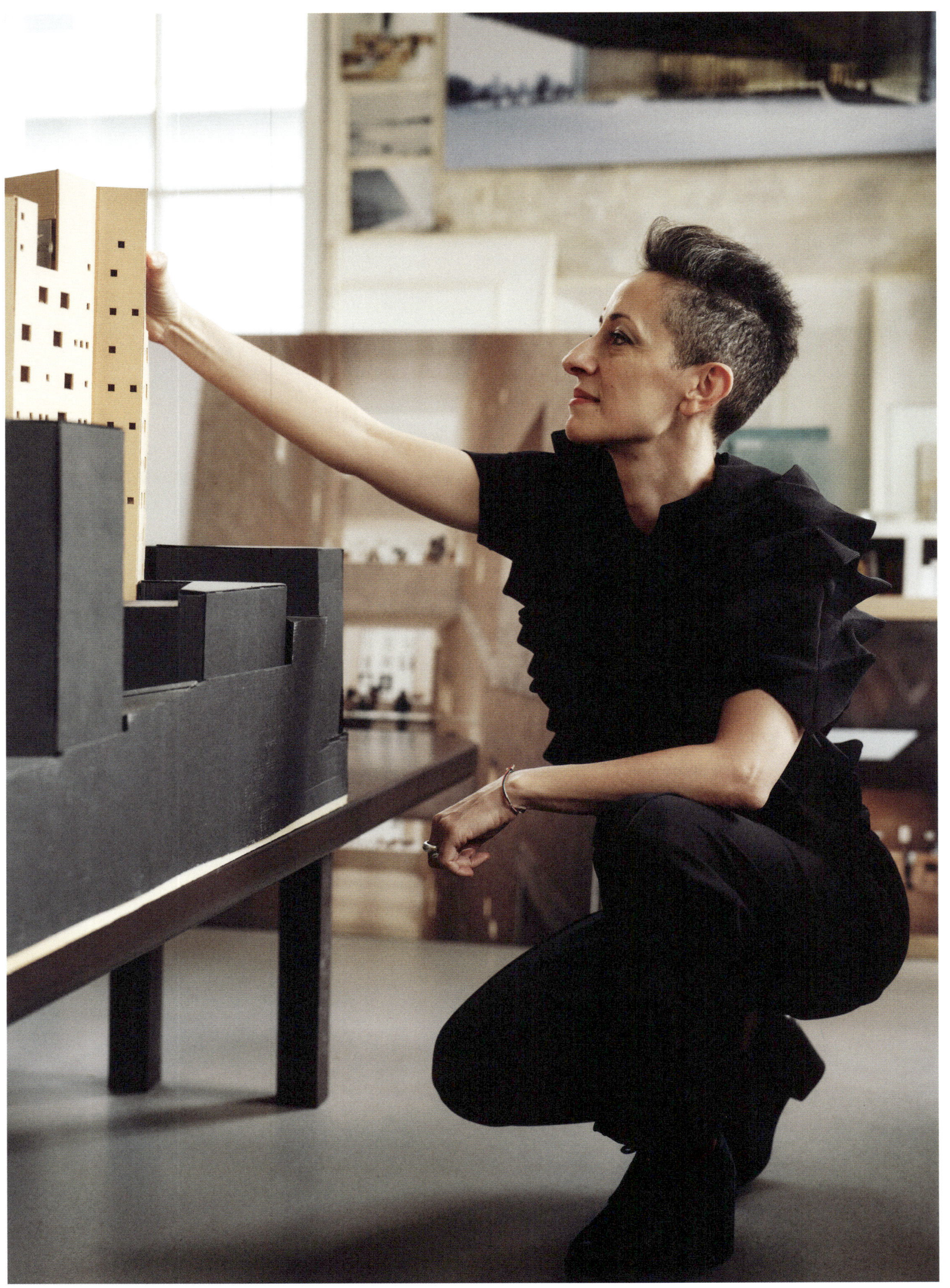

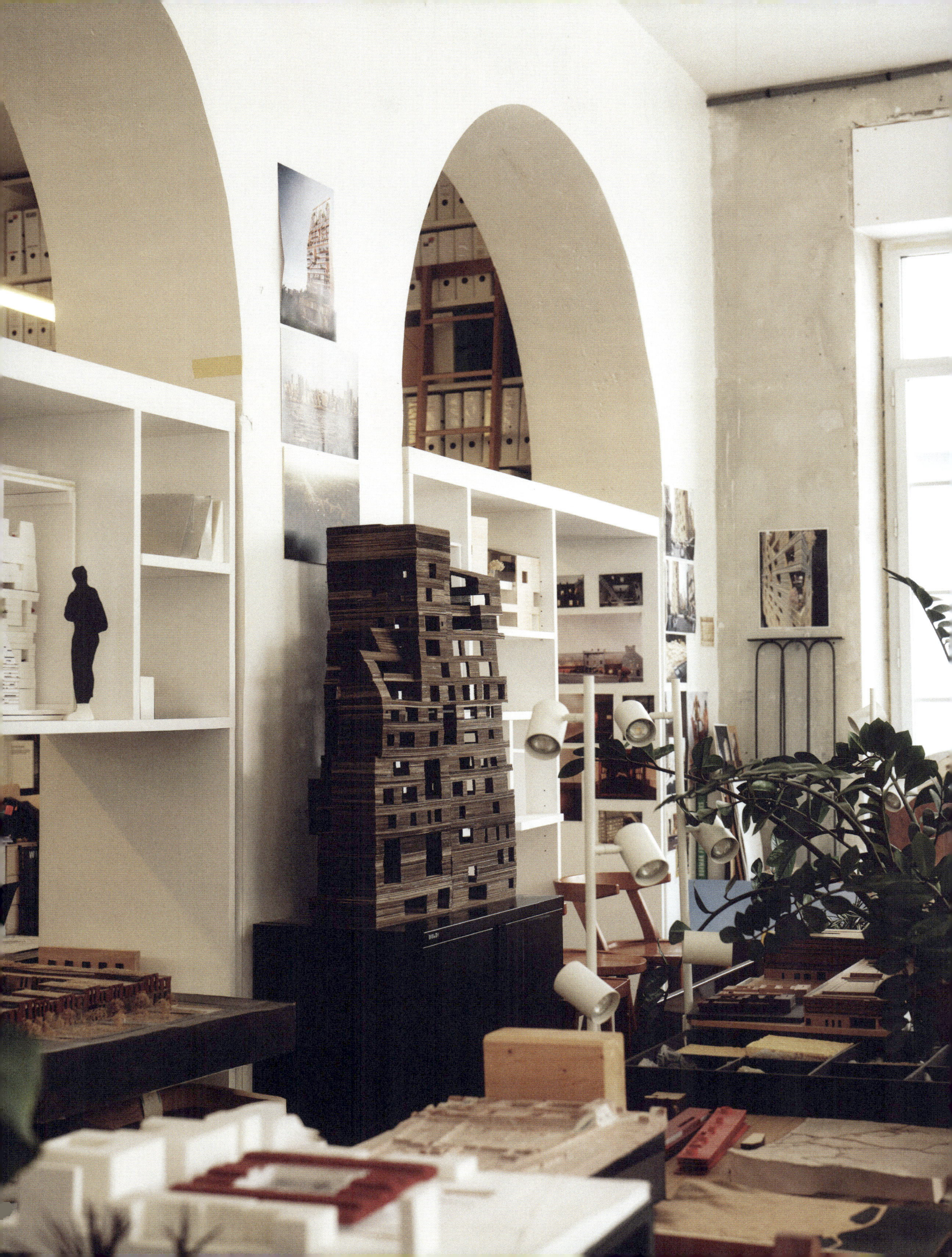

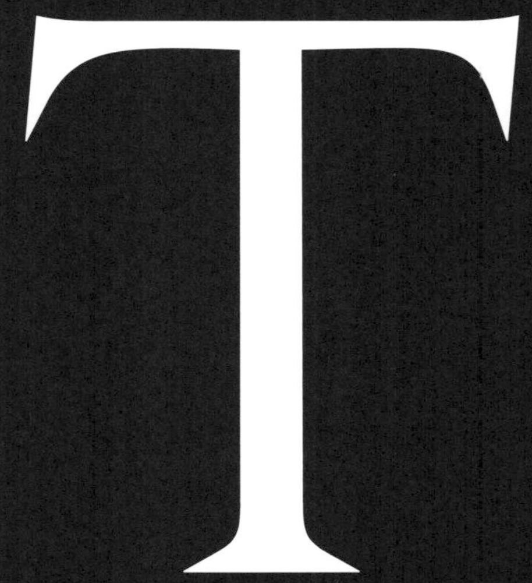

Words
Elle Hunt
Photos
Alicia Dubuis

T he OnePlus Photography Awards were established in 2021 with the goal of celebrating the art of smartphone photography. Open to everyone with a smartphone, rather than just OnePlus users, the awards seek to create a global platform for photography, highlighting the technical capabilities of the phones we carry with us and their role as creative tools. Here, we speak with two of this year's winners about the images that set them apart.

MUKUL MAHANT—GOD'S OWN MOUNTAIN
OnePlus Group, Silver Award, Night and Low Light Category
Using OnePlus 13

The Gonbo Rangjon peak in the Zanskar region of Ladakh, India, is sacred to the local Tibetan Buddhist communities and is known as "God's Own Mountain." Mukul Mahant traveled there from his home in Kullu in the neighboring state of Himachal Pradesh in April 2025 with the intention of shooting the mountain against the Milky Way. The resulting image was shot after midnight, on one of the darkest nights of the year, as temperatures dropped to about 15 degrees Fahrenheit.

EH: How did you feel when you found out you were a winner?

MM: I was not expecting it, to be honest. It's my first major honor. Before I got the email, I never called myself a photographer—I was just someone who liked taking pictures. Now, maybe that will change.

EH: How did you get started in photography?

MM: My father gave me a DSLR as a graduation gift in 2014. I worked with that for four or five years, so I knew the basics of how to expose pictures, shutter speed, aperture. Around 2019, I got my first phone with a nice camera [the OnePlus 6T]. Eventually I stopped using my DSLR, because my smartphone was a lot easier to carry, and it let me take more pictures and share them. Nowadays phones are up there with DSLRs, in terms of image quality. You don't have to spend thousands of dollars on a camera and different lenses; you can do pretty much everything with a nice phone.

EH: What are some of the challenges of shooting in the dark?

MM: As a photographer—or someone who just likes to take pictures—you need to first visualize the kind of frame you are looking for, especially for night photography. It's a different process compared to shooting during the day as you need to expose the image for longer. For the stars to appear, there needs to be minimal light from the surroundings and minimal air pollution. That's one of the challenges with astral photography: You end up in the middle of nowhere. Another factor is weather—if there is even a single cloud in the sky, the image won't be as clear.

EH: What was the process of taking your winning shot?

MM: I had been to this place in 2021, and had an idea that it would be good for the Night and Low Light category because there is no light pollution there. There are roads, and small tribal villages in the area, but they are far apart. And when I took this, there was no moon, so the maximum number of stars were visible. I brought a friend with me, because I did not want to be alone outside at night in the dark—it's a perfect habitat for snow leopards. We scouted a few possible locations and just after midnight, we went out. It was very cold, but I was prepared.

EH: What did you like about this image?

MM: I submitted 15 different pictures in the category, but this one is framed particularly nicely: The road leads the eye to the mountain, which is in the middle of the frame and acts like a bridge between the upper half (the Milky Way) and the lower half (the road).

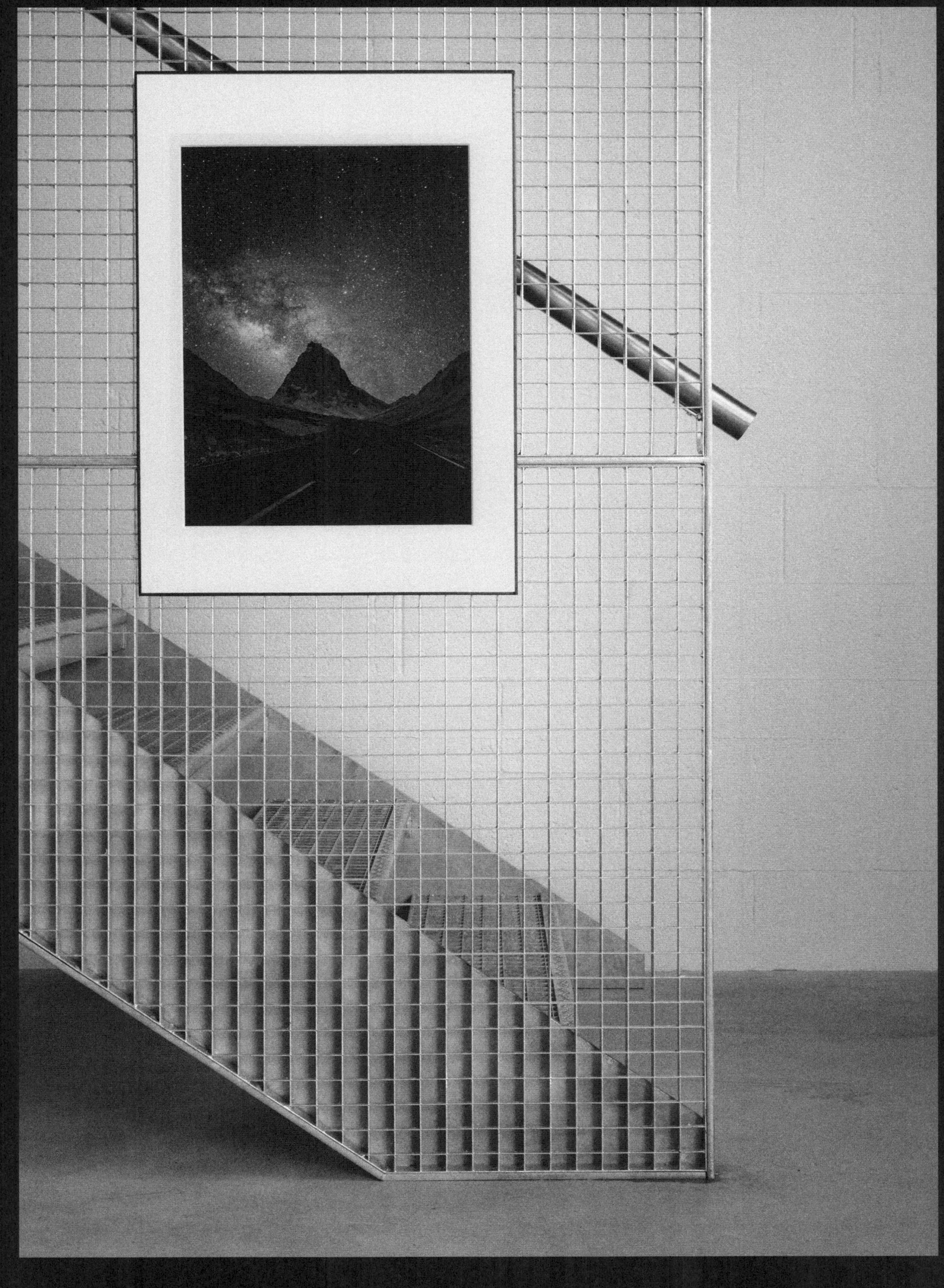

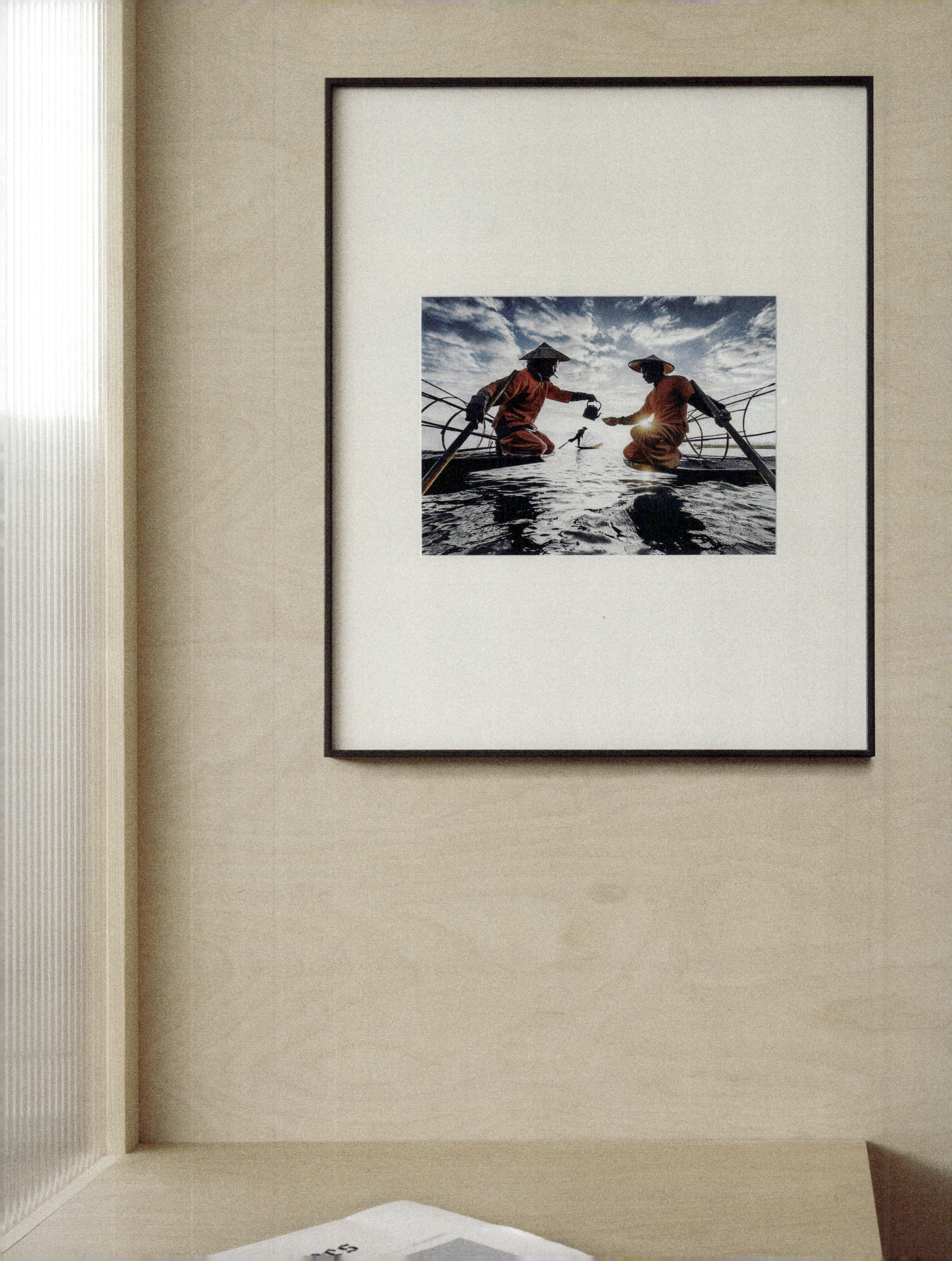

Myat Zaw Hein's winning image, *Traditional Life on Water*, shows two Intha fishermen dressed in traditional attire sharing tea at dawn on Myanmar's Inle Lake. It captures a peaceful moment of camaraderie before the day gets underway; behind them, another fisherman demonstrates the Intha people's world-renowned "leg-rowing" technique, which involves wrapping a leg around the oar to propel the boat along.

ELLE HUNT: When did you start taking photos?

MYAT ZAW HEIN: I started my photography journey in 2015. Since then, I've participated in many local and international photography competitions, and have been fortunate enough to win some awards. I currently use both a professional camera and a mobile phone in my practice.

EH: What is the story behind this photograph?

MZH: This photo was taken during a trip I took to Inle Lake, one of the most famous places in Myanmar, together with my friend and fellow photographer, Min Min Zaw, in January 2025. It took us a day to get there, and then we spent three days taking photographs. This photo was taken on the day we were due to return home. It had rained the night before, and in the early morning the sky was cloudy. I was worried about the weather, but we stuck to our plan and took a motorboat to the spot we had chosen on the lake to prepare. Fortunately, around 7 a.m. the clouds began to clear and the sun rose beautifully over the eastern mountains.

EH: What were the challenges of shooting on water?

MZH: We collaborated with the local Inle fishermen to bring my vision to life, creating two or three different compositions— it's particularly easy to do this with a phone, as it's more convenient to use. That's why I value mobile photography; there's no longer a need to invest in expensive cameras and lenses to achieve high-quality shots.

EH: What did you like about this composition in particular?

MZH: While shooting, I was focused on making the image reflect the beauty of Inle Lake and the traditions of the local people, and the culture of sharing in particular: One fisherman is sharing his tea with another, while a third approaches from afar, all under the glowing sun. I took a lot of photos on the trip, but this one is my favorite.

This story was created in partnership with OnePlus. Founded on the mantra "Never Settle," OnePlus creates exquisitely designed devices with premium build quality and high-performance hardware.

"I stopped using my DSLR, because my smartphone was a lot easier to carry."

HOME

Words
George Papam

ALEKOS FASSIANOS

Inside the artist's atelier on the Greek island of Kea.

Photos
Bill Stamatopoulos

TOUR

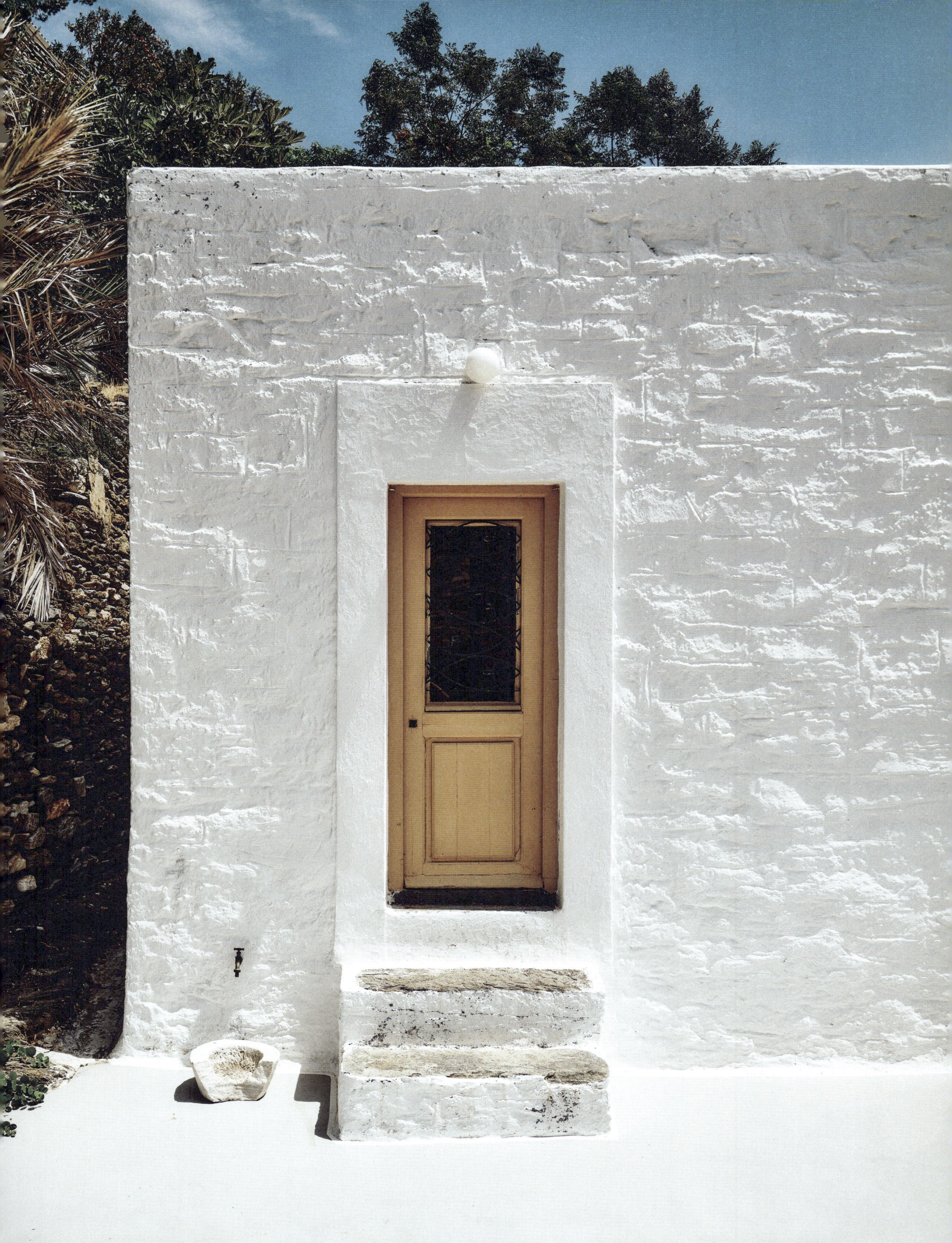

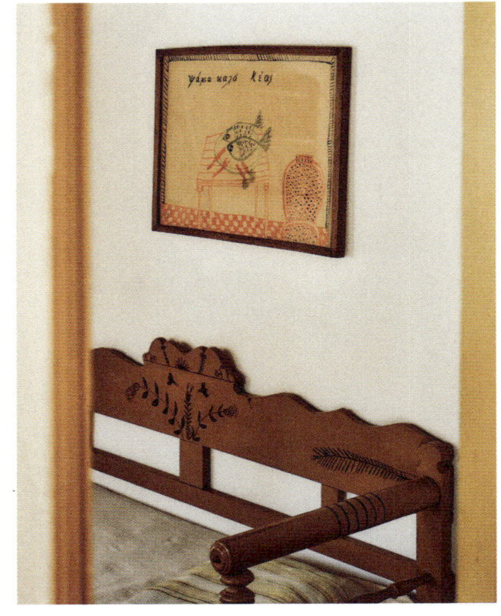

The island of Hydra was the established haven for writers and artists in 1960s Greece, but Fassianos did not appreciate the number of foreigners and intellectuals that were drawn to it. He preferred a quieter and more grounded place, away from the bustle of the art scene and, most importantly, somewhere with several accessible beaches where he could fish. He bought the house in 1967 and returned there every summer, taking welcome breaks from busy Athens and rainy Paris, until 2021, the year before he passed away. Every summer since, following the pattern of the artist's visits, the Fassianos estate has opened the studio to the public.

Two large fish on a plate, served on a table beside a single chair, seem to await a lone guest on a checkerboard tiled terrace. Drawn with playful watercolor strokes of red, green and blue, on a scrap of paper that the artist likely had to hand, the scene has a disarming simplicity. At the top, in the artist's handwriting, it reads: "Good fish of Kea." It welcomes you as you step over the threshold of Alekos Fassianos' house: A homage to the Greek island it sits on—and its fish—that captures the unpretentious spirit of the artist.

Perched high on the northern hillside of Kea's capital, Ioulida, the house was Fassianos' summer retreat and studio for over 50 years. The artist—who is celebrated in Greece for weaving folk traditions and the dreamlike quality of Greek mythology with the everyday—had studied painting and lithography in Athens and Paris, and was practicing between the two cities when he first visited the island in the mid-1960s. He was deeply impressed.

Kea, also known as Tzia, is the westernmost of the Cyclades islands in the Aegean Sea, and the one closest to Athens. To this day—and in contrast to many of the better-known islands nearby—Kea has not been overwhelmed by tourism and maintains some of its industrial identity—something that appealed to Fassianos at the time. Back then, the island sustained a lively farming sector and was home to tanneries and a large enamel homeware factory.

G oogle Maps is of little use as you approach the house through Ioulida's labyrinthine alleys but traces of the painter begin to appear along the way: One of his signature profiles carved in stone relief at the school's wall; a fading six-winged figure with Fassianos' characteristic brushstrokes on a green door; a dragon of black metal standing guard on the house's courtyard gate. Fassianos wished to be known as an artist of the people and shared his art with fellow villagers: When the priest asked for the six-winged icon, or when the butcher and a neighbor asked for a mural on their wall, Fassianos was glad to spend hours painting in the town's alleys. He befriended and worked alongside local craftsmen, lingered in conversation at the town's coffee shops and even persuaded some of his Athens friends, such as the painters Nikos Stefanou and Vassilis Sperantzas, to join him on the island. In short order, he formed a deep bond with Kea and its people.

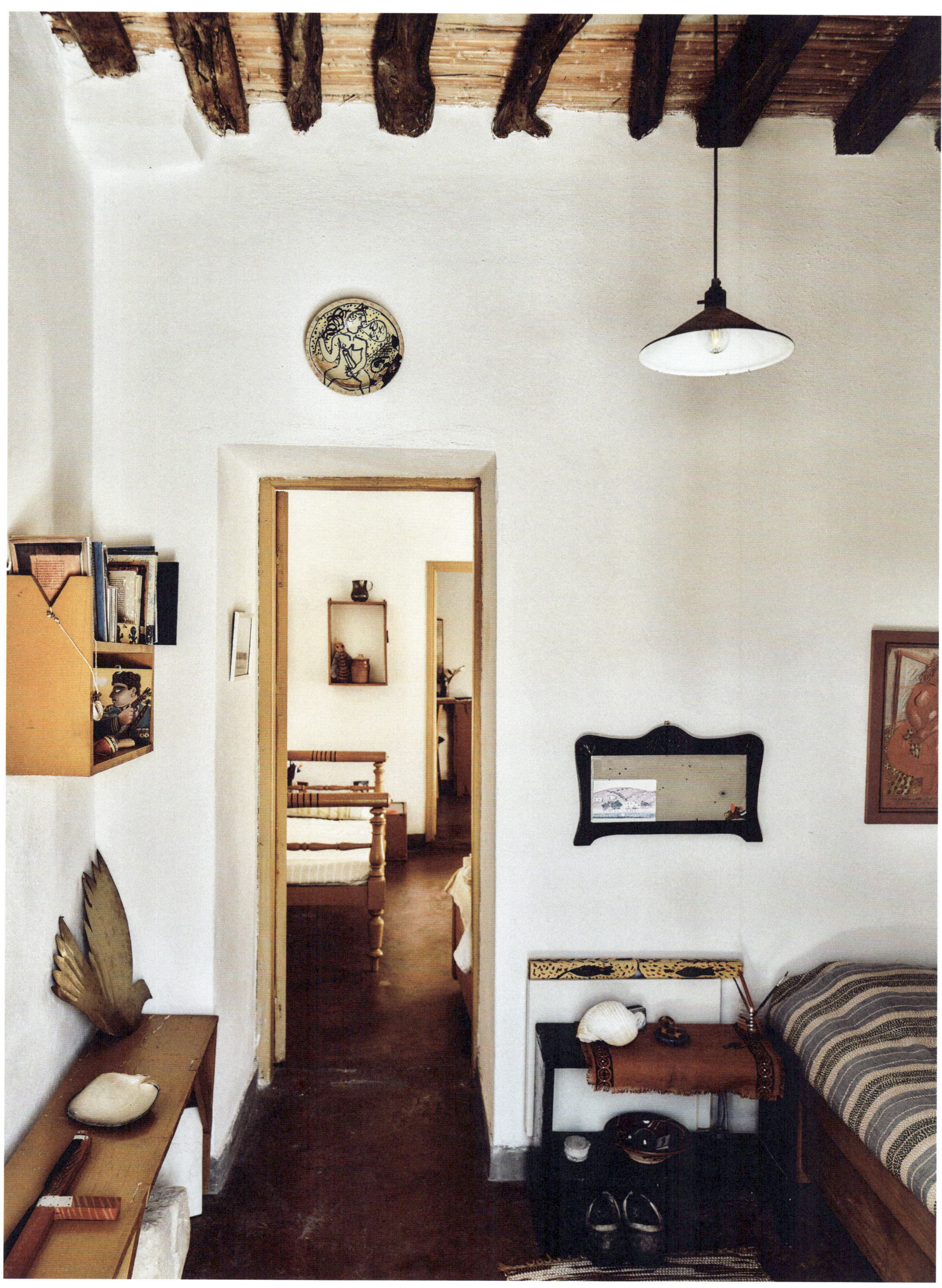

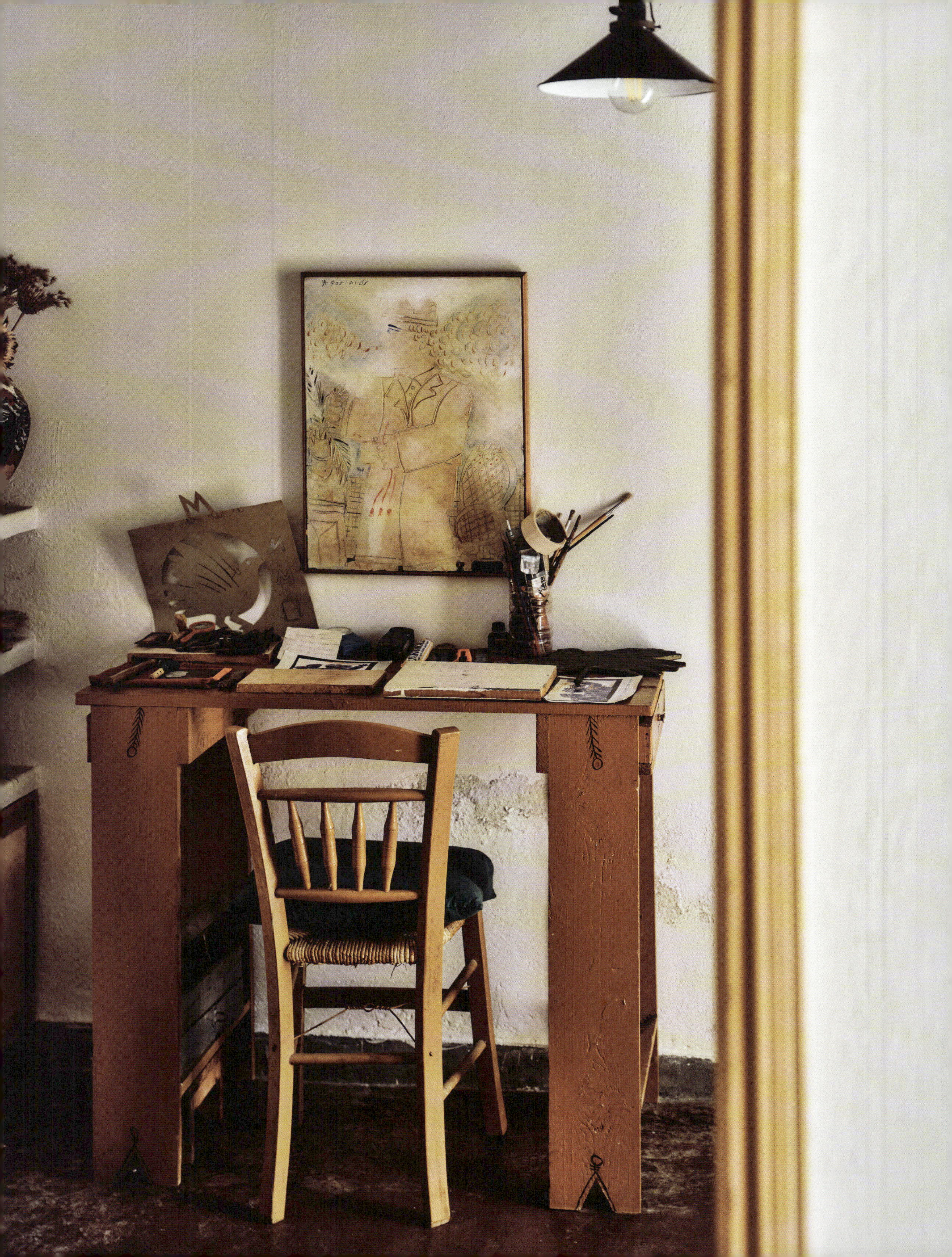

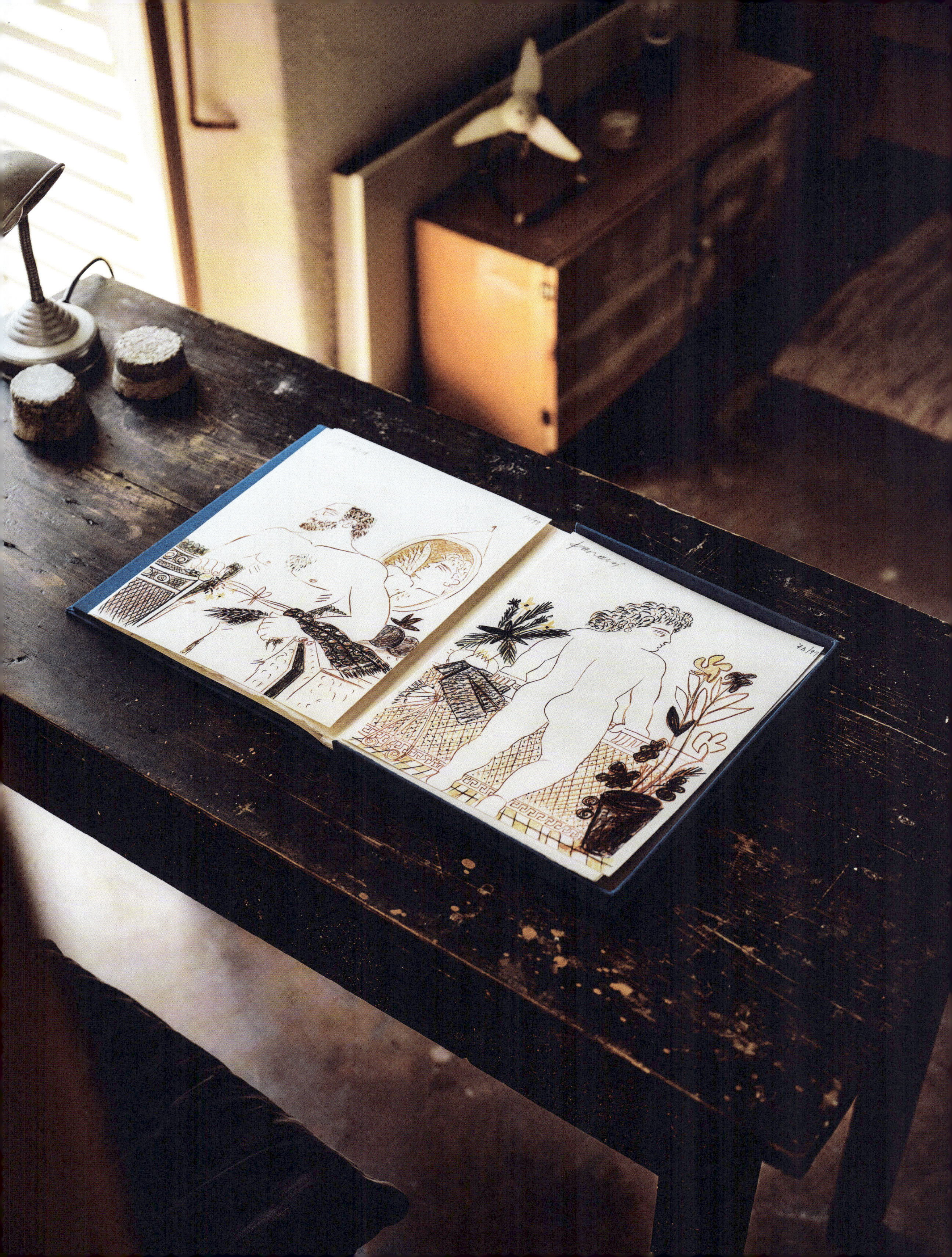

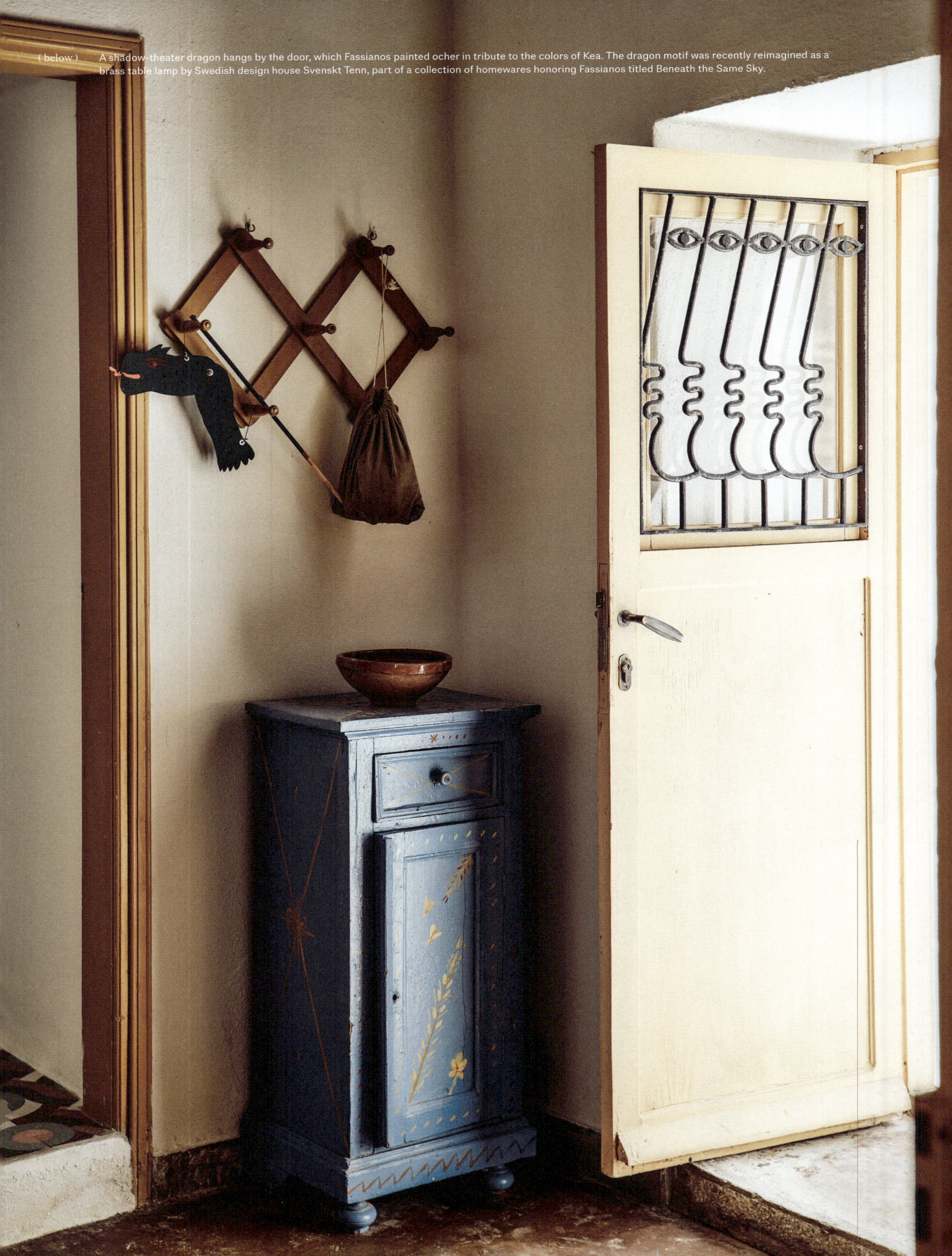

(below)   A shadow-theater dragon hangs by the door, which Fassianos painted ocher in tribute to the colors of Kea. The dragon motif was recently reimagined as a brass table lamp by Swedish design house Svenskt Tenn, part of a collection of homewares honoring Fassianos titled Beneath the Same Sky.

Although he soon acquired a second house in the coastal village of Ksyla for his fishing excursions, and later another property in Ioulida for his family, his main home on the island remained his first house and atelier. Viktoria Fassianou, the artist's daughter, has spent every summer on the island since early childhood and remembers how her father preferred to pass the nights alone, working in the house, even when his family was visiting.

The building, in its form and layout, is typical of the modest houses in Ioulida, which evolved from the forms of rural houses on the island. In the 19th and 20th centuries it was typical for Kean farmers to raise a modest dwelling in the main village, as a place to gather on Sundays and feast days—a kind of vacation home, though with the relationship between town and countryside inverted.

The entrance opens to a small living room that divides the house in two: On one side there is a bedroom and on the other a working space, which in turn opens to a small kitchen. None of the four rooms are large—between 50 and 100 square feet—but outside, the terraces more than double the footprint of the house and embed it in the network of levels, stairs and verandas that comprise the settlement of Ioulida. Facing south and west, they overlook Ioulida and the hills opposite, and allow the gaze to reach as far as the sea. Fassianos, who loved to paint on the ground, could often be seen out here, working on larger pieces.

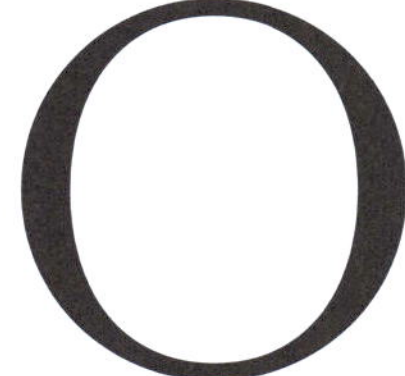

Over the decades, Fassianos kept interventions to a minimum, wanting to maintain the identity and simplicity of the house's architecture. He resisted the addition of roof tiles, a feature foreign to the island but adopted by many as a convenient substitute for the traditional flat roofs built of wood and earth. The matrix of branches and reed that still line the ceiling only add to the house's character. It was with equal fervor he searched for and applied traditional colors on doorframes and shutters, and he took care to maintain the original flooring.

His determination has meant that a remarkable example of Kea's traditional architecture has been preserved and yet, plain and unassuming, the house offers a quiet backdrop for the countless works and artifacts that populate it to this day. As Theodora Patiti, an artist from Kea who works for the Fassianos estate, explains, nothing in the house was curated to create a particular narrative after his death. Instead, most items have remained exactly where Fassianos left them: the painted desk, where he drew; the notes to friends, scrawled on planks because the house had no telephone line—acts of fidelity more than conservation.

Other than a few items made by local friends or guests—such as a plate drawn and gifted to Fassianos by Yannis Tsarouchis, or some drawings by the local folk artist Delapitsas—everything that can be seen today was either created by Fassianos or carries, in some way, his presence. The artist's paintings can be found on nearly every wall, but it is the small things that catch the eye: everyday objects, toys, improvised creations, various hand-decorated pieces. The sofa, the desk, the night table and the cupboards have all been adorned with flower motifs and fish; vases and ceramics are embellished with the faces with flowing hair that he was known for. A self-made speargun lies next to a makeshift toy windmill improvised from cans, and shadow-theater dragons of varying sizes and materials are hung here and there.

" Most items have remained exactly where Fassianos left them."

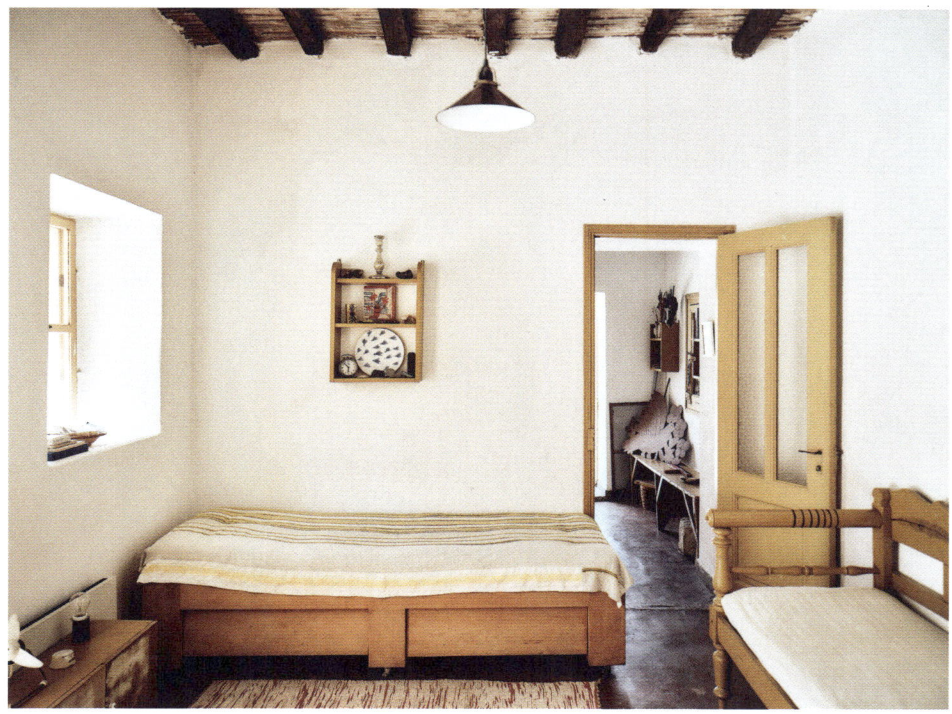

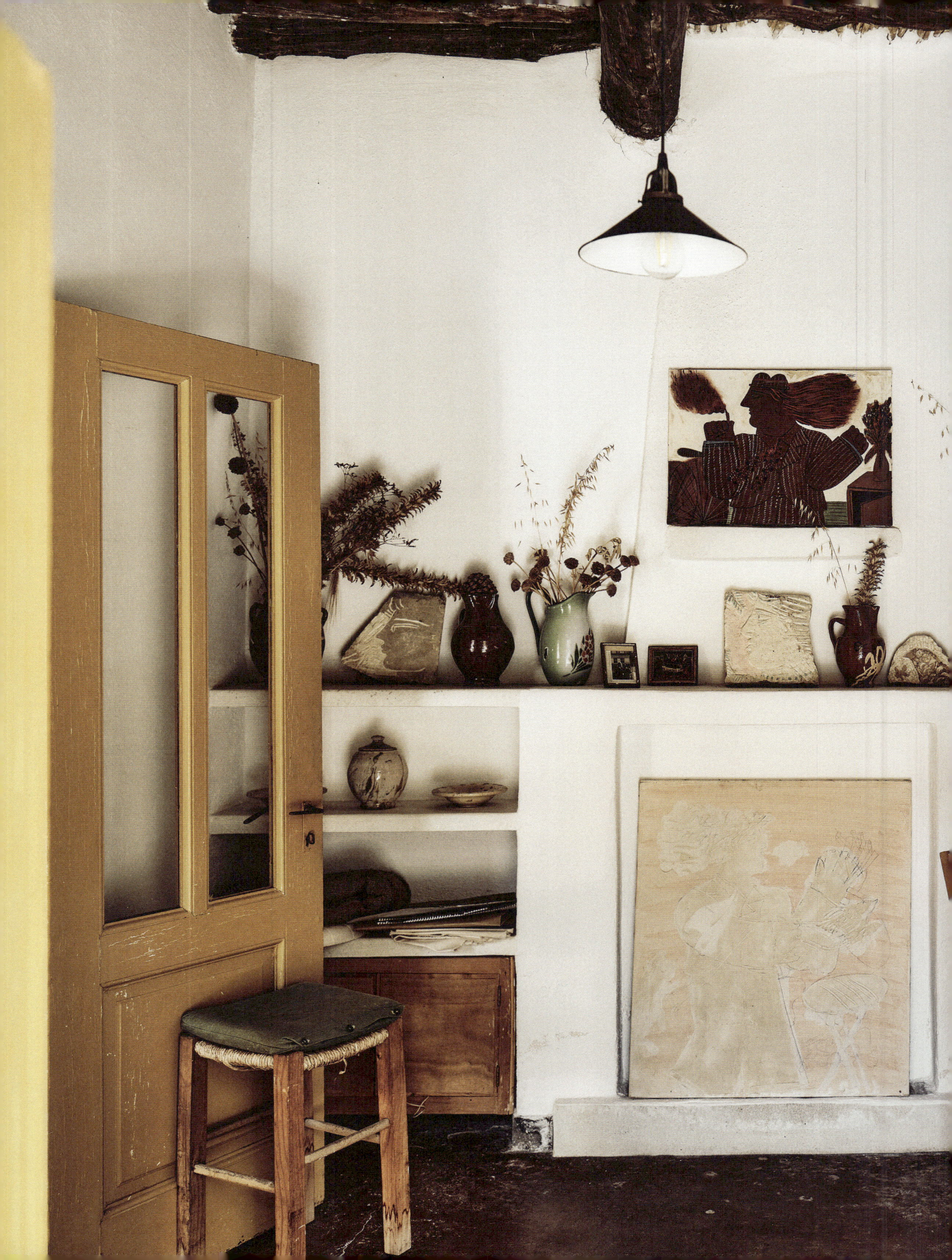

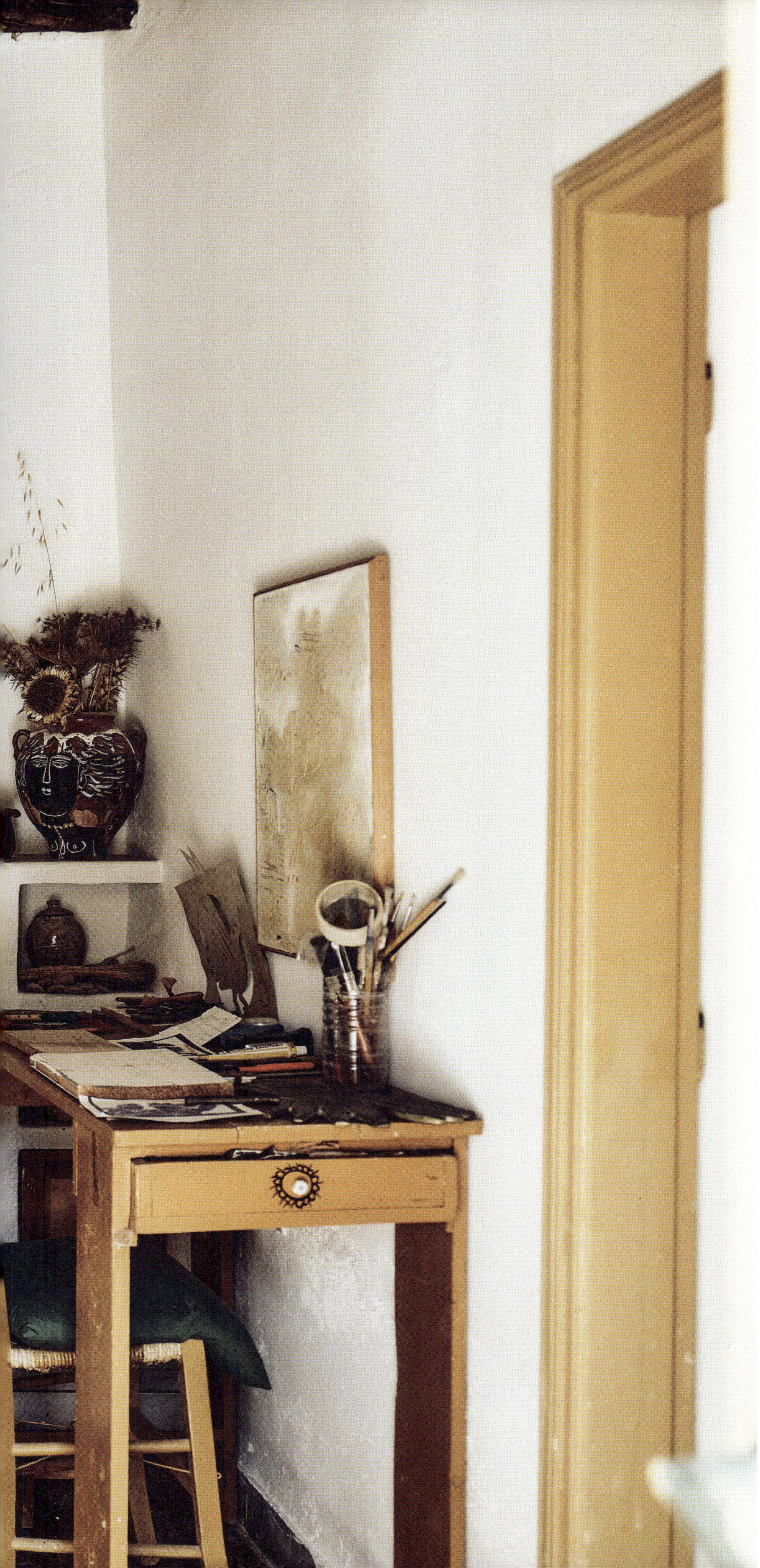

This domestic practice was central to Fassianos' conception of both art and life. In a 2002 interview, recalling the ascetic room where the poet Odysseas Elytis once wrote, Fassianos summarized his view plainly: "The greatest wealth is the little room, your desk, your bed, the objects you have behind and in front of you. And so I paint the little nightstand beside my bed; my chair; the things I know. And the greatest wealth is this: To create your world, to enclose yourself around it, and then to radiate outwards."

" The greatest wealth is this: To create your world."

Tellingly, many of the small works clustered around the rooms are studies of Kea itself: paintings of the houses in Ioulida, or of the island's landscape and sea— subjects he would later repeat in many of his better-known works.[1] But there are also countless meticulous observations of the island's minute nature: its birds, bugs and insects, its fish, fruits and herbs. He even gathered these drawings into three books dedicated to the island: *The Small Things of Kea*, *The Antiquities of Kea* and *The Fish of Kea*. These drawings and artifacts, crafted with curiosity and affection, seem to be trying to bring all of Kea into the house and, conversely, to make the house a part of Kea.

(1) Perhaps one of Fassianos' best-known, if not most-seen, works can be found at Metaxourgio Station on the Athens Metro. In 2000, he was invited to paint two large-scale murals, which he titled *The Myth of My Neighborhood*. One depicts an outdoor cinema, a passing cyclist and a folk singer; the other shows a fruit market, with a grocer weighing vegetables on a scale.

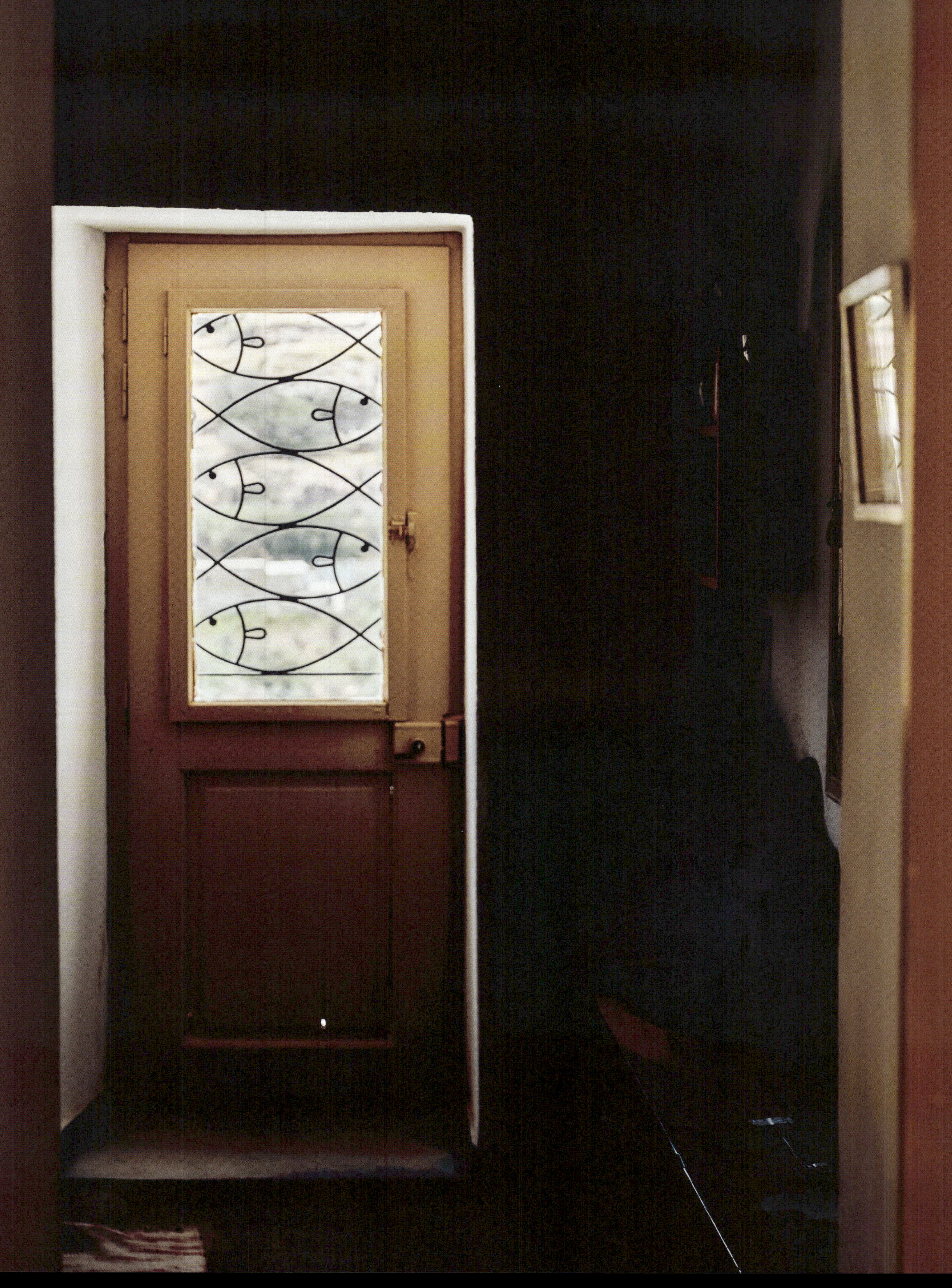

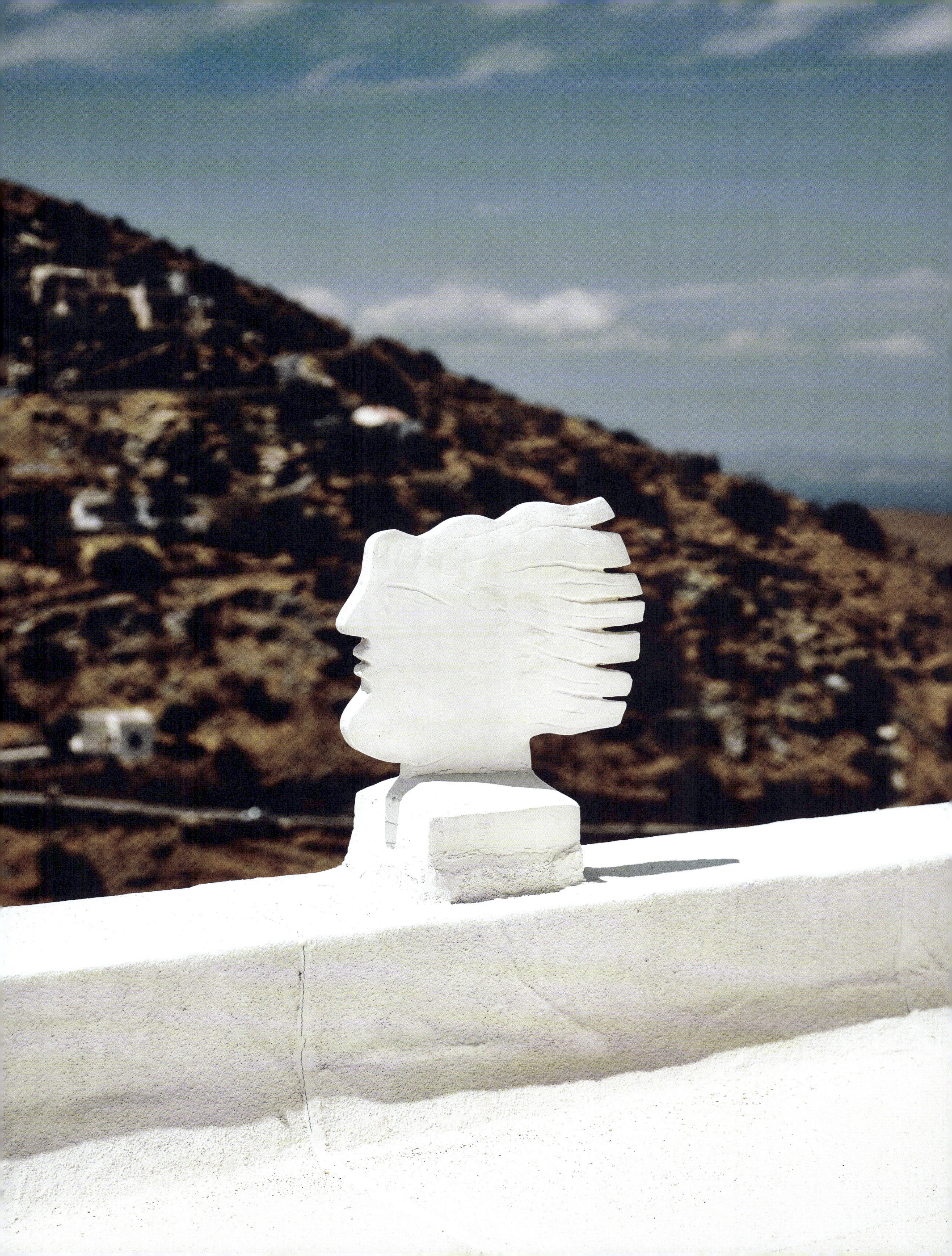

THE ANXIETIES OF THE ULTRA-RICH

How do you start closing the wealth gap? Convince the rich to do it themselves.

Words
Hettie O'Brien

Earlier this year, 47,000 Norwegians won the lottery. Many won the equivalent of hundreds of thousands of dollars; some even became millionaires. The good news had been delivered by a text message from the state-owned gambling operator, Norsk Tipping. Three days later, it sent another message: The company had made a mistake, mangling the currency conversion from kroner to euros, and most were only a few dollars richer. Many spoke to the media about their excitement and subsequent disappointment. For Lise, who had spent the time thinking about how she was going to spend $185,000, "it was a very fun minute."

Lise had found herself playing a real—if short-lived—version of a game that almost everyone has played at some point: If you won the lottery, what would you do with the money? Most answers tend to be quite similar. A new house for yourself, or your parents. An upgrade of your old car. That piece of furniture you always wanted but couldn't justify buying. If you won millions, perhaps you'd quit work and tell your boss what you really thought of them, or take all your friends to a villa in the South of France. You might even buy the villa.

Once you got used to being rich, however, the nicest thing would probably be the ability to detach yourself from ordinary problems. Everything on your to-do list can be made more bearable with money: You can either pay someone to make a situation go away, or upgrade to a better version of it. Activities like cooking, DIY and even some aspects of parenting could all be made to disappear. But would this make you happy? After all, if you could pay someone to fulfill each of your needs, there would be no reason to learn how to fulfill those needs yourself, and this, in turn, could leave you feeling alienated and useless. You might come to miss the satisfaction of completing mundane tasks.

Such was the experience of Iris Brilliant, who grew up in the San Francisco Bay Area, where her father founded and later sold a tech company, allowing her family to enter what she describes as "affluent culture." Although they didn't go skiing, have a cabin on Lake Tahoe or "fly private," Brilliant never doubted that her family was "comfortable." They socialized with other tech founders (her father was friends with Apple cofounder Steve Jobs), her parents had staff and she didn't need an after-school job. "I never even had to make my own bed," she says.

You would be forgiven for envying her situation but Brilliant's wealth also created a sense of failure. "It made me feel kind of weak and stupid," she explains. Cordoning yourself off in a bubble of privilege, she found, has the effect of depriving you of the sense of achievement and the unpredictable, often life-changing encounters you get by having to do something yourself. The mechanic at the repair shop could turn out to be a soulmate, for example, or at least the source of an interesting conversation. It's telling that poet Philip Larkin likened having money to the isolating experience of looking at a town from behind a window: "It is intensely sad."

THE RICHER TESE PEOPLE WERE, THE LESS GENEROUS TEY BECAME.

When Brilliant arrived at college, she found that she had few of her roommates' life skills. "All I really knew how to do was write a five-paragraph essay, how to get really good grades and how to do multiple-choice tests well," she says. "But I didn't understand how the world worked." The experience made her reflect on her wealth and privilege, and she resolved to give much of her inheritance away. After college, she joined Resource Generation, a charity that works with rich young Americans. Her clients included families with more than a million dollars in assets; Brilliant's job was to persuade them to give their wealth to charities and nonprofits, tackling inequality one rich family at a time.

Brilliant found that most families were keen to talk about philanthropy, but she noticed something strange: The richer these people were, the less generous they became, and the more inclined they were to hoard their wealth, as though they were scared it might one day disappear. She believes this is partly due to "lifestyle creep." Once a person gets used to certain luxuries—having a driver, flying first class, maintaining a yacht—it becomes more difficult to let these luxuries go, and they end up spending more to sustain them. Such accretive entitlement is neatly exemplified by the indignant reaction of Roman Roy, the petulant son of the patriarch in the HBO drama *Succession*, when the new owner of his father's company attempts to take away his private jets. "The PJs? No."

Money can also have a numbing effect on a person's sense of gratification, even if they do manage to meet their ever-more-demanding needs. Sooner or later, acquiring expensive things becomes a substitute for enjoying those things, as there is always someone with a bigger house or fancier jet to compare yourself to. Rachel Sherman, a sociologist at the New School for Social Research, spent eight years interviewing high-net-worth couples in New York, and found that many of them were "upward-oriented," comparing themselves to those who had more money, not less. "It is easy to be fascinated by the details of my interviewees' lifestyles," Sherman later wrote in her 2017 book, *Uneasy Street: The Anxieties of Affluence*. Yet she found that these lifestyles also became deadeningly familiar: expensive art, Carrara marble countertops, multiple properties that were being continually renovated, children at private schools—if anything, their similarities made them downright dull.

Indeed, extreme wealth—and the tendency to insulate yourself from the rest of society—often results in a more boring existence. The world is full of interesting people, people so funny that they make your sides ache; people who live wild, creative lives, or have a brilliant way of telling stories. Yet those with deep pockets tend to only socialize with other, similarly wealthy people, who, relatively speaking, form a rather limited circle. Perhaps this is down to a fear of feeling inauthentic. A person who is invited to participate because of their money rather than their talent or personality can seem like a slightly tragic interloper.[1] Lauren Sánchez Bezos may have been on the (digital) cover of *Vogue*, but everyone knows it was because her husband is a billionaire (the Amazon founder Jeff Bezos). But if most of the people at your party are multimillionaires, you never have to wonder if they only want you around because of your wealth.

Such isolation also does funny things to a person's psychology. Sherman discovered that rich people who socialized mostly with other rich people often viewed themselves not as wealthy, but as middle class. And it is not hard to imagine how such upward-oriented people might cease thinking about "downward" people; how, as they pull further away from the rest of society, they would give up on the idea of owing anything to that society, and on the idea of society itself.

Brilliant is among a handful of people who are trying to tempt the rich back down to earth. She founded her own coaching business in 2018 and now works with a handful of exceptionally wealthy families, encouraging them to forge new relationships with money, and ultimately to give far more of it away. She's not interested in vanity philanthropy of the type that produces endless reports speculating on the probable causes of poverty, or new charities and foundations that bear their owners' names. Instead, she prompts her clients to seek out existing organizations with a track record of working within communities.

Gaining control of your wealth can be a challenge. Susanna Penfield, the head of relationships at Chosen Family Office, a financial advisory group that encourages the wealthy to redistribute their money, inherited a million dollars in a trust fund at the age of 21. She was, by then, an activist working on racial and climate justice, and wanted to give her money to causes she cared about. "I quickly learned that trust funds are not set up to serve the beneficiary, but rather the trustee," she says. The trust had the final say, and rejected her proposals because they threatened its bottom line. She petitioned her family members to dissolve the trust. Finally, after four years, they agreed.

The rich own most of the world's wealth—the top 10% own more than 75%—and influencing their decision-making is fast becoming a global necessity. For people like Brilliant, convincing the affluent that lots of money makes a person miserable is not just about helping them "step off the gilded throne and come back to people, come back to reality, come back to the world," but a vital step to solving this chronic and ever-growing inequality: "Even if it's hard at first, it's really good for the soul."

---

(1)   Clay Cockrell, a therapist to the ultra-rich, believes that the isolation of the 1% stems partly from an ingrained suspicion of others. "I hear this from my clients all the time," he told *The Guardian* in 2021: "'What do they want from me?' or 'How are they going to manipulate me?'"

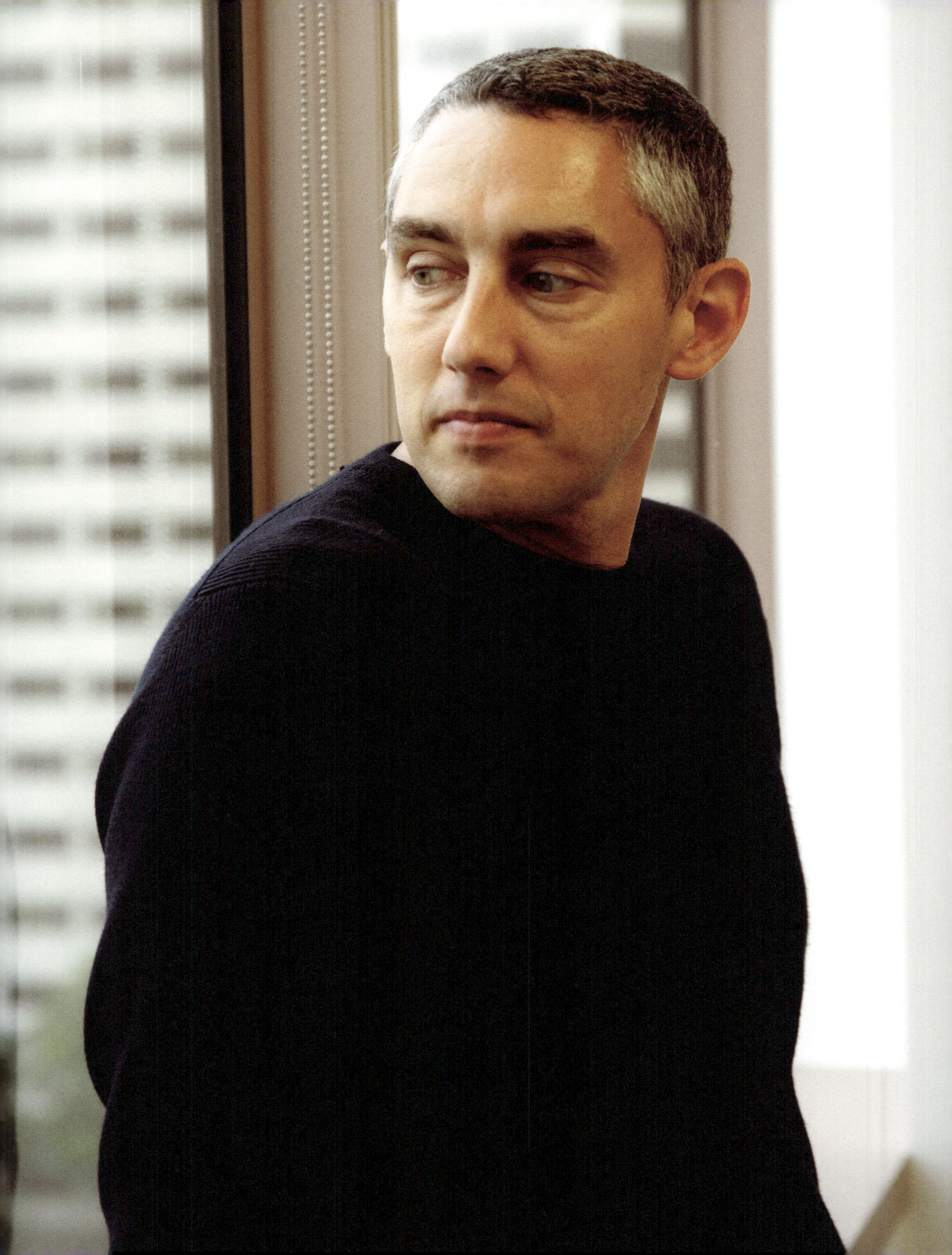

ELIE HASSENFELD

Words
Elle Hunt

Photos
Julien Sage

ELLE HUNT: You founded GiveWell after trying and failing to get information from charities about how they spent donations. What did you want to find out?

ELIE HASSENFELD: It was just really hard to get good answers. I think this has changed now, but back then, I could call up an organization working on water and they would say "$20 provides a child with water for life." I'd be like, "That sounds amazing—how do you know? What data do you collect? If you dig wells, do you go back a few years later and check if they're still there?" And at that point, they'd just shut down. They didn't have answers to those questions, and I think the reason was donors weren't asking them. But without those answers, how can you know that your money's doing a lot of good?

ELLE: How does GiveWell evaluate charities for cost-effectiveness?

ELIE: Our focus is really on identifying the organizations or programs that are having the very best impact per dollar. Organizations have to jump through a lot of hoops at the early stages, and those that are wasteful or inefficient aren't going to even pass our first filter. We rely on research from global health and development researchers who are not tied to any charitable organization, and who are looking at what programs reduce malaria, or improve water quality, or increase incomes. That becomes a building block in our analysis: What's the evidence that this program is effective?

Then it's about getting data from the charities: All right, you're delivering childhood immunizations, but what's your monitoring? We're looking for organizations that are ready and willing to be very transparent, who have bought into the idea that being open and truthful is in their interests.

Back in 2006, Elie Hassenfeld was 25 years old, a recent college graduate and working in finance. Conscious of his good fortune, he and a few friends decided to give some of their earnings to charity, but when they started looking into potential causes, they discovered that the process was surprisingly opaque. "It was very hard to get good information about what organizations do, and how well it works," he says. "There's a lot of marketing, a lot of claims—but very little evidence."

Hassenfeld and Holden Karnofsky, a friend and colleague, soon became "obsessed" with how to ensure their donations made the greatest possible impact. In 2007, having seen how little information charities disclosed, the pair decided to found a nonprofit charity evaluator. Since then, GiveWell has researched, evaluated and recommended charities to "help donors decide where to give;" it also receives donations to its own giving funds, which are allocated to specific funding opportunities at vetted charities that have been assessed as high impact.

"The idea was to create something that could serve donors like us—people who had a little extra money, who wanted to give and be confident that the places they were giving to were doing a lot of good," Hassenfeld says.

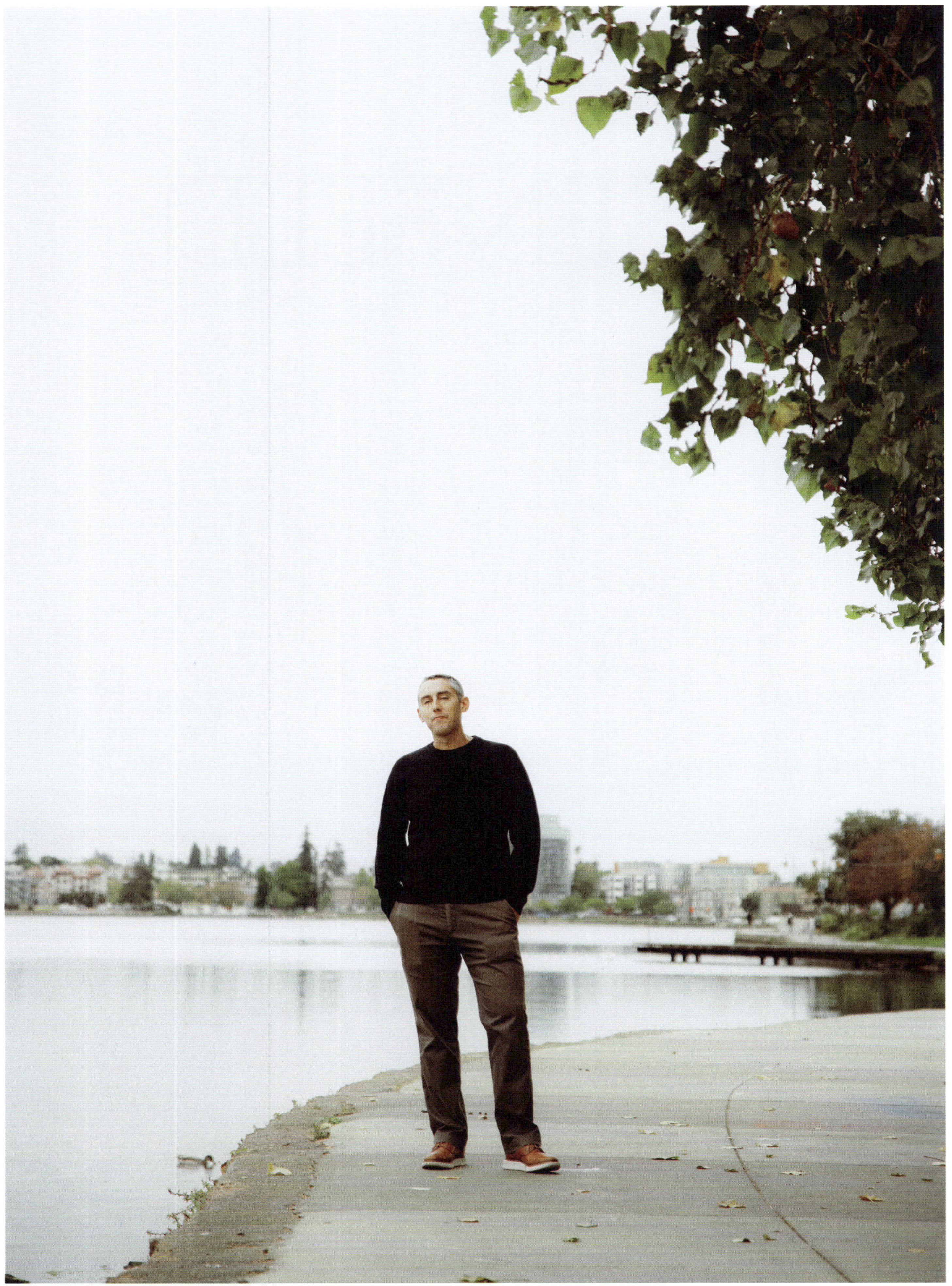

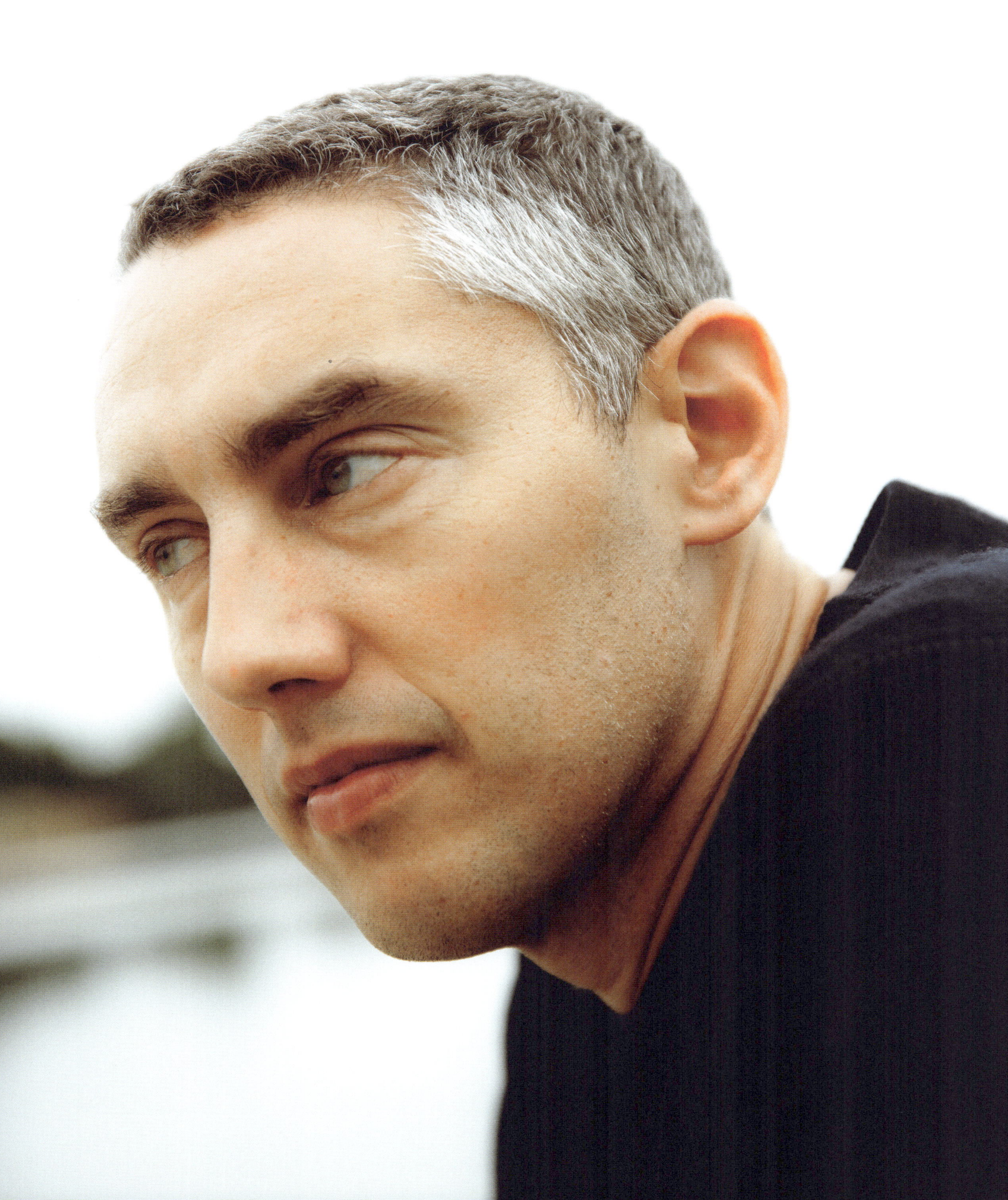

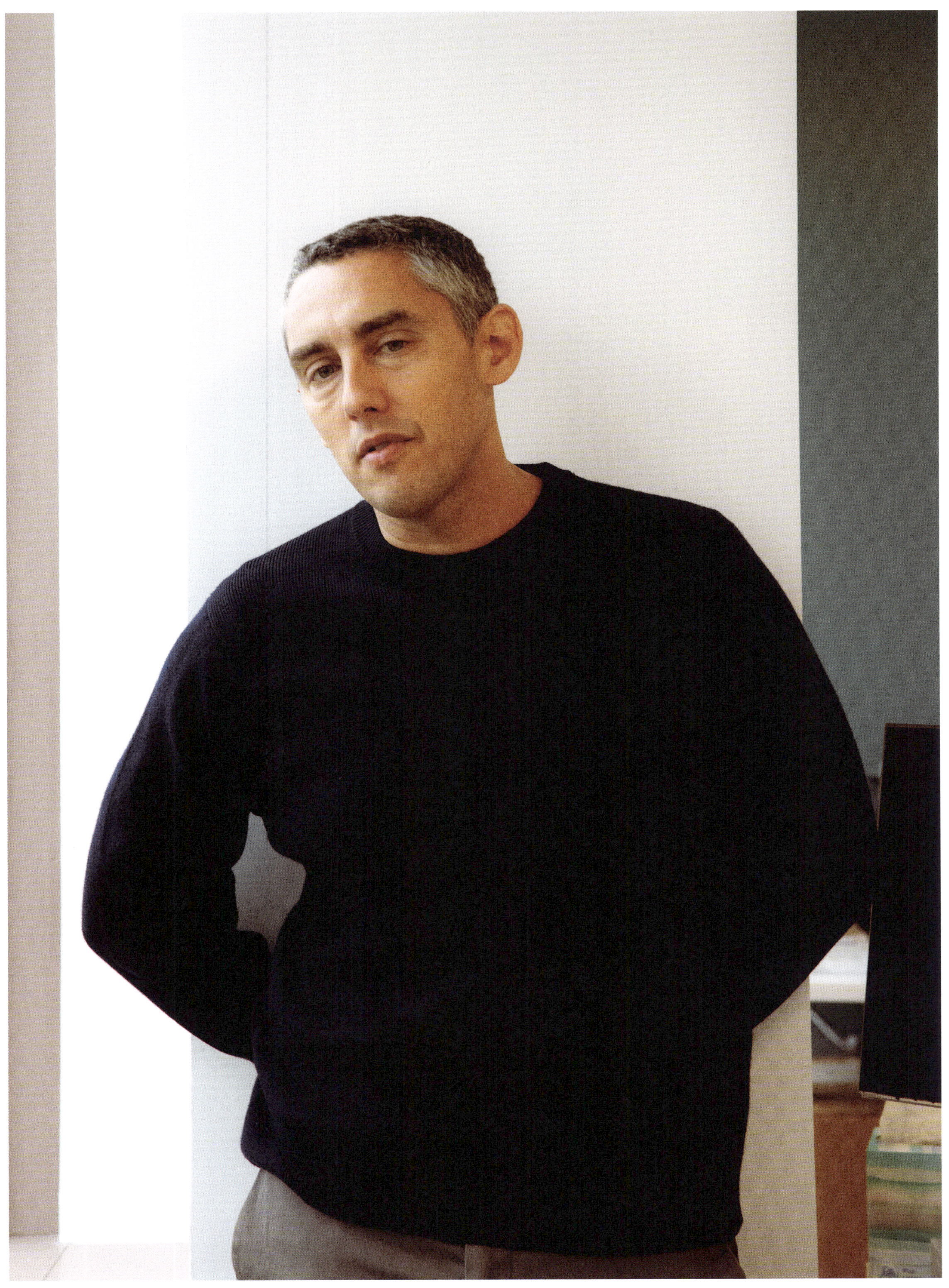

ELLE: Many people think of giving to charities in moral or emotional terms, not financial ones. Has that been a check on how much good charities can achieve?

ELIE: The core message—that charitable dollars can do a huge amount of good—is correct. Many living in high-income countries truly have so much more wealth and resources than people in low-income countries. But what needs to be added onto that message is that it's really hard to do a lot of good, and you need to apply a serious level of analysis and diligence to do so.

What is bad about many of the slogans used by charities to get people to donate is that they gloss over how hard it is to know that you're actually achieving the greatest impacts possible. For example, we provide a lot of funding to programs that work on malaria. One very basic question is how many people die from malaria in a given location, in a given year, but there's not a straightforward answer, because we don't have great data. That's just one of 20 or 30 things you need to know to be able to say "X dollars has X impact."

ELLE: Are we obliged as donors to ensure that our contributions make the biggest possible impact?

ELIE: All things being equal, I would say it's always better to have more impact than less—if it costs one organization $100,000 to save a single life, I'd rather give that to another organization that will use it to save 20 lives. But things are not always equal—there could be a case where it's really hard to measure the effect of giving, but the potential impact is big.

I certainly don't think that just having a measurable quantity is sufficient, but it can be helpful to check what you're being told is actually represented in some data. We're very guided by quantification, and I think that's appropriate when trying to help people who live thousands of miles away, in a very different context. If we can collect information rigorously, at least that is a check on our own assumptions about what works.

ELLE: What's one charity you want to single out for setting the standard?

ELIE: One of our top-rated charities is Malaria Consortium, which distributes preventative malaria medication to children under five across Africa.[1] This program has an immense body of evidence behind it, with randomized control trials showing that when you distribute this medicine and kids take it, it reduces malaria cases by about 50%. Lives are saved even with smaller amounts: One cycle of preventative treatment costs $7, so $70 is protecting 10 children from malaria. We've been recommending them for nearly 10 years, because the evidence is strong; we've seen their program on the ground and they provide really high-quality data.

ELLE: If you had to choose, would you rather have more people giving smaller amounts, or higher earners giving more?

ELIE: If push came to shove, I would choose to have more money than less money, but I would rather it came from a greater number of people. Having more people giving is good for two reasons. One, it means a more stable donor base, which is critical for organizations. But it also helps to build community around the idea of effective giving. I wish people talked about charitable giving more, and even about how much they give. It's not really socially acceptable at the moment, but I think it would be helpful if people saw what others were doing.

Sitting where we do, it's easy to look at the billionaires and the uber-wealthy and say "They should take care of all that—they're rich, I'm not," but in many ways, you're much closer to the billionaires than you are to a subsistence farmer in Malawi who has to go a couple of days without meals because the rains were not good this year. When I'm there, it makes me feel very wealthy to know that with $7, I can provide this preventative malaria medication, and with $20 to another organization, I can get an additional child immunized— all these things are valuable, even for small amounts of money.

" How can you know that your money's doing a lot of good?"

(1) Malaria kills about 600,000 people every year, nearly 75% of whom are children under five. In addition to the seasonal malaria chemoprevention (SMC) program recommended by GiveWell, which provides children with antimalarial drugs, Malaria Consortium also supplies insecticide-treated nets and trains healthcare workers.

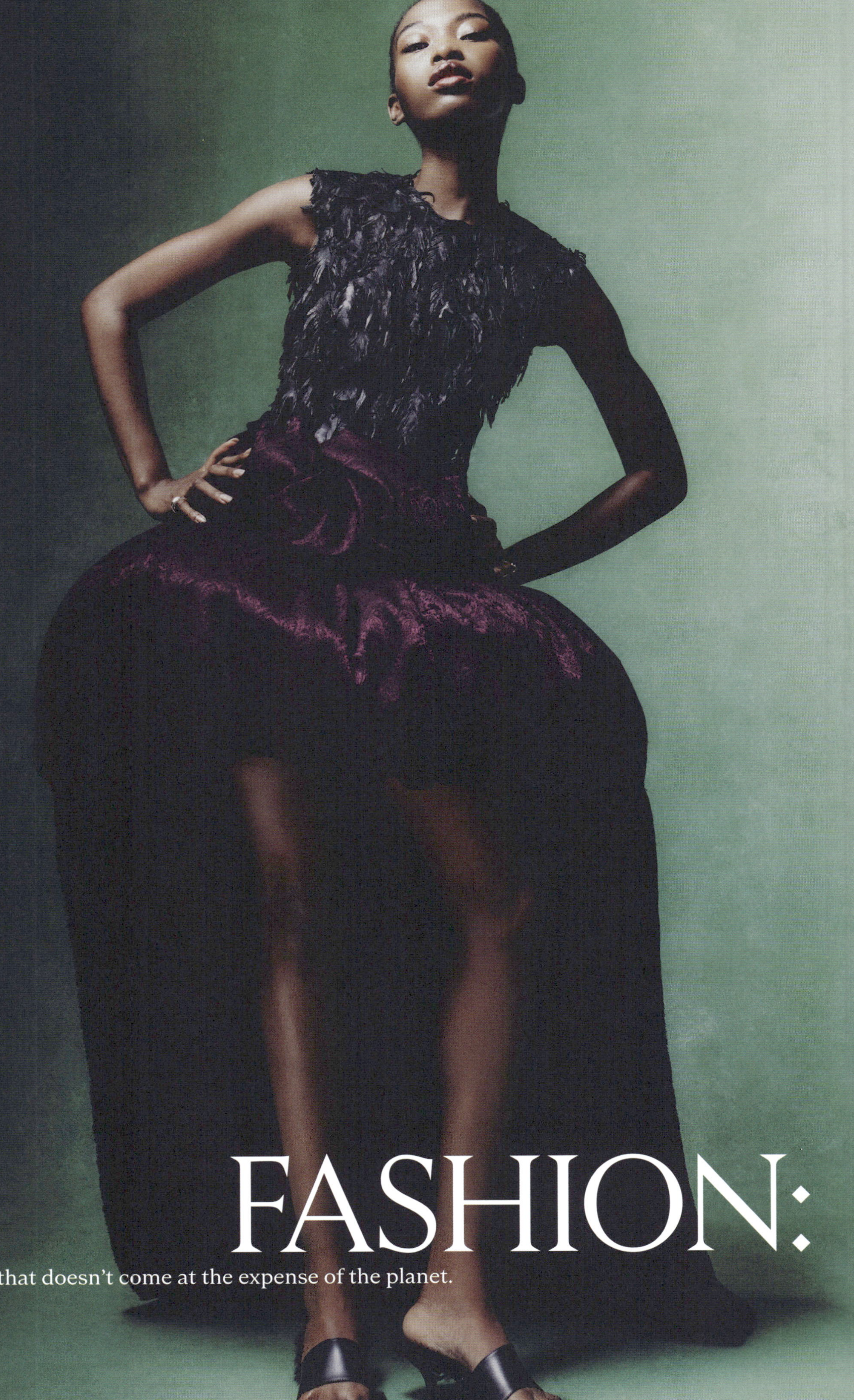

FASHION:

Eveningwear that doesn't come at the expense of the planet.

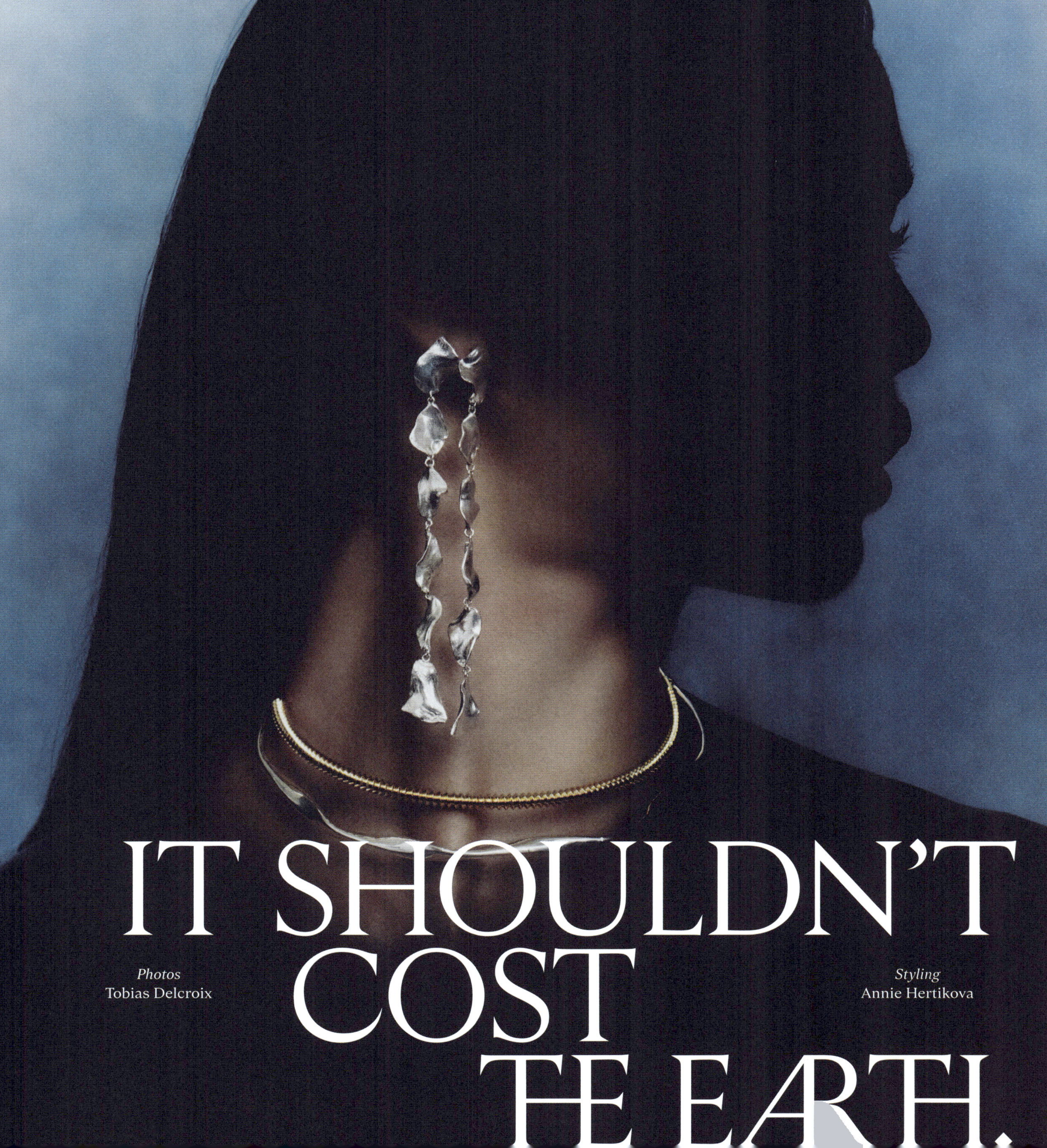

Photos
Tobias Delcroix

Styling
Annie Hertikova

IT SHOULDN'T
COST
TE EARTH.

(below)   Chizoba wears a dress by TALLER MARMO and coats by KASSL EDITIONS and RÓHE. KASSL EDITIONS are
            B Corp certified, meaning they meet rigorous social and environmental performance standards.
(opposite) Elysia wears a dress by PHOEBE SCOT and earrings by TOM WOOD. The dress is made from shredded denim and recycled paper.
(previous   Chizoba wears a top by TAUS, a dress worn as a skirt by HECTOR MACLEAN, shoes by FILIPPA K and rings by
left)   YSSO and ANUKA. All HECTOR MACLEAN pieces are produced from dead stock or scrap fabrics.
(previous   Elysia wears earrings and a silver necklace by ANUKA, and a gold necklace by RACHEL BOSTON. RACHEL BOSTON
right)   uses 100% recycled precious metals for their pieces, reducing the demand for newly-mined gold and platinum.

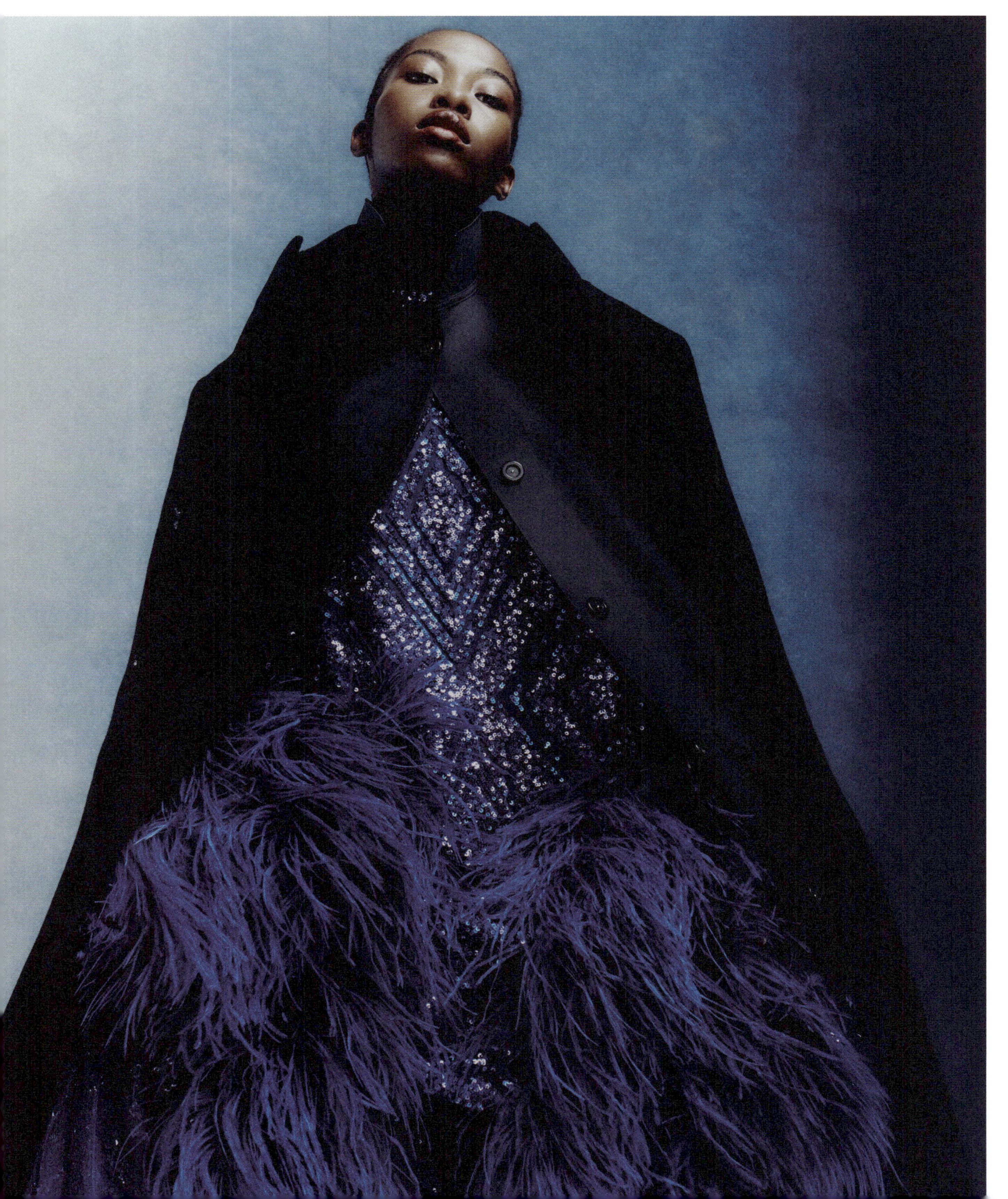

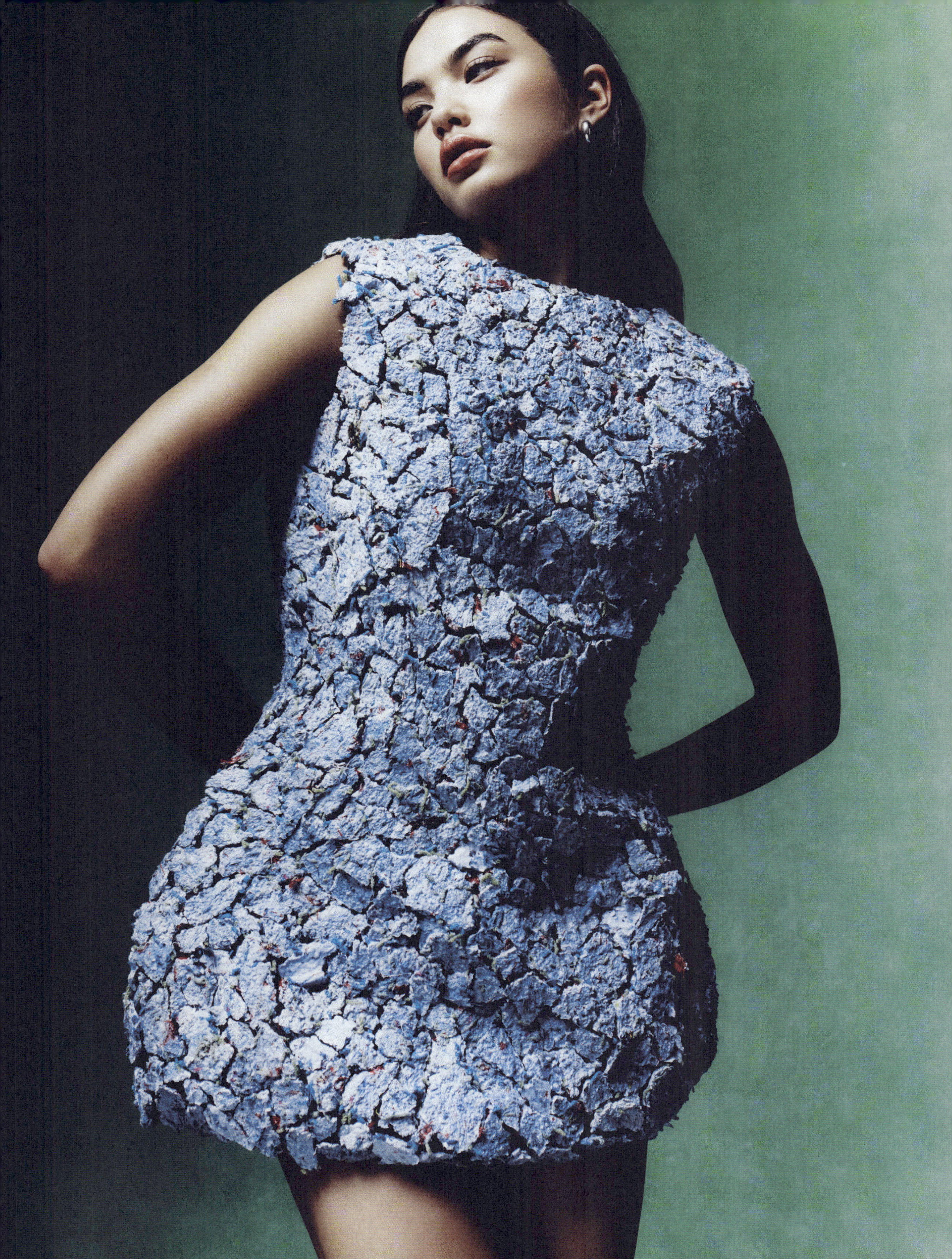

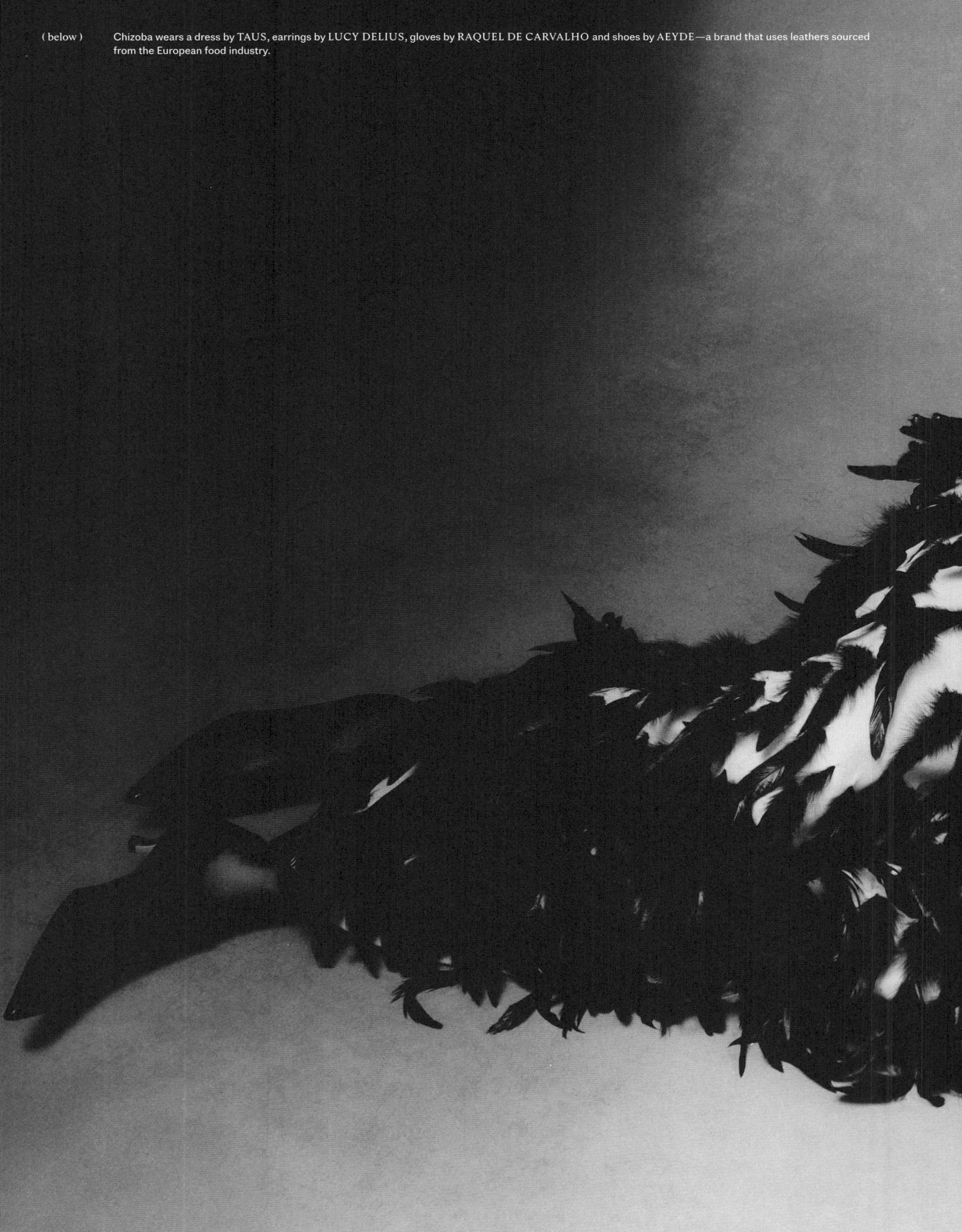

(below)   Chizoba wears a dress by TAUS, earrings by LUCY DELIUS, gloves by RAQUEL DE CARVALHO and shoes by AEYDE—a brand that uses leathers sourced
from the European food industry.

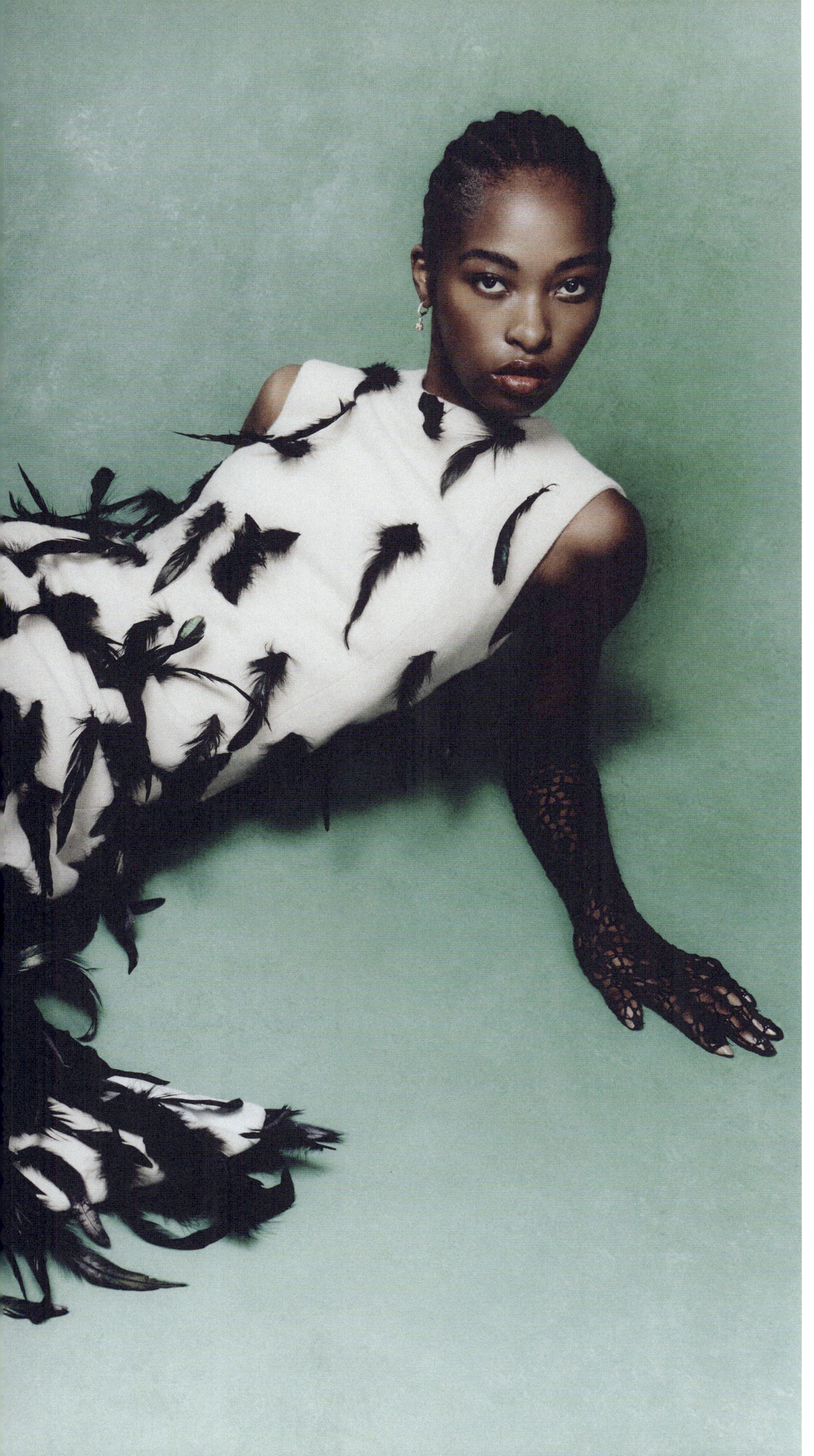

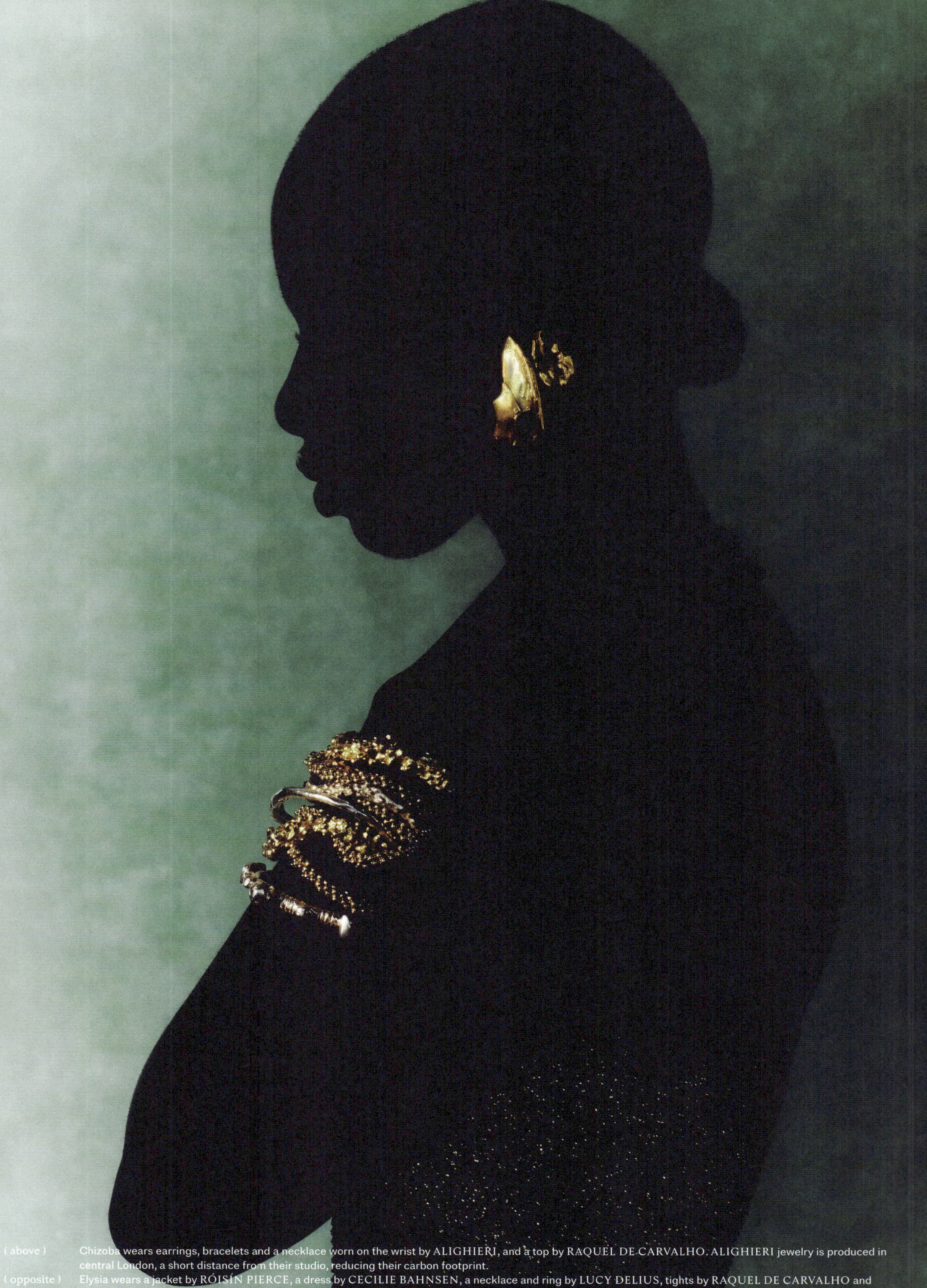

(above) Chizoba wears earrings, bracelets and a necklace worn on the wrist by ALIGHIERI, and a top by RAQUEL DE CARVALHO. ALIGHIERI jewelry is produced in central London, a short distance from their studio, reducing their carbon footprint.
(opposite) Elysia wears a jacket by RÓISÍN PIERCE, a dress by CECILIE BAHNSEN, a necklace and ring by LUCY DELIUS, tights by RAQUEL DE CARVALHO and boots by AEYDE.

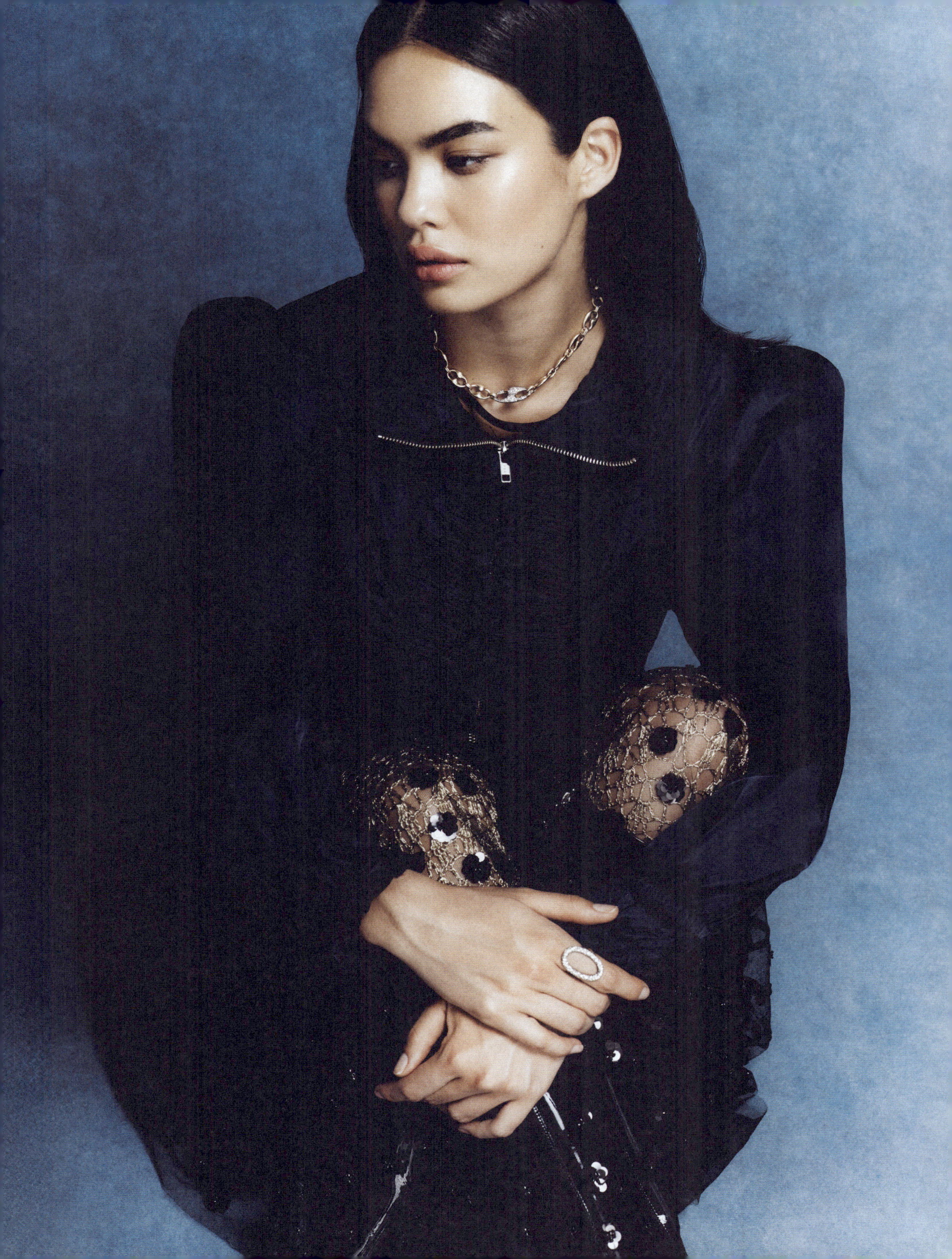

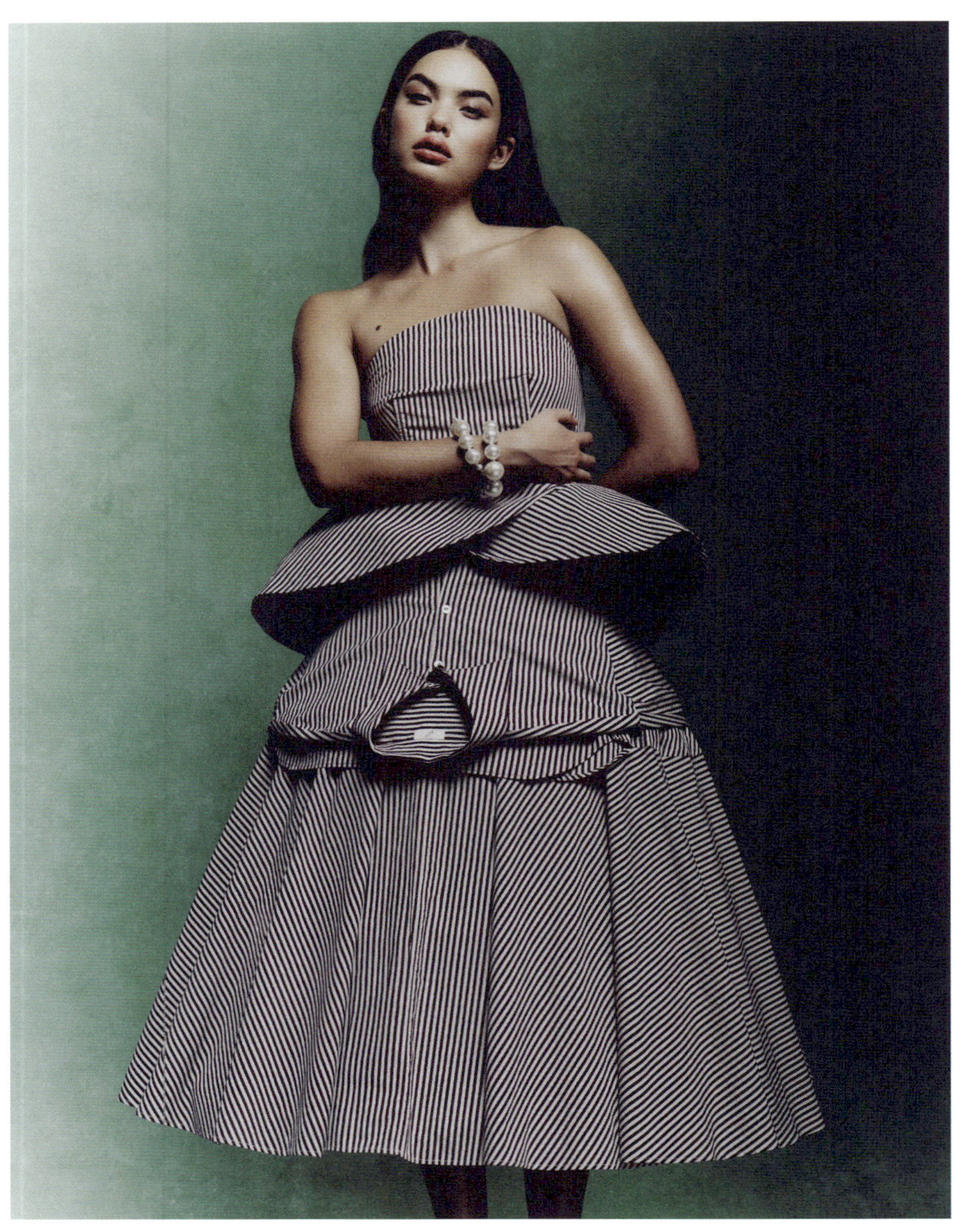

(above)   Elysia wears a full look by BITE STUDIOS and a necklace worn as a bracelet by COMPLETEDWORKS. BITE STUDIOS uses organic cotton that is produced using sustainable agricultural practices and techniques that reduce water and energy use.

(opposite)   Chizoba wears a top and shorts by POLA WIŚLICZ, earrings by BAR JEWELLERY and a coat—worn as a skirt—by GANNI. GANNI's Fabrics of the Future program researches and tests innovative new sustainable materials.

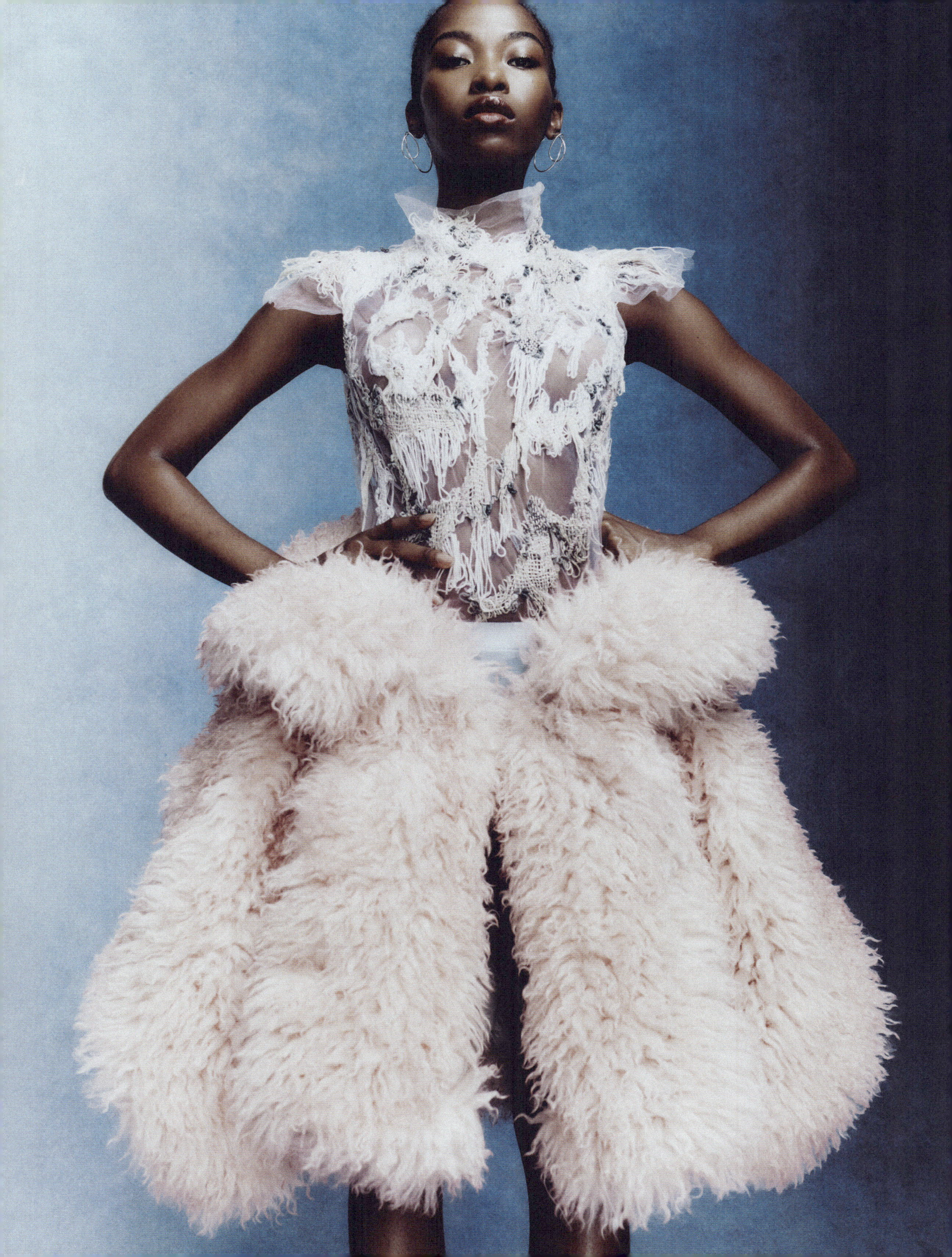

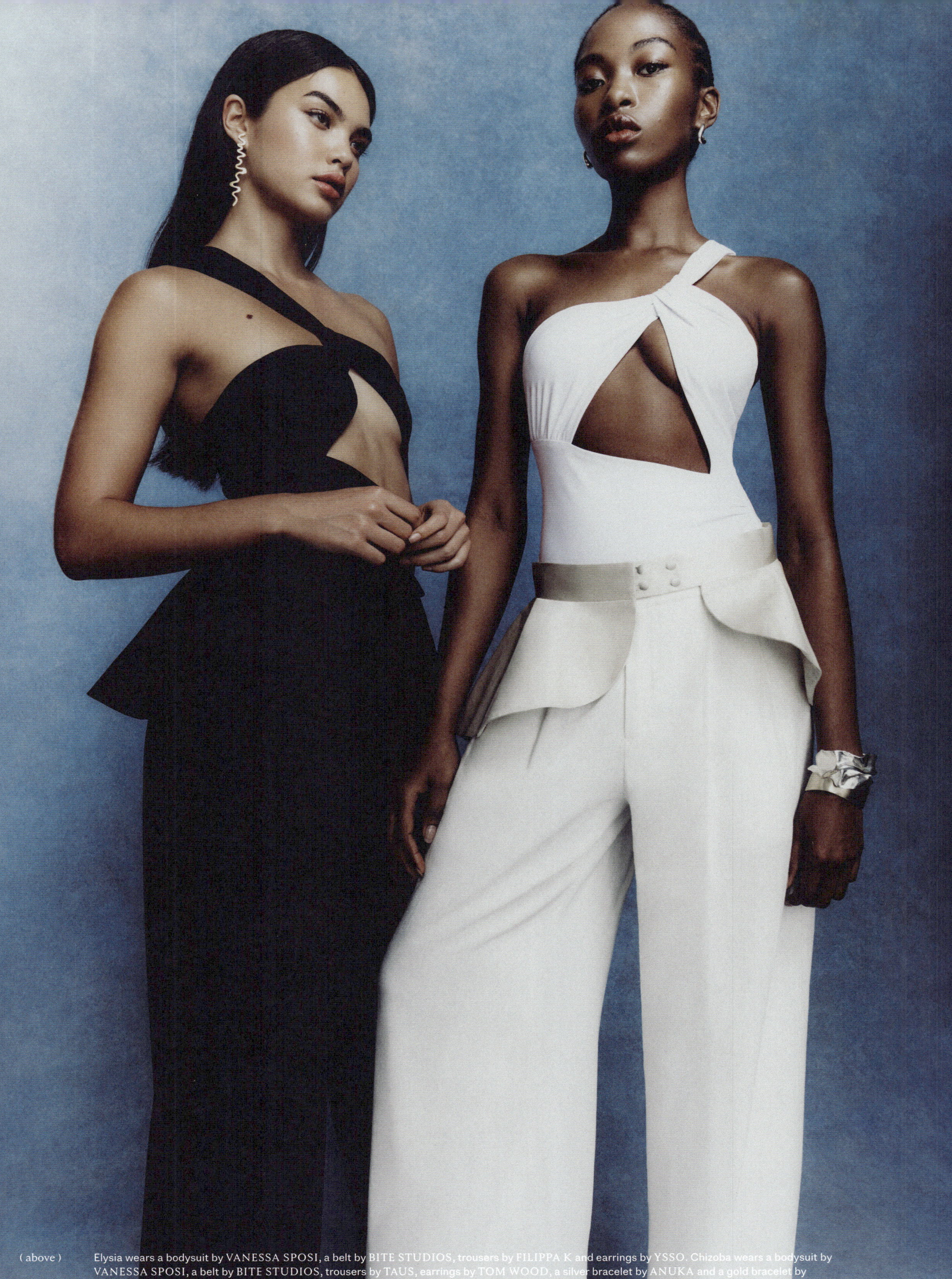

(above)   Elysia wears a bodysuit by VANESSA SPOSI, a belt by BITE STUDIOS, trousers by FILIPPA K and earrings by YSSO. Chizoba wears a bodysuit by
VANESSA SPOSI, a belt by BITE STUDIOS, trousers by TAUS, earrings by TOM WOOD, a silver bracelet by ANUKA and a gold bracelet by
COMPLETEDWORKS. ANUKA is a B Corp certified company that uses Fairmined gold, which supports artisanal miners and their communities.

98 Otegha Uwagba
108 Health Is Wealth
116 For Love, Not Money
126 Jo Ellison
134 Rich
146 Expensive Mistakes
154 Accountable Aspiration

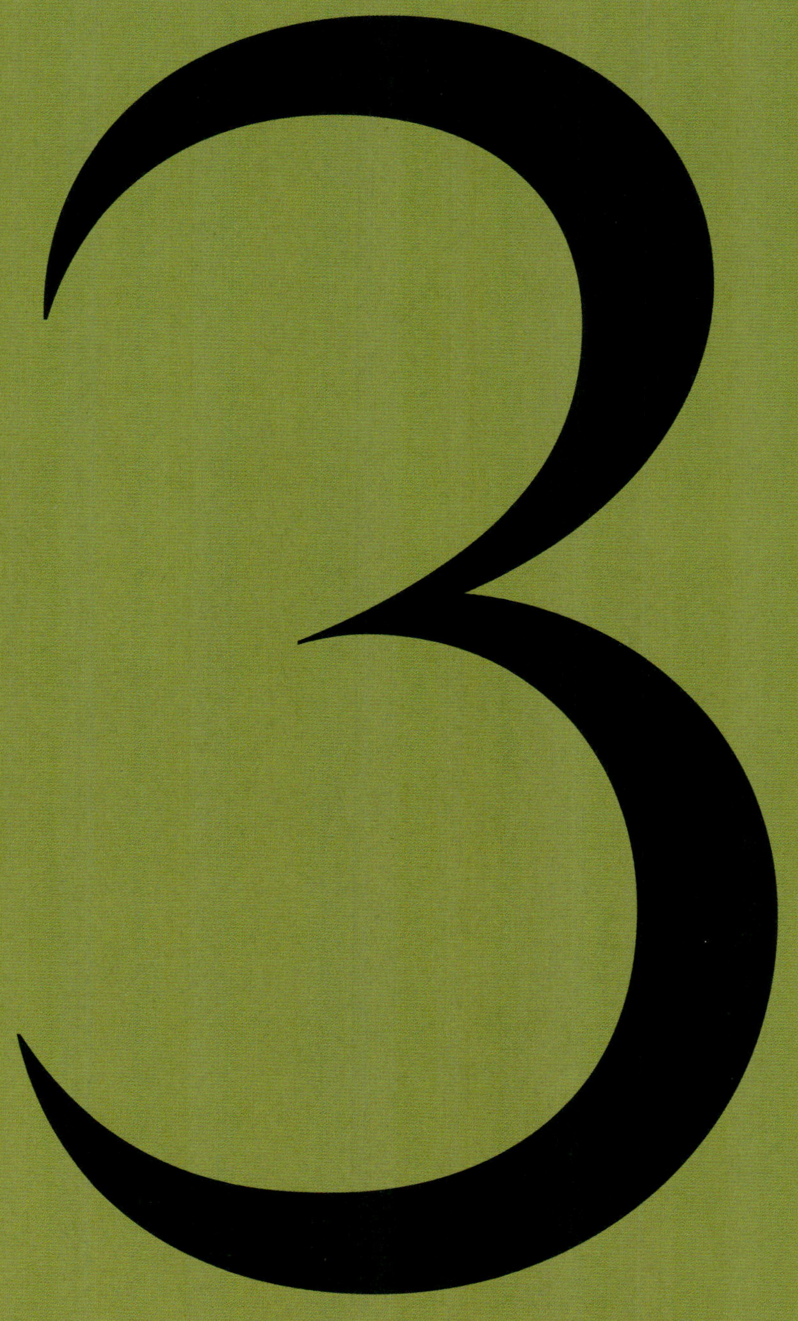

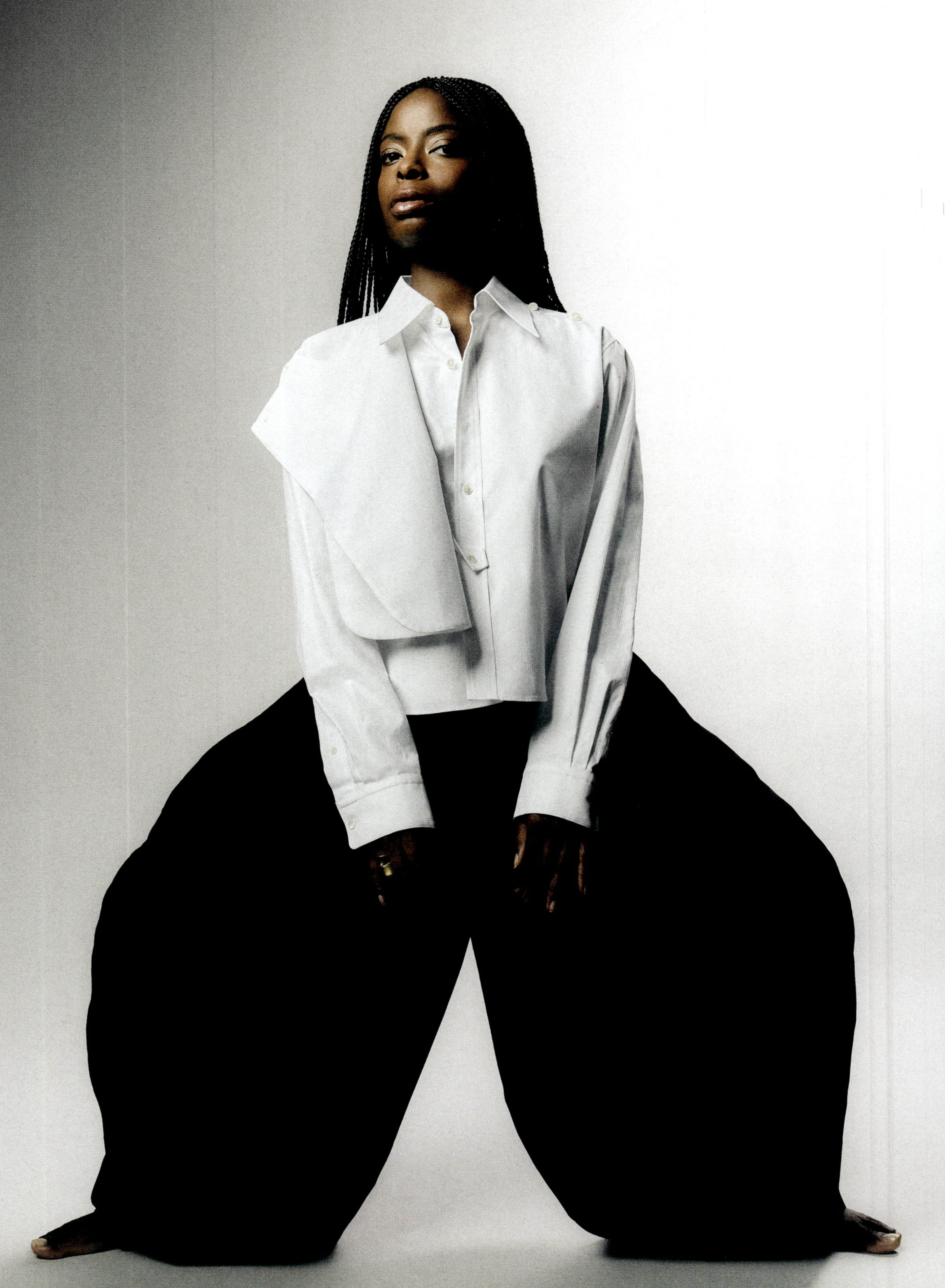

OTEGHA

Words
Allyssia Alleyne

Photos
Joe Whitmore

Styling
Aartthie Mahakuperan

On a world where inherited wealth increasingly determines who gets ahead.

(opposite) Uwagba wears a shirt and trousers by TOGA and a ring by COMPLETEDWORKS.
(overleaf) She wears a dress by TALLER MARMO and a ring by TOM WOOD.

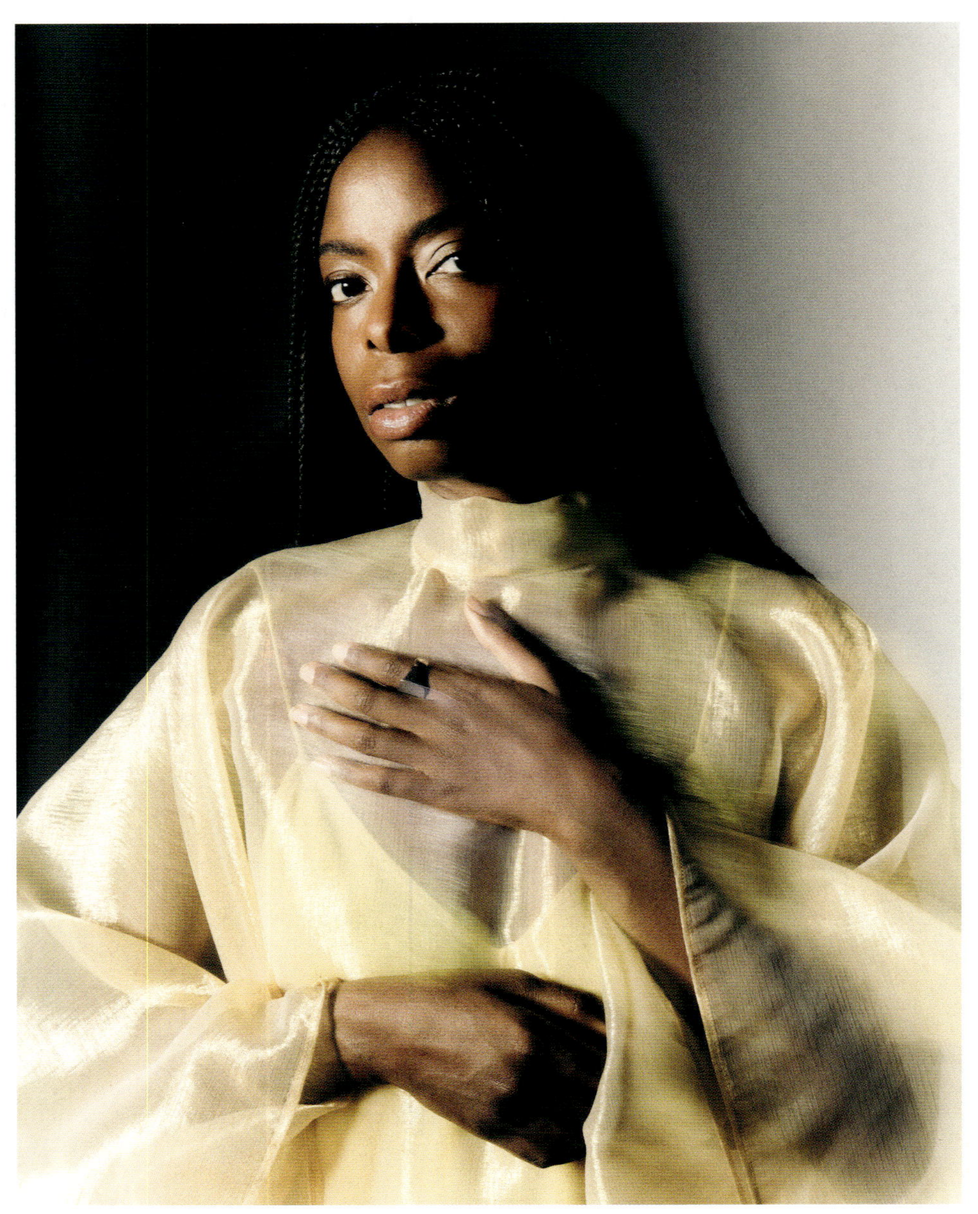

UWA

"Because I bought my flat when interest rates were historically low and they are no longer historically low, I'm going to have to pay more each month. And that's fine, I can afford it—I'm resentful of it, but it's fine," she says with a grin. "In my 20s, an unexpected £80 [$100] penalty would ruin my week. Now I'm much more equipped to handle the financial unpredictability."

The story of how Uwagba came to buy the apartment forms the triumphant final chapter of her 2021 memoir, *We Need to Talk About Money*. In it, she traces her journey from demoralized public school student to private school scholarship kid to underemployed Oxford graduate; and her later experiences with the casual sexism of media boys' clubs, a rotation of nightmare living siutations, and the on-and-off-again financial precarity of her 20s. Personal anecdotes are intercut with observations about liberal guilt, the beauty tax, the #GirlBoss and "the right type of Black."

Throughout, she reflects on the impact growing up in a modest Nigerian immigrant household (her family moved to the UK when she was five) has had on her attitudes toward money. When she didn't have it, she felt like a failure. When she did, she was vigilant—pathologically saving and afraid of spending.

"I thought, I cannot be the only person who has a relationship with money that's this complicated and this emotionally fraught and anxiety-ridden," she says, recalling the moment she conceptualized the book in 2017. "I remember making notes on my phone that were literally something like, 'A book about women and the emotional turmoil of money told through my own stories. Part memoir, part cultural commentary.'"

The book became a *Sunday Times* bestseller, in the process subverting the chic-and-successful-girl-about-town facade Uwagba had been projecting on social media and in glossy magazine profiles. Having founded Women Who in 2016, a now-defunct community supporting women working in creative industries, she'd made a name for herself with articles, speaking gigs and a podcast that centered on money, careers and feminism.

T

he longest sections of her first book, 2017's *Little Black Book: A Toolkit for Working Women*, pertained to money management and negotiating salaries. Her second book, *Whites: On Race and Other Falsehoods* (2020)—released months after the murder of George Floyd and the protests and performative allyship that followed—approached the topic from another direction, reflecting on the mental labor required of Black people to navigate whiteness and suggesting that true racial equality requires a redistribution of wealth, power and opportunities.

But though she seemed to have her life together when she first conceived of *We Need to Talk About Money*, she explains that

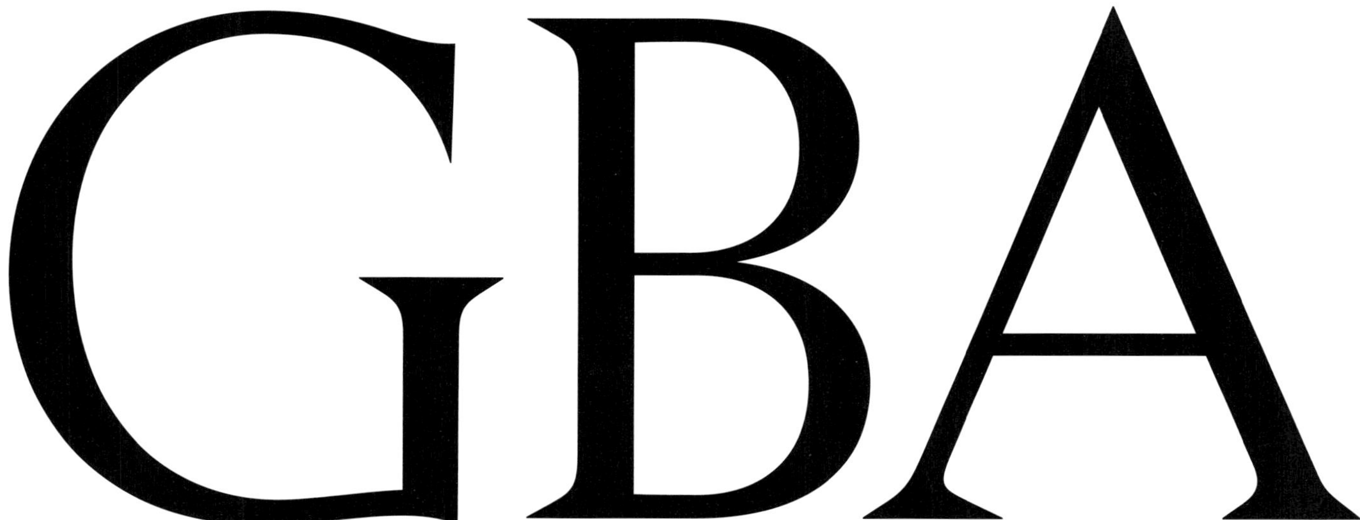

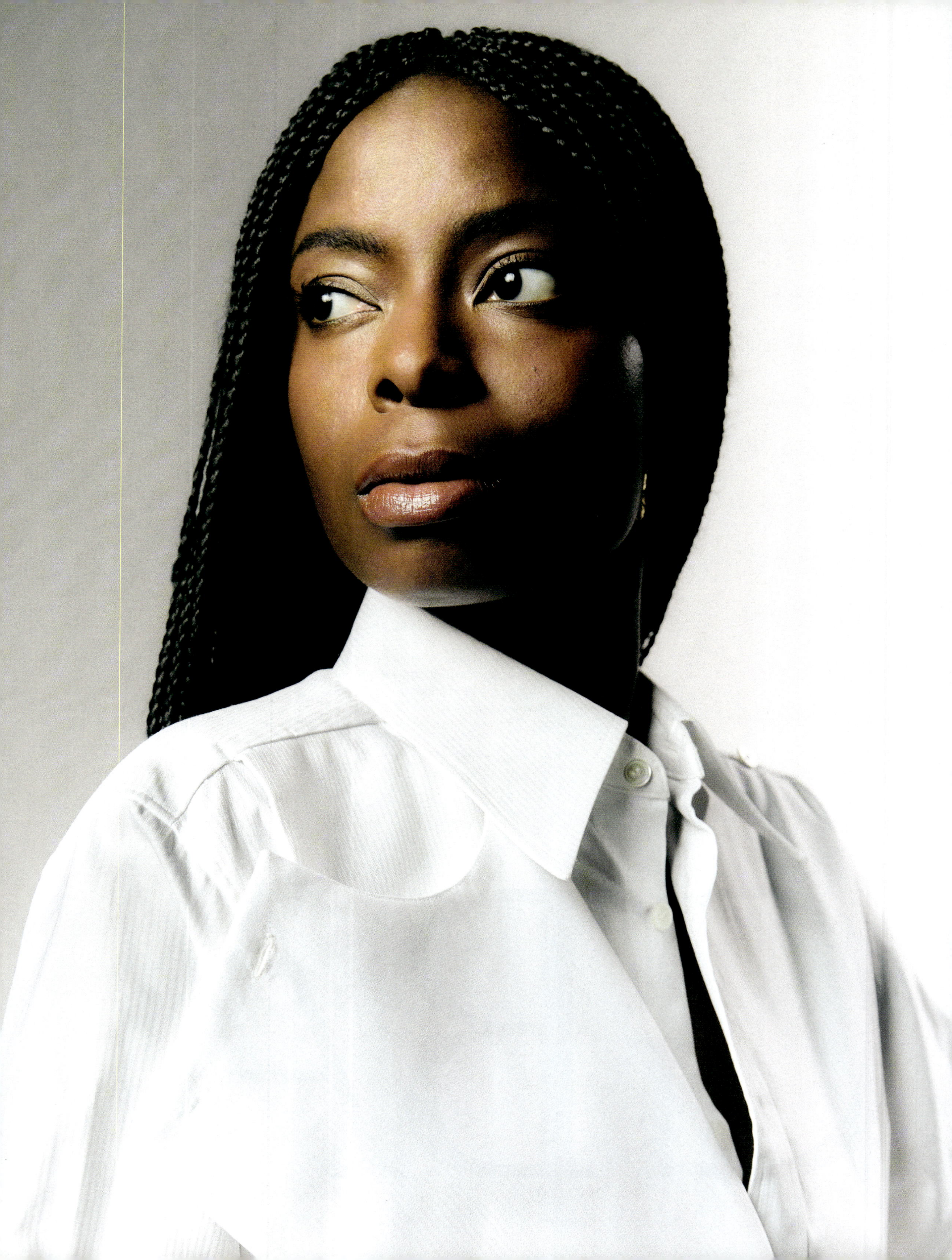

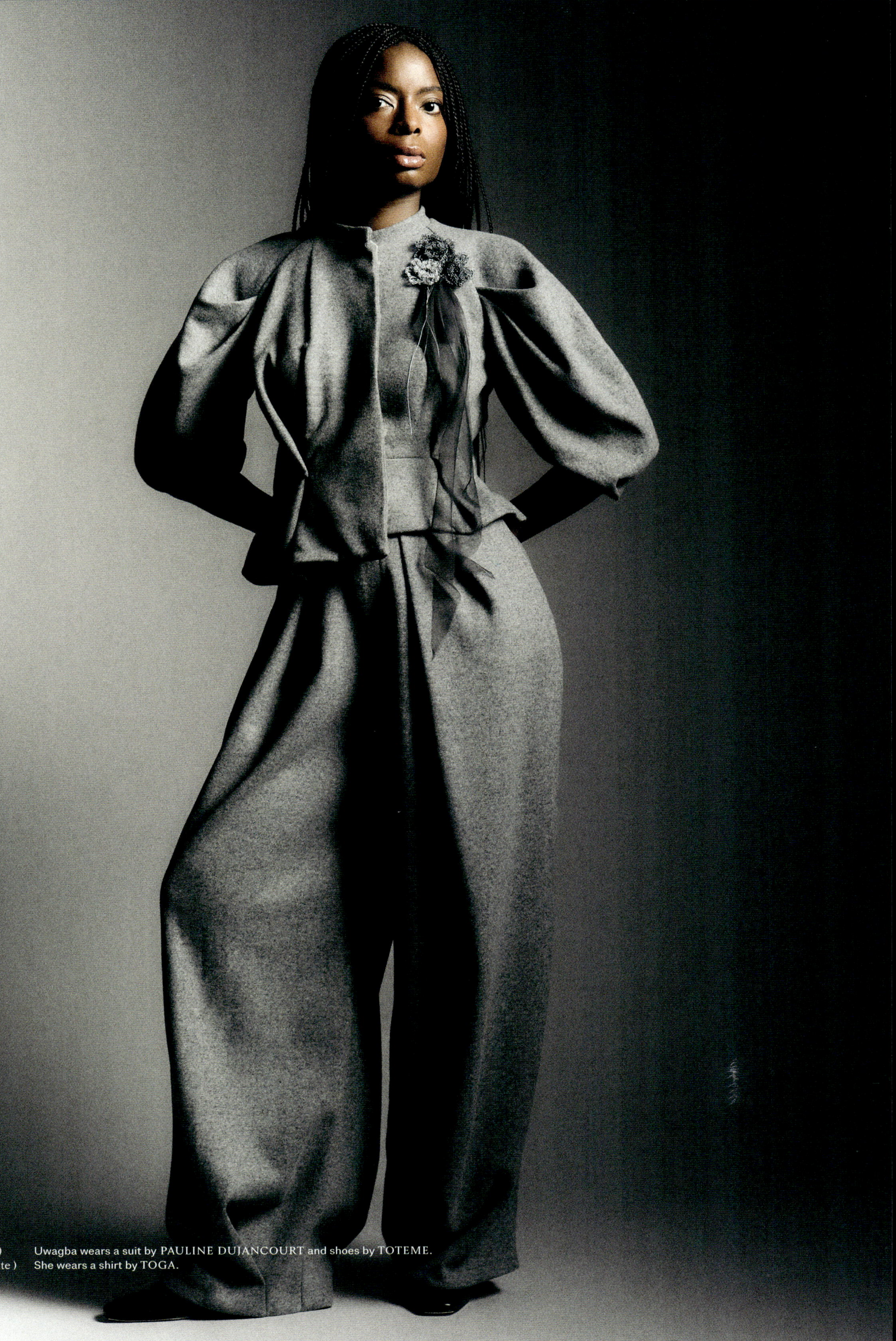

(above)   Uwagba wears a suit by PAULINE DUJANCOURT and shoes by TOTEME.
(opposite)   She wears a shirt by TOGA.

she was actually living at home with her parents in South London and earning very little. The future was a blur; homeownership was an impossible dream.

It was only when royalties from her first book rolled in that the dream came into focus. Even then, buying her first apartment, just as she turned 30, necessitated not only years of "penny-pinching and counting and planning and worrying," as Uwagba writes, but also having to endure COVID-era restrictions on house viewings, deceitful real estate agents and lenders who doubted her viability as a self-employed solo buyer. In doing so, she joined the minority of Black Africans (22% versus 68% of white households) and millennials (39%) in the UK who own their homes.

T

he roots of our problematic relationships with money—intergenerational wealth transfer, workplace sexism, austerity politics—is something she comes back to repeatedly in *We Need to Talk About Money*. But that hasn't stopped people from trying to cast Uwagba as a millennial Suze Orman, doling out advice to the masses sporting Ganni and Loewe. Editors and producers still reach out for her quick tips for financial success and fighting the system; they're looking for pat behavioral solutions to the systemic issues she describes. "They want the neat bow, the happy ending," she says. She routinely declines.

"It's impossible to give one-size-fits-all money advice," Uwagba says. "Is this person married or divorced? How old are they? Are they renting or homeowning? Are they Black or white? I decided around the time that I was writing this book that that's not what I was interested in doing with my platform."

"A lot of the book is like, 'Do as I say, not as I do,'" she continues. "Here are some mistakes I made; here are some ways in which I was naive. Here are things that I wish I'd known or done differently." Your boss could be passing you over for opportunities because you aren't white or male, she suggests, or your progressive friends are probably too embarrassed to tell you that parental help, not sensible saving, is what landed them their new apartment.

"So, in that sense, I hope it's informative or educational, but I never set out to write a how-to," she says. "I can't help you with that situation personally. But hopefully, now that your eyes are open to it, you might start thinking about how you can make some changes."

The success of *We Need to Talk About Money* presaged a wider change in how—and how much—we talk about money. "The cultural conversations have really changed," Uwagba says. "Back in 2017, 2016, people were not talking openly about money and what they were being paid, and even I wasn't really sharing figures with friends in terms that I do—and I think we all do—much more freely now."

Indeed, Refinery29's wildly popular Money Diaries series, in which working women track their spending over the course of a week, has bred legions of imitators offering insights into the habits of normal people. But this shift is particularly obvious on social media, where regular people cheerily confess how much they're paid, how much they pay in rent and how much they have in savings. In 2024, TikTok reported a 373% annual rise in financial content, and a recent survey found that 59% of 18-to-30-year-olds follow a "finfluencer." What was once personal finance, Uwagba says, is now public information—often framed as a lifestyle topic.

"I just have some reservations about how much depth some of these conversations actually contain. Some of it feels quite surface level and designed so some media outlet can drive clicks with a splashy headline—"Here's how I managed to buy my first flat when I was just NINETEEN." And then there are a lot of unqualified people doling out financial advice with the aim of building their own platforms, and of course monetizing that."

"But I'm pretty financially literate," she concedes. "I imagine for a lot of people—who haven't spent years researching and writing about this topic, and don't necessarily feel on top of their finances—that content is actually really helpful."

This understanding of how others navigate the murky waters around money was heightened through her own writing on the topic. In the book, Uwagba recounts an astonishing conversation in which a friend

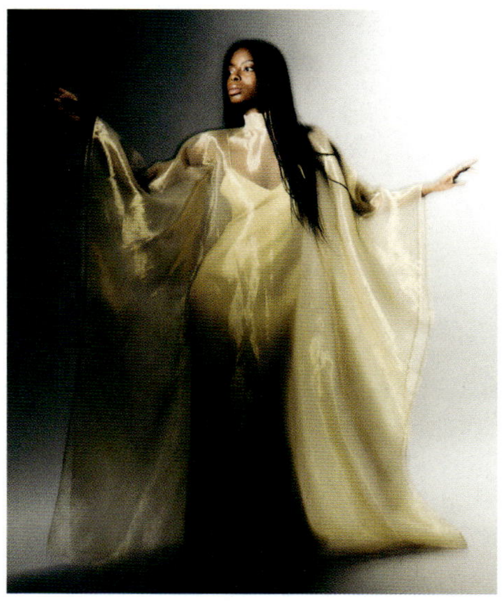

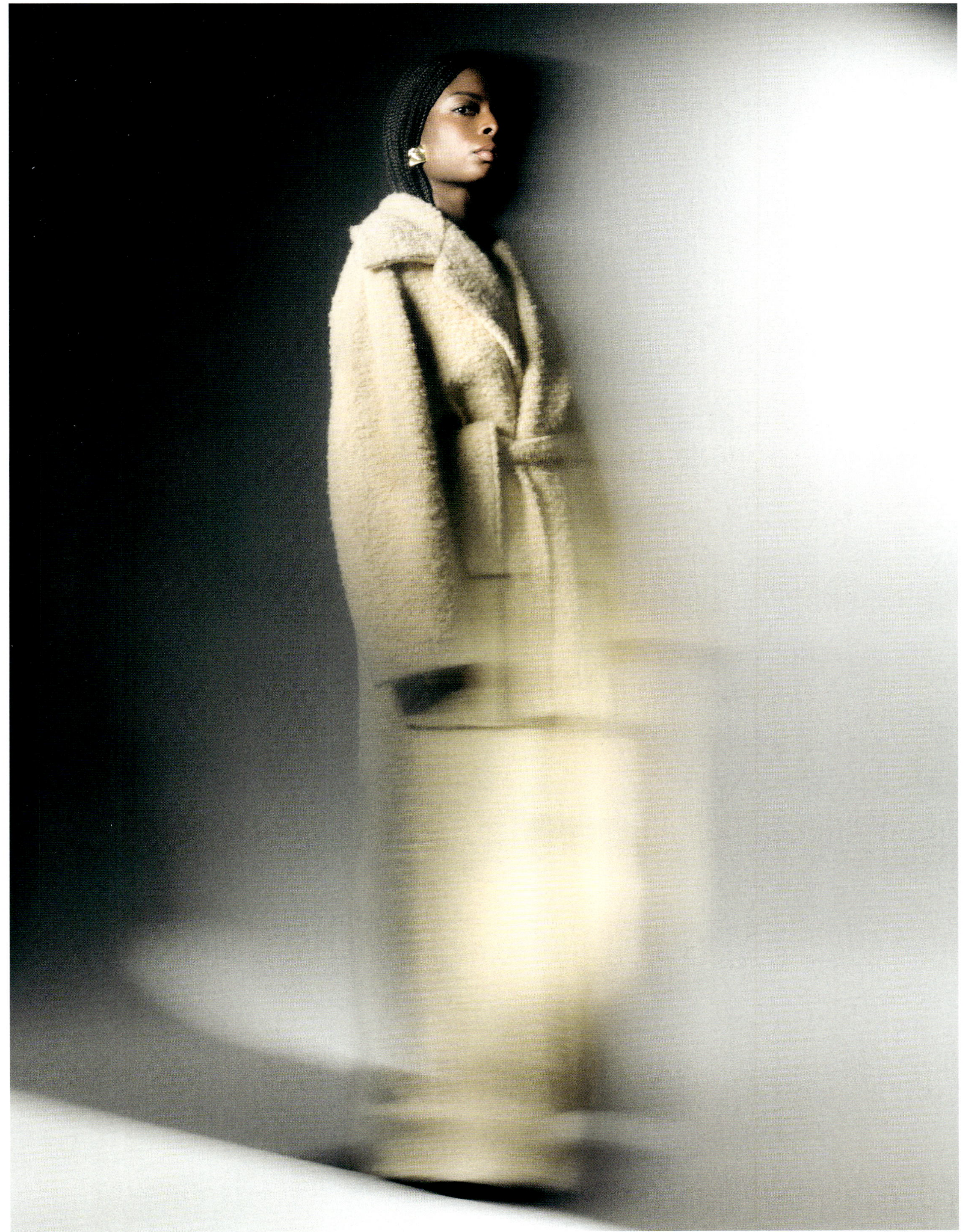

(above) Uwagba wears a coat by RAY CHU and earrings by COMPLETEDWORKS.
(opposite) She wears a dress by TALLER MARMO and a ring by TOM WOOD.

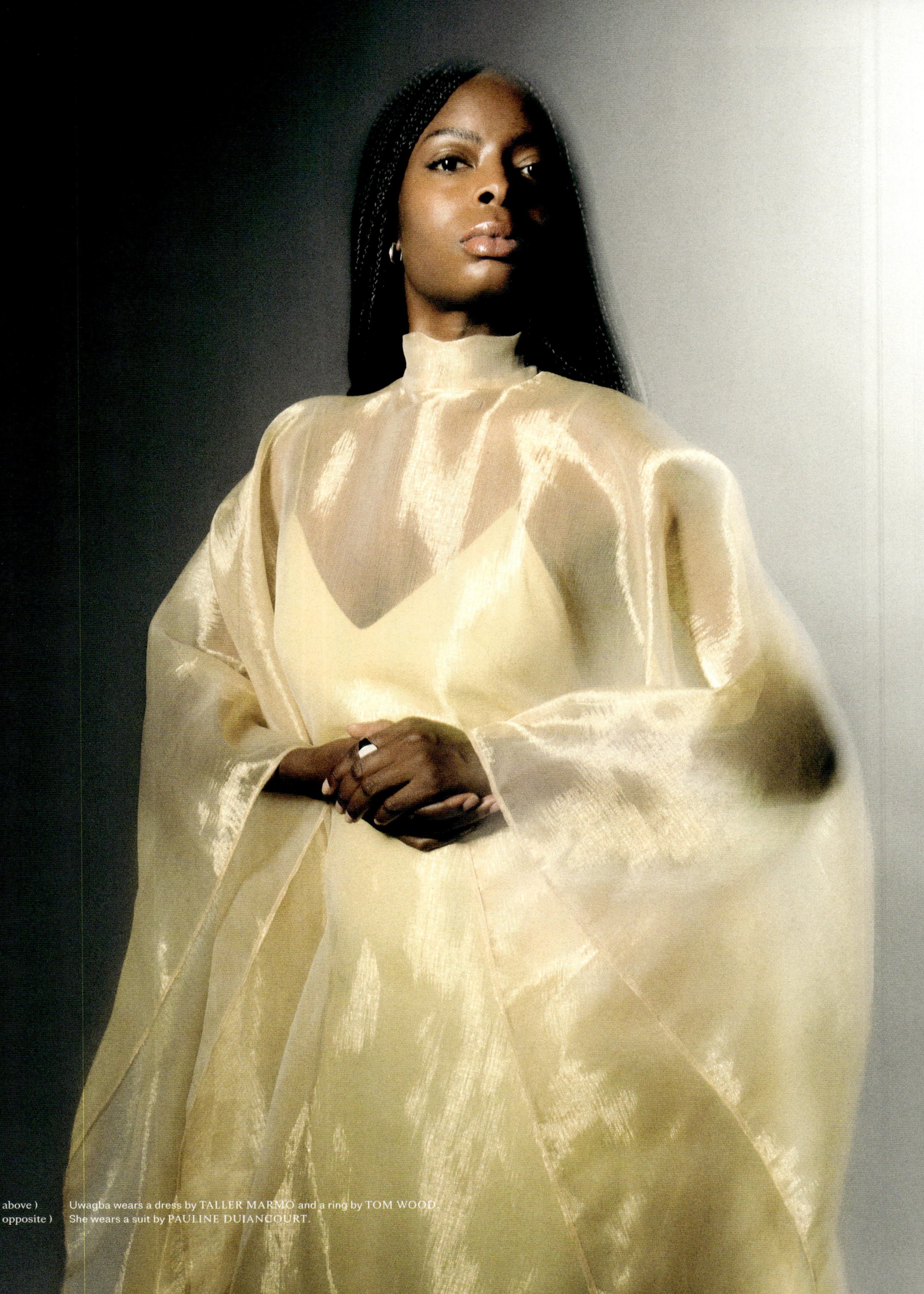

(above)   Uwagba wears a dress by TALLER MARMO and a ring by TOM WOOD.
(opposite) She wears a suit by PAULINE DUJANCOURT.

confessed that she'd been lying about having a mortgage when her parents had in fact bought her apartment outright, and there are others in her life whose behavior with money seems antithetical to her own—the well-off friend who is unfailingly stingy, the struggling friend who insists on putting her card down for rounds of drinks.[1] "I was wondering why people behave the way they do about money. Like, what caused that?" she says. "Everyone has their own neuroses, so I try to be open-minded."

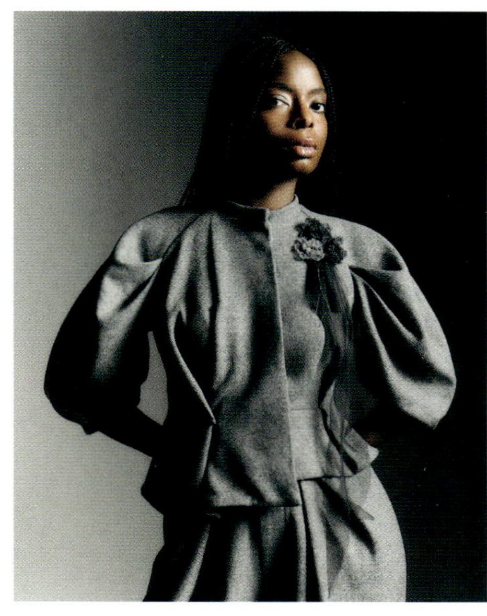

U

wagba has undergone a number of changes of her own since writing the book. No longer hypervigilant about money, she now allows herself to indulge in vacations, designer clothes and nice dinners without the nagging guilt. After extensive, expensive home renovations, she's made peace with living without the iron safety net of cash savings that was once sacrosanct.

"You can't be as vigilant when you're a homeowner.... I had to really get comfortable with large sums of money leaving my account seemingly at random," she says, recalling the gas leaks, unexpected repairs and maintenance charges that have piled up on top of her mortgage payments. "And I say this with the knowledge and the privilege that I do have the funds to sustain that.

"My relationship with money is ever-evolving. I think I'm definitely better with it now than I was a decade ago. But as you grow older, there are new challenges and also new goals. What I'm also trying to do is not get sucked up into the mentality of always wanting more."

Today, Uwagba has largely moved on from money as a subject. The writer who once quipped "Money influences everything. Give me a topic, and I will bring it back to money," is now pursuing other concerns. With several celebrity profiles under her belt (Fran Lebowitz for the *Sunday Times*, Naomi Campbell for *Harper's Bazaar*, Lashana Lynch in *Tatler*), she's leaning further into the zeitgeist. She's been publishing her monthly Add To Wishlist newsletter on Substack since 2023, mixing fashion and homeware recommendations with cultural criticism and personal essays; and in September, she became a *Grazia UK* columnist, offering up commentary on TV, movies, books and celebrity goings-on. Recent bylines include a dispatch from a luxury digital detox in Thailand and a report on the surprising vogue for ugly clothes. "You can make a very lucrative living out of rehashing the same opinions day in, day out," she explains, "but I am fundamentally a writer, and I have different interests."

This is not to say that Uwagba has shaken money completely. She's currently working on a novel looking at class within the Black community, privilege and integrity that touches on the topic; and she's written a screenplay loosely based on her time working at toxic London ad agencies in her 20s.

Now, five years on from *We Need to Talk About Money*, she's still gratified any time a new reader reaches out to her to talk about how her writing has impacted them. "I've had numerous people message me and talk about real changes they have made in their lives off the back of reading that book, whether it's quitting a job or going toe-to-toe with their boss or colleague, or asking for a pay rise. People are learning something from this."

Uwagba is still happy to share financial advice with friends, but knows her limits. "I was actually leaving voice notes with an industry friend yesterday who's dealing with a contractual issue," she says. "She told me, 'I picked up your book! I just put it on my bedside to read it to help me!'"

"I was like, that's lovely and actually very sweet. But that is not going to help you—get a lawyer!"

(1) From 1980 to 2020, UK house prices trebled in real terms. Even modest council homes bought under Margaret Thatcher's right-to-buy scheme—by a generation with free education and attainable homeownership—now fetch seven figures in some London neighborhoods, transforming modest past purchases into vast inheritances.

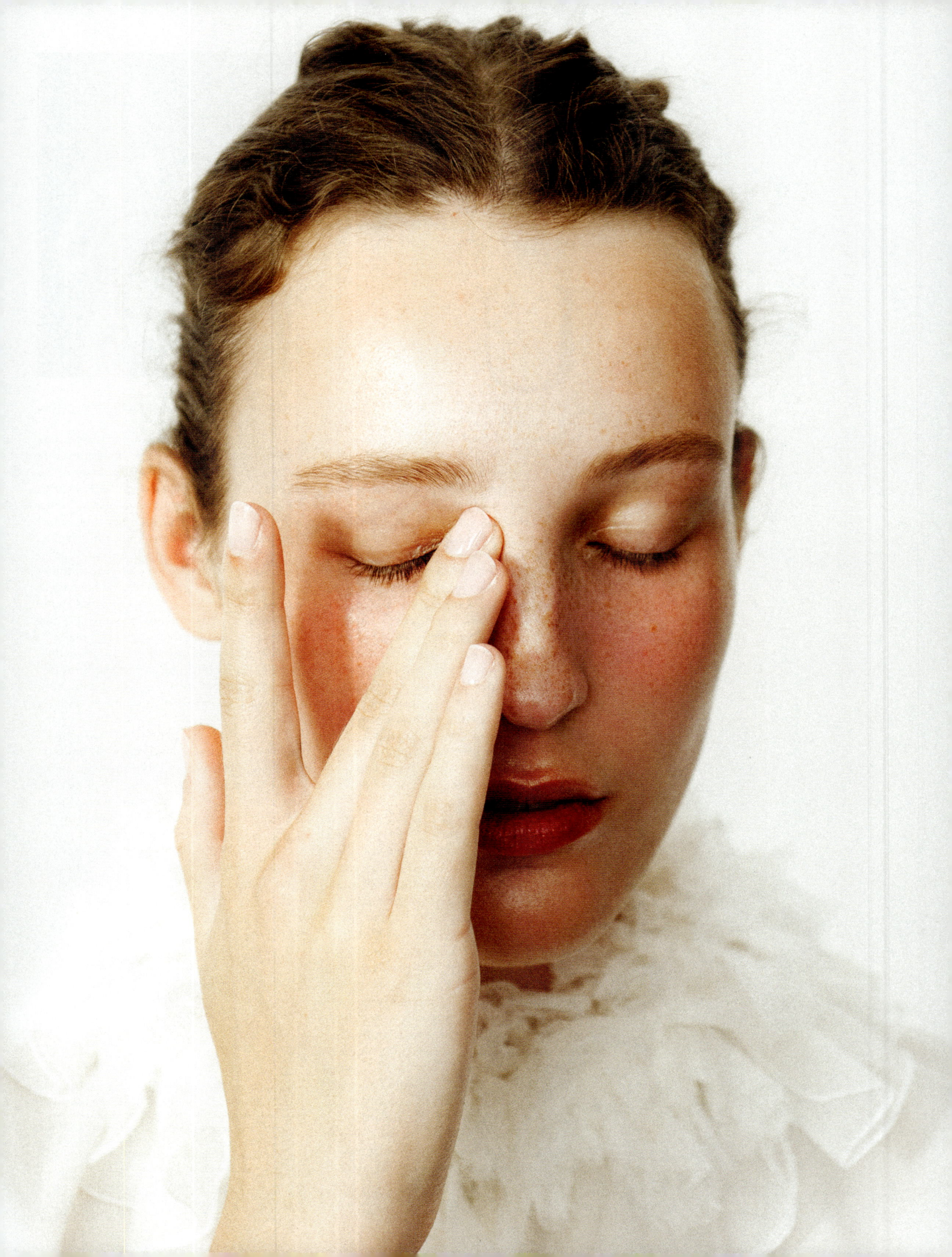

Cold comfort—a style guide for convalescence.

FASHION: HEALTH IS WEALTH

Photos
Guillaume Garat

Art Direction
Joséphine Daru

Styling
Maureen Barbier

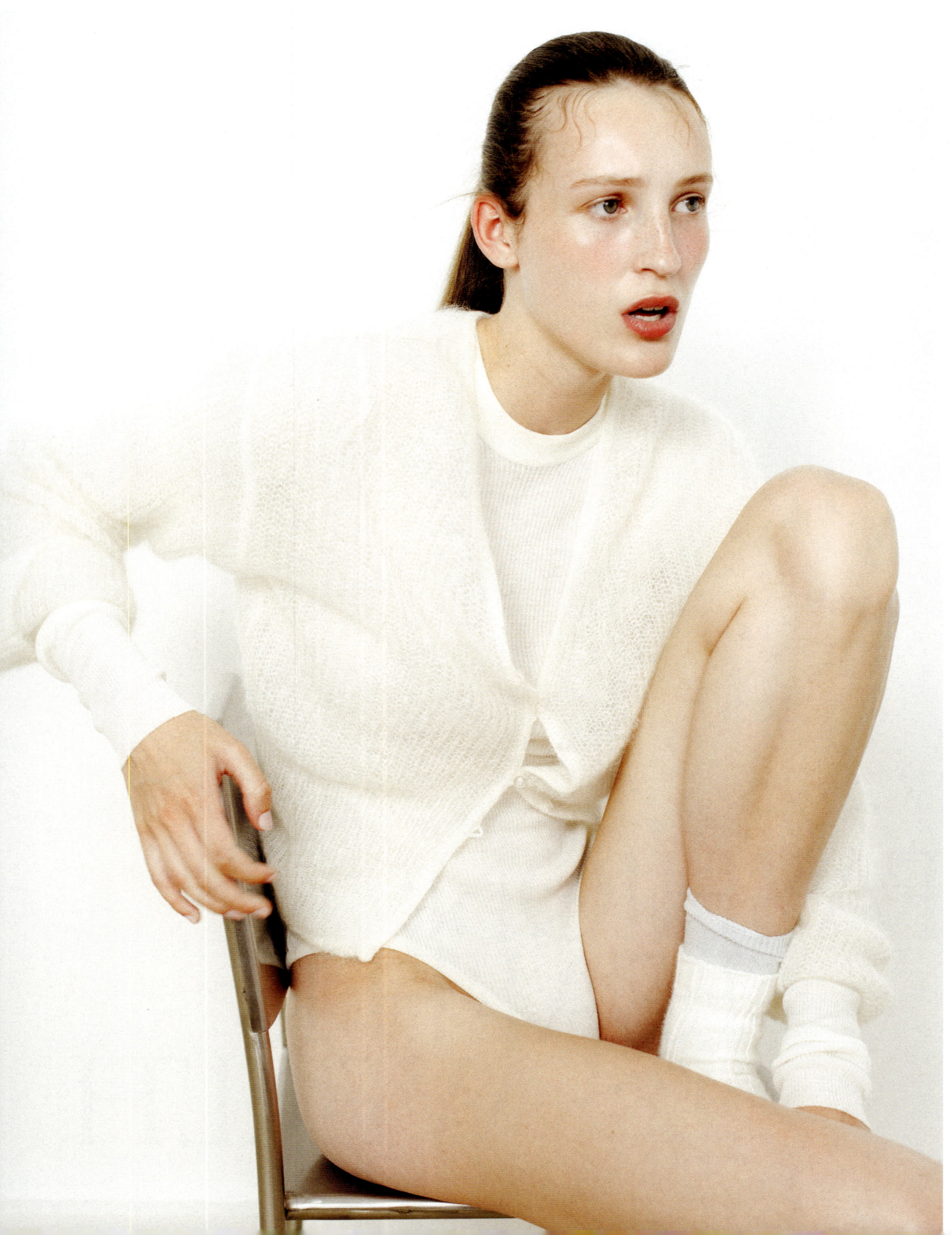

Set Design: Camille Pouyat. Model: Emily Bennett.

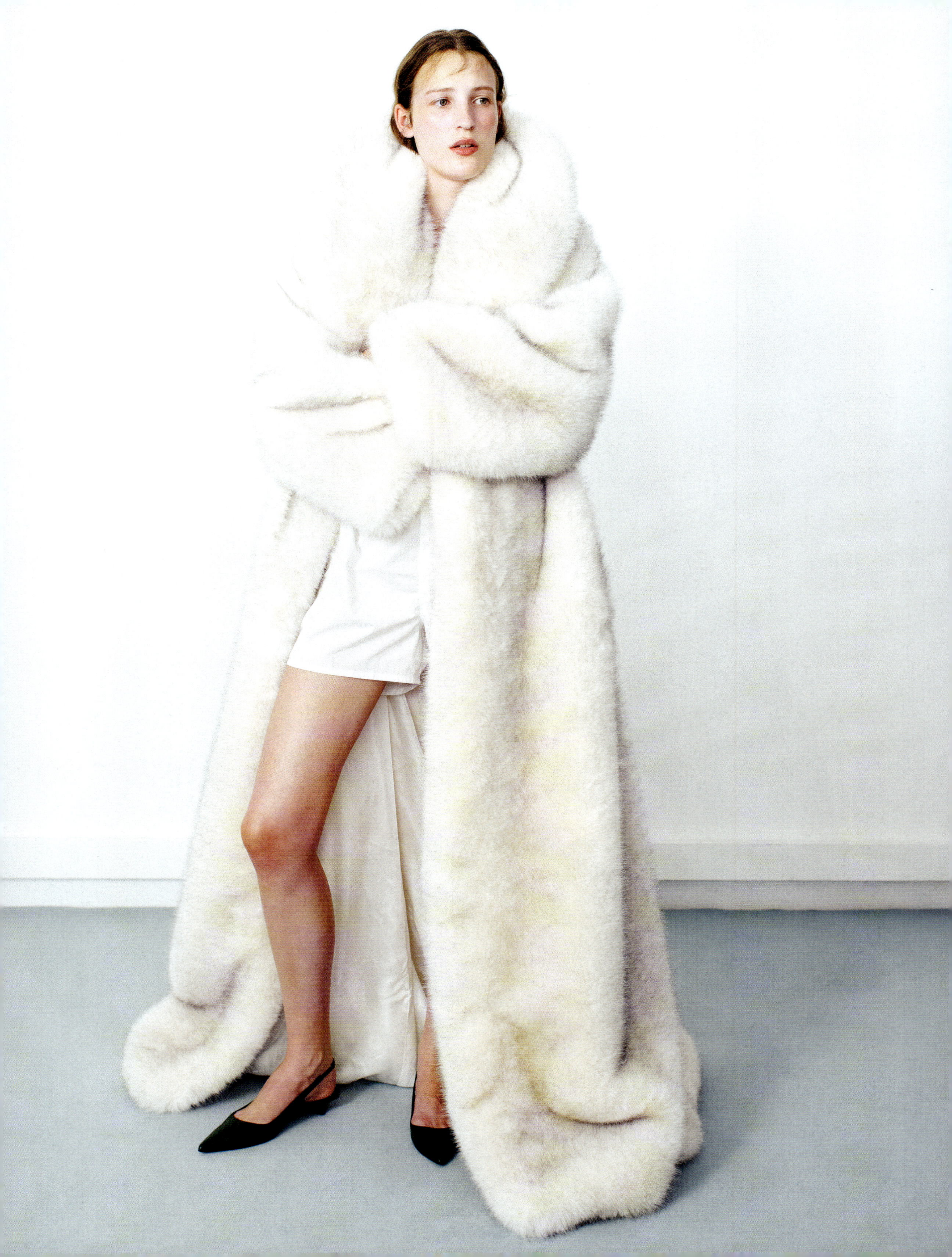

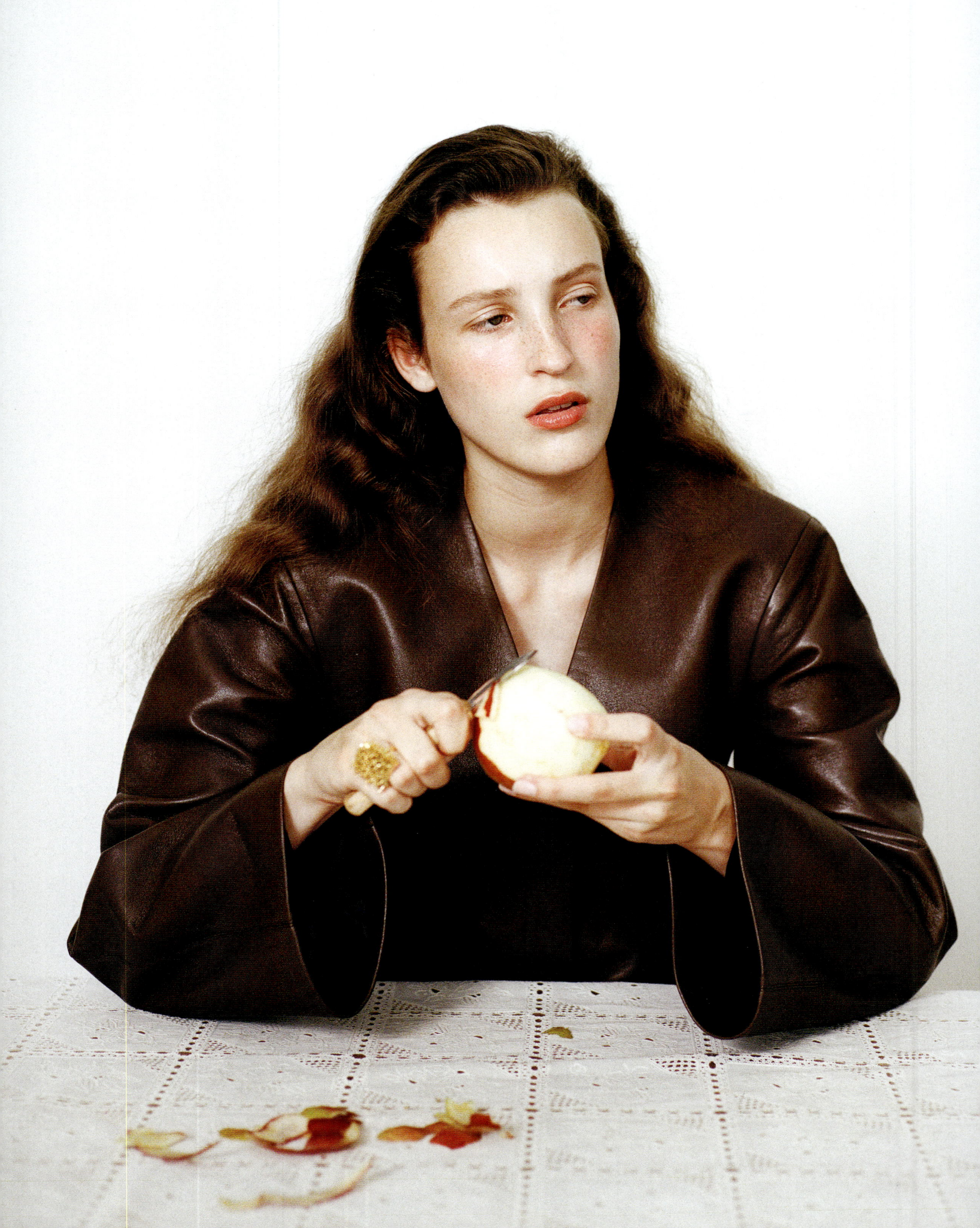

(below)   Emily wears a shirt, tunic and skirt by ISSEY MIYAKE, rings by CELINE and cashmere socks by FALKE.
(opposite)   She wears a jacket by NANUSHKA and a ring by WENS.

Hair: Damien Lacoussade. Makeup: Ellen Walge. Nails: Romane Martini.

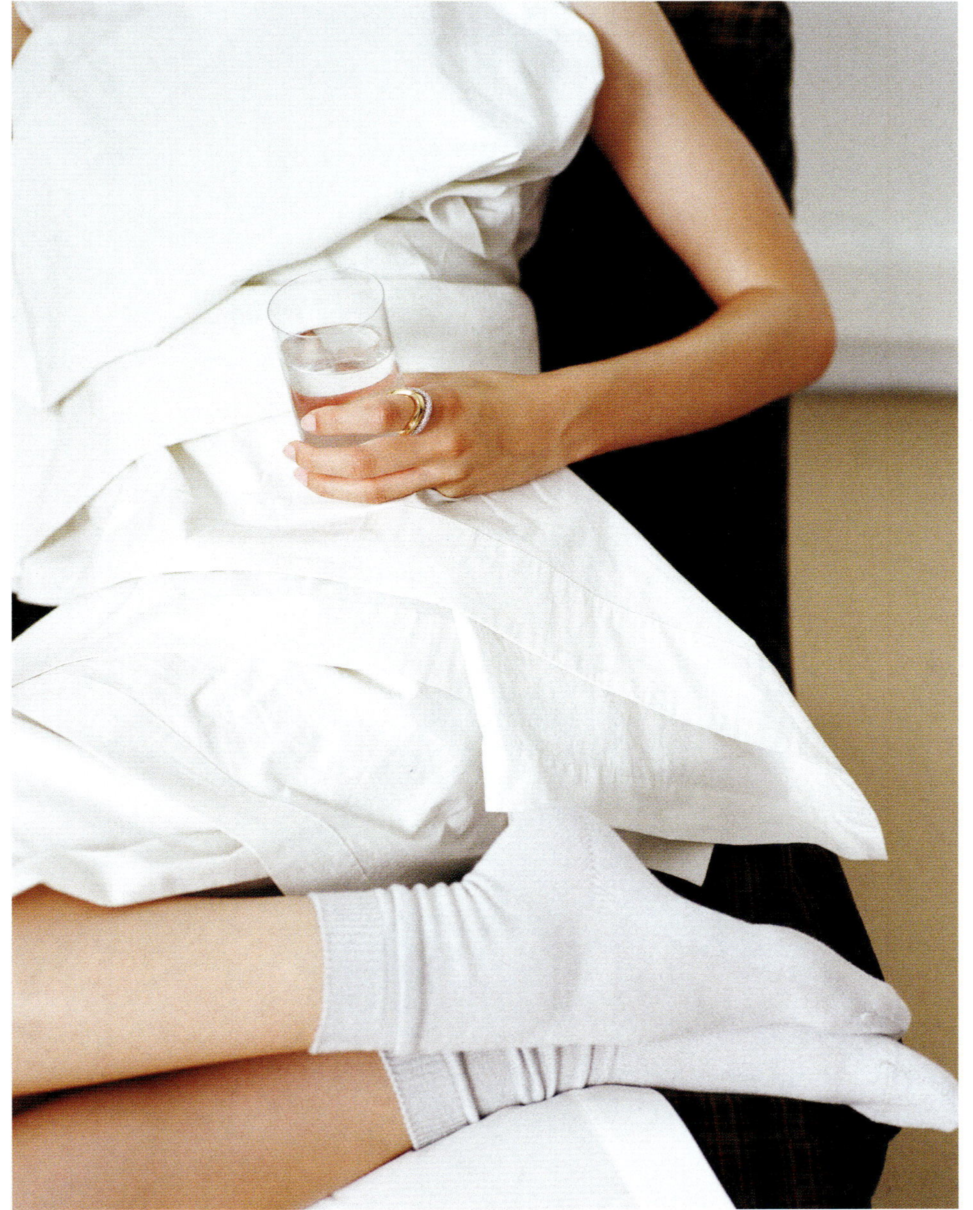

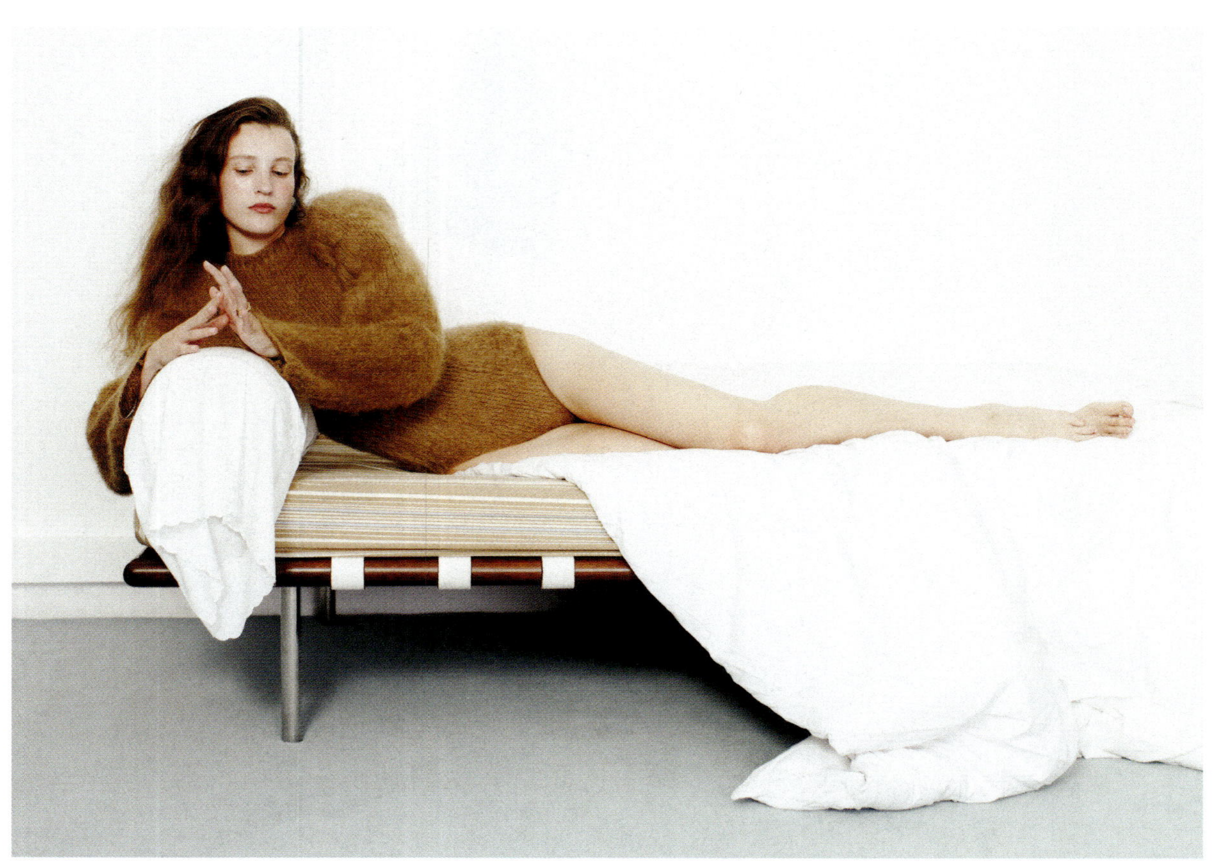

(above) Emily wears a bodysuit by ACNE STUDIOS, rings by REPOSSI and earrings by WENS.
(opposite) She wears a faux fur coat by ELIE SAAB and rings by COPIN.

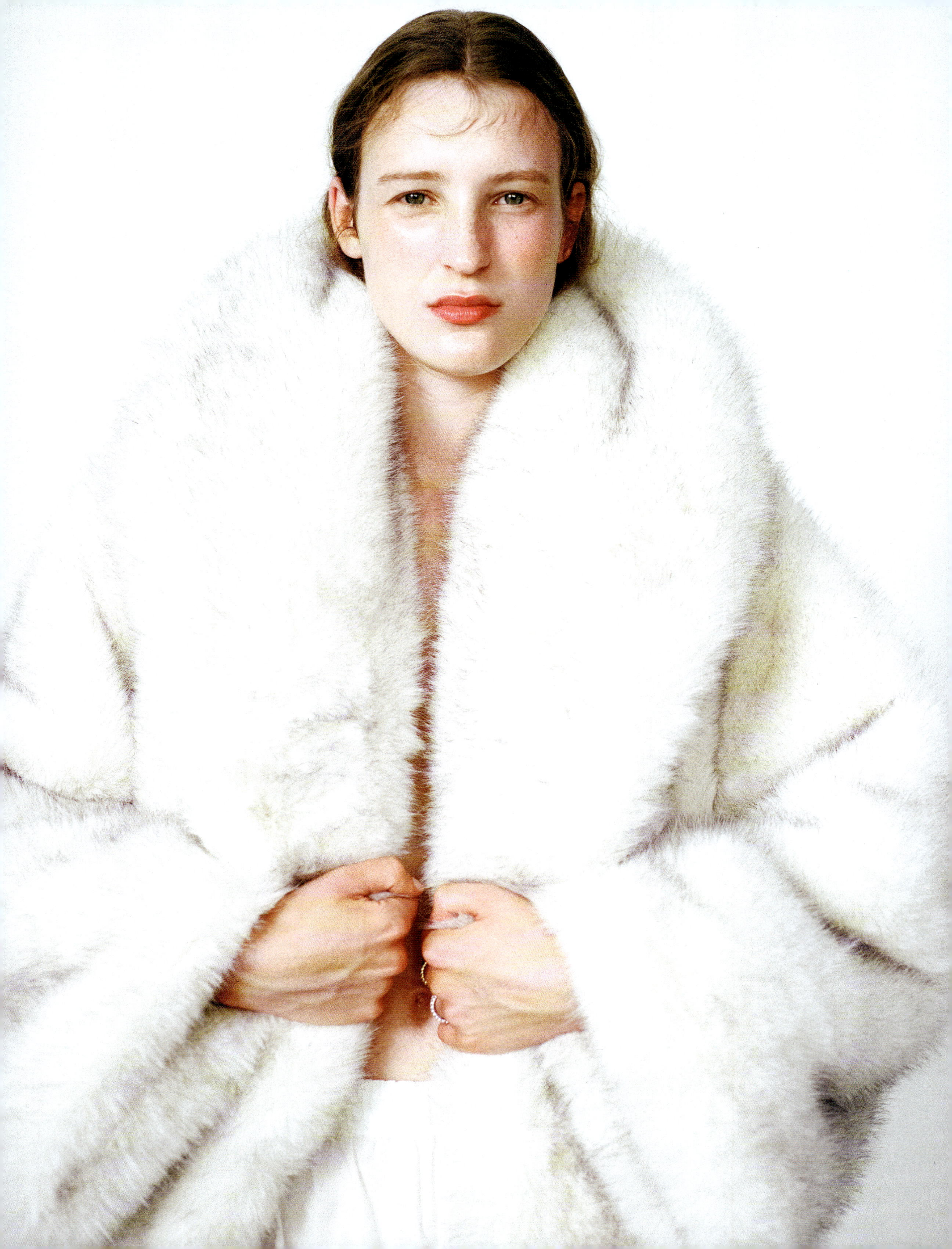

FOR LOVE, NOT MONEY

Five Scandinavians choosing purpose over profit.

Words
Benjamin Dane
Photos
Cecilie Jegsen

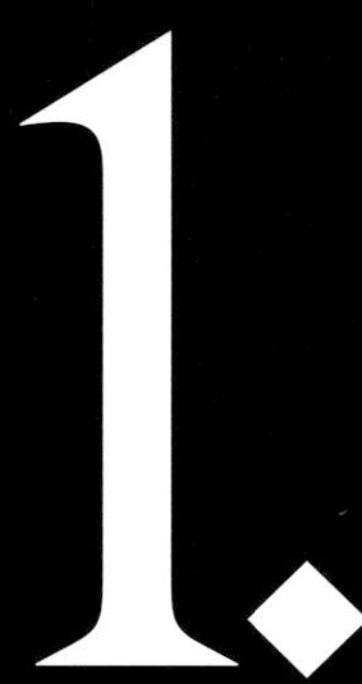

1. Degrowth: Isangs

What does it mean to build a business without chasing growth? For Sundra Essien, founder of Copenhagen-based hair- and body-care company Isangs, the answer lies in redefining the meaning of success. Her shop runs on principles of degrowth: no advertising, no plans to scale up and physical limits built into production. Instead of expansion, she prizes relationships, craft and impact.

BENJAMIN DANE: The idea of degrowth sounds appealing in theory, but how does it work in practice?

SUNDRA ESSIEN: That's the question, right? I've had this conversation for years. The response is always the same: nice idea, doesn't work. So, part of this is just my stubborn way of saying—Well, I'll show you. And really, it's not that radical. Most of human history has been slow-growth or no-growth: local bakers, cobblers, small shops that never franchise. Degrowth for me is simply designing limits into the business—working at a scale that is sustainable, not chasing expansion for its own sake.

BD: How did your background shape the choice to start Isangs on these principles?

SE: I studied business, then law, worked as a corporate lawyer, moved into human rights, spent time on a permaculture research farm in Belize and taught at Copenhagen Business School. But I wanted something more tangible. I've always loved chemistry—my mom was a chemistry teacher—and hair and body care touches everyone. It's an interesting way to introduce ideas like overconsumption and supply-chain issues through a familiar product. People don't expect to have a discussion around degrowth in a soap shop, and that disarms them in a positive way.

BD: If not by revenue or expansion, how do you measure success?

SE: You could call it qualitative growth instead of quantitative growth. We're growing in our relationships, knowledge, craft; in how we spread information. It doesn't translate into bigger profits or larger spaces, but into better processes and richer conversations. We deprogram consumers one person at a time—because we've all been trained to always want more. If someone comes in and already has a product at home, we'll tell them: Use that first.

BD: How do you handle demand if more people want your products?

SE: We've built slow growth into everything. Production is limited to the shop. Soap is handmade and cured for weeks, so capacity is capped. We don't advertise; it's all word of mouth. Employees aren't trained to push sales but to build relationships. We also rarely release new products—we've been selling the same deodorant for seven years.

BD: To what extent do you see Isangs as an experiment?

SE: Very much so. It's an experiment and a playground. When people say it can't work, this is how we show them it can. Sometimes experiments fail but that's part of it. Most businesses fail, growth-centered or not. You have to be naive enough to believe you'll make it, but realistic enough to know failure is always possible.

BD: If you did face failure, would you ever compromise by scaling up to increase income?

SE: No. Growth doesn't necessarily solve problems—it often creates new ones. Expanding means more expenses, more entanglements. I prefer subtraction over addition: reducing costs and complexity instead of chasing more money.

BD: How has running Isangs for more than a decade changed your ideas of wealth and value?

SE: It's been a feedback loop. My parents both grew up poor—in Texas and in Nigeria—but chose to live within their means. I carried that into the business, and the business feeds it back to me. When people tell me something resonated, when we spend an hour with a customer, laugh or cry with them—that's real value. Growth would actually prevent those moments. For me, success is building a life and a business small enough to sustain.

—

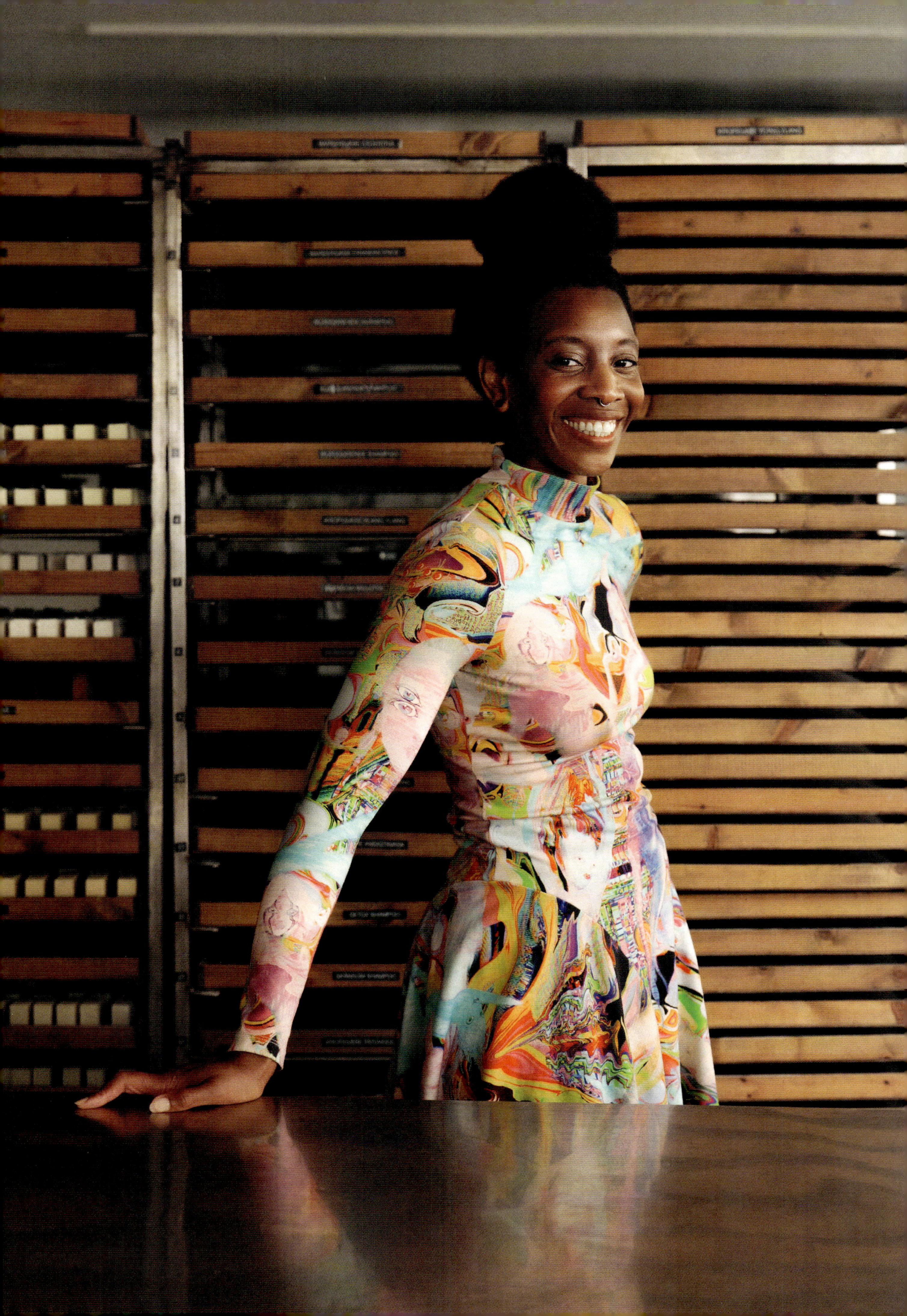

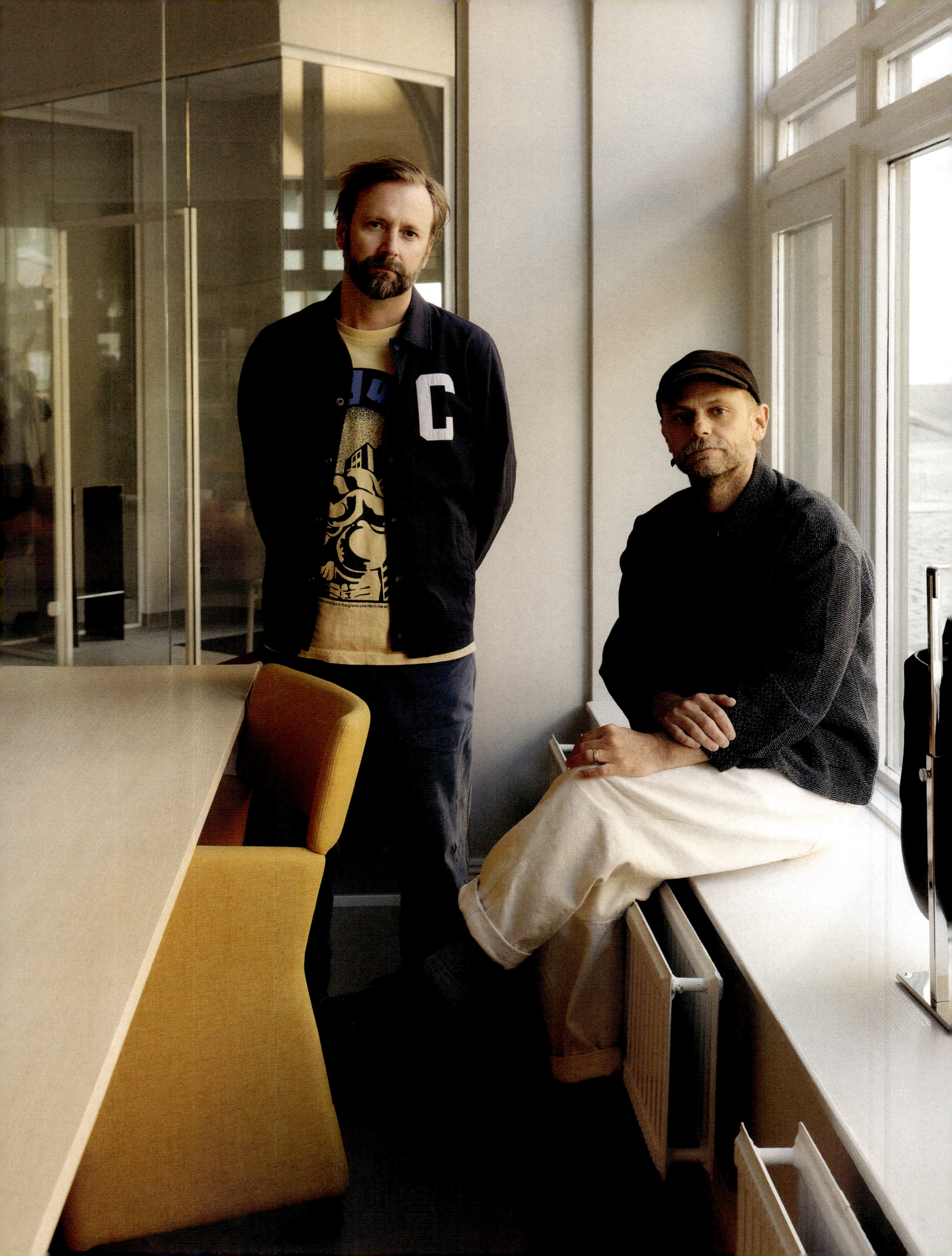

In 2023, Swedish accessories brand Sandqvist cut their workweek from five days to four—without reducing salaries. The move was first suggested by the company's CEO, Caroline Lind, and quickly embraced by founders Daniel Sandqvist and Sebastian Westin, who saw an opportunity to improve employee well-being and rethink how time is valued at work. Since then, the change has reshaped the company culture and even the founders' own relationship to work.

BENJAMIN DANE: Why did you decide to introduce a four-day workweek at Sandqvist?

DANIEL SANDQVIST: When our CEO came to us with the idea, we were drawn to it—one of the motivations for running our own business has always been freedom. The possibility of having more time was something we wanted to pass on to our employees. But the main motivation was employee well-being—reducing the stress of everyday life when you're juggling kids, shopping, cooking and work.

BD: How did your employees react when you announced it?

SEBASTIAN WESTIN: We shared the news in our monthly gathering and there was a lot of gratitude—some people even teared up. Of course, there were also questions—how it would work, whether deadlines could still be met—but we had prepared carefully. We'd studied other examples and tested scenarios internally.

BD: And how does it work?

DS: It's flexible. Some people take Fridays off for a long weekend, others spread the hours out and work shorter days. It depends on your role. If you're in sales and go to a trade fair, you might work longer hours that week. But when the workload is lighter, you can enjoy the extra time. It's not a strict one-day-off policy—it's about finding balance.

BD: Were there challenges in the transition?

SW: Definitely. Some people found it stressful at first as they felt they had to do the same amount of work in less time. We worked through that by sitting down with individuals, reviewing workloads and even bringing in external consultants to help people find better ways of organizing their time. It's also about flexibility: Some jobs simply can't be compressed in the same way as others, so we had to adapt.

BD: What about the benefits—were there any surprises?

SW: At first there was excitement, then a period of stress as people adjusted. But after a few months, many employees experienced a second wave of happiness. One colleague told us he almost felt like he was cheating at first—having Fridays off felt unreal. But once he settled into the rhythm, he was delighted to have more time with family or to go fishing.

DS: Personally, I've also noticed that the best ideas often come when I'm not at work. Having that extra time off seems to make everyone more creative.

BD: How has it affected productivity and company culture?

SW: We received a flood of job applications after the change. Our bimonthly employee surveys also show that we've succeeded in improving well-being, and productivity hasn't dropped; in some ways it's gone up, because meetings are shorter and people use their time more wisely. The bigger shift is cultural: People value their time more, and they value each other's time too.

BD: Do you think the four-day week could be a model for other companies and industries?

DS: I think so—or at least I hope so. We've had a lot of interest from other companies asking about our experience, even from politicians looking into the idea. Of course, every business is different, but in industries where people work physically hard and risk burning out early, shorter workweeks could make a real difference. It might also help companies that struggle to attract staff, because people value this kind of benefit highly. For us it works, but we stay humble about the fact that it may not be a one-size-fits-all solution.

Four-Day Week: Sandqvist

2.◆

Not for Profit: Svenskt Tenn

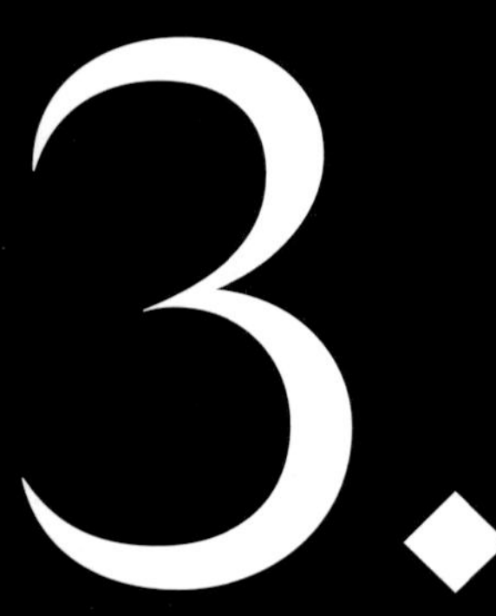

3.

Since 1975, the Swedish design house Svenskt Tenn has been owned by the Kjell and Märta Beijer Foundation, a charity that promotes scientific research. Today, every krona of profit made by the much-loved store, which was originally founded in 1924, goes to support research in areas such as sustainability, genetics, biomedicine and pharmaceuticals. For Maria Veerasamy, the CEO of Svenskt Tenn since 2011, the structure means balancing commercial success with a higher purpose: to sustain craftsmanship, uphold timeless design and fund knowledge for the future.

BENJAMIN DANE: What does it mean in practice for Svenskt Tenn to be owned by a nonprofit foundation?

MARIA VEERASAMY: We are a profitable company, but the difference is what happens with the profit. All of it goes to research through the foundation. Profitability is still expected—without it we cannot ensure the long-term stability of the company, nor provide grants and sustain our suppliers, many of them small Swedish workshops. It's a very unique way of running a business.

BD: How does this structure affect your role compared with a traditional luxury brand with shareholders?

MV: My responsibility is not to people who want to earn money; it is toward the history of the company. The foundation bought Svenskt Tenn to keep it forever, so everything is long-term. If sales are lower one year, that can be accepted if the quality is maintained. But you are challenged in another way: Are you making the best decisions for the future of the company? That is the perspective.

BD: I understand that when you started you were told you had to think in centuries.

MV: Yes, the chairman said: You need to make decisions that will last 300 years. At first, I thought he was crazy, but it really shifted my mindset. If we start something new, it might be a 20-year project. That is very different from most companies, where a CEO stays three or four years and then moves on. Here you can build quality over a lifetime.

BD: Can you share examples of the projects that the foundation has supported with Svenskt Tenn's profits?

MV: The foundation funds a wide range of research into the environment, food systems, animal welfare and medicine; the researchers often tell us they can work more freely than in commercial projects. As an example, they have studied the nutritional value of food, and how speeding up food production reduces quality. Another project looked at keeping calves with their mothers longer, and what that means for both animal welfare and milk production. They have even developed methods to study horses' movement to detect health problems.

BD: How does the ownership model influence the culture of the company?

MV: People feel pride. There is a higher purpose. We make sure that the staff knows where the money is going by arranging talks—recently, we met a researcher working with AI in cancer studies. For me personally, my joy is when I see a supplier with a young apprentice in the workshop. Without those projects Svenskt Tenn is nothing—we need the crafts. Because we don't have to compromise on quality, we can support that.

BD: How does it affect your approach as a design brand?

MV: We don't work with seasonal collections, and we don't do sales or discounts. That means when we collaborate with a new or young designer, we can give their work the time it needs. The Dagg vase, which is now one of our most iconic pieces—and even featured on Swedish postage stamps—barely sold in its first couple of years. That kind of patience is rare in this industry, but for us it's natural. We don't panic if something isn't an immediate success; we believe in quality and longevity, and we trust that the right customers will see that too.

BD: Could this be a model for others in the industry?

MV: I hope so. The big companies have so much money. It would make a real difference if they produced even one or two products locally and helped to safeguard crafts. I believe high-quality crafted objects are the future.

—

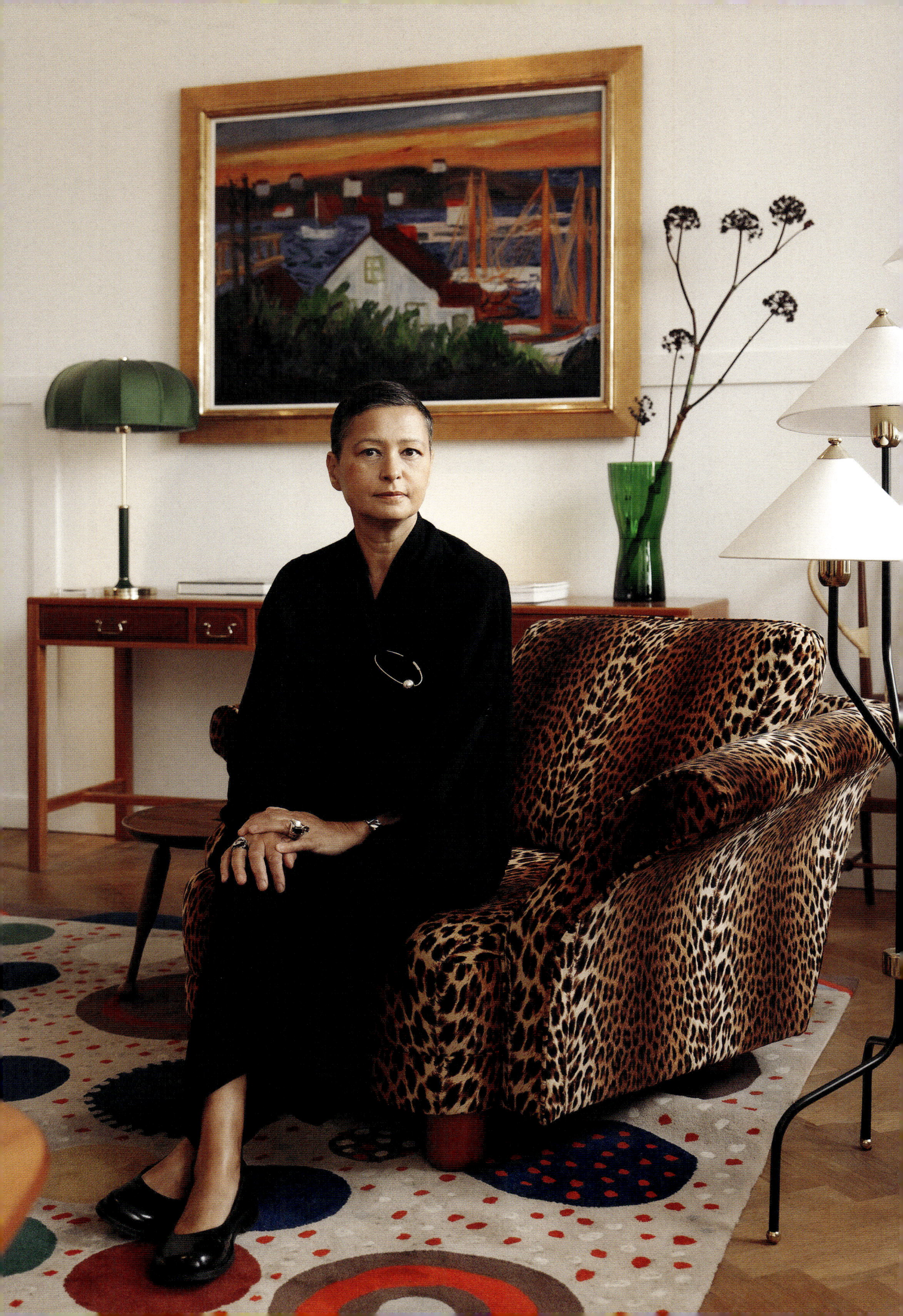

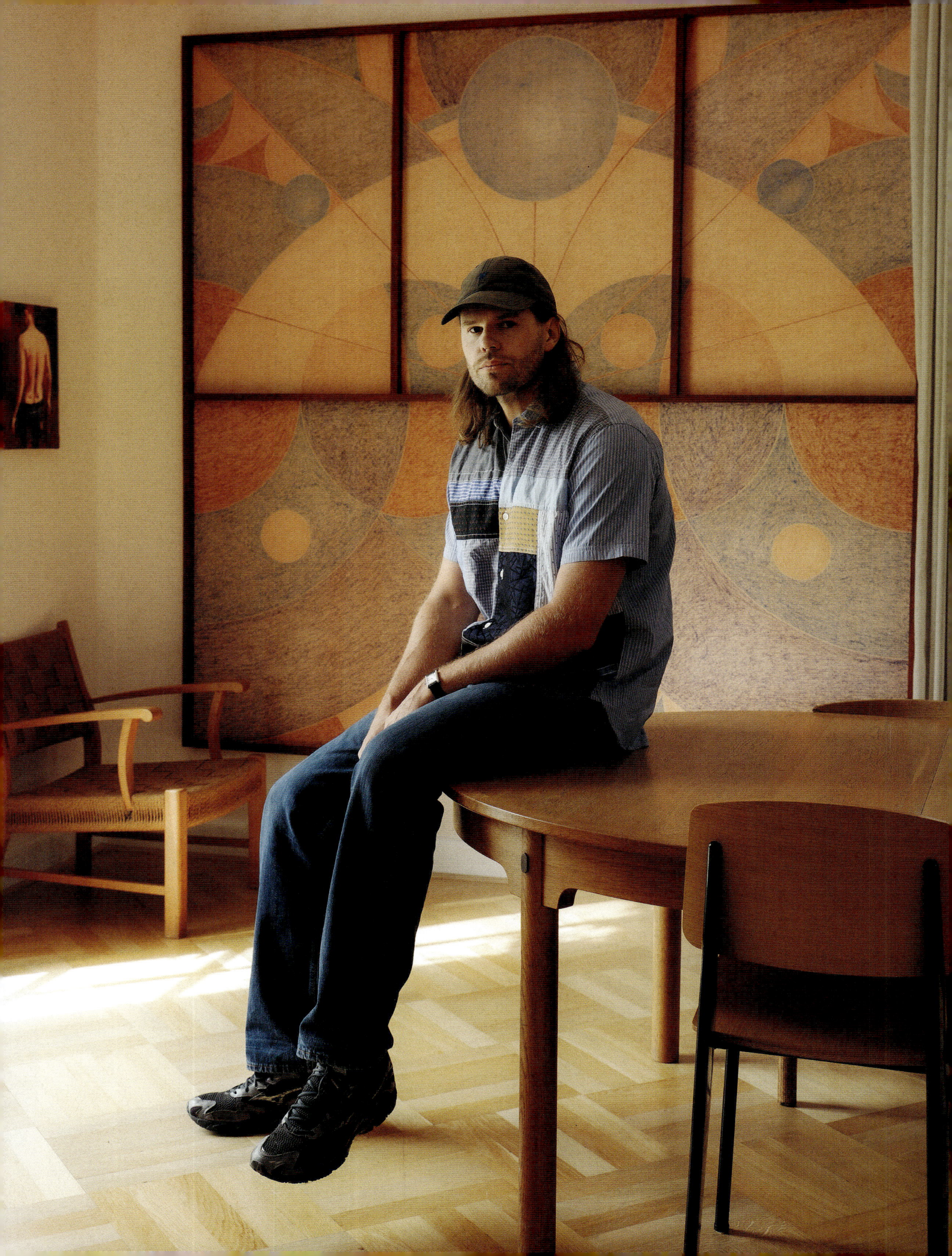

Patronage:
Mikkel Hansen

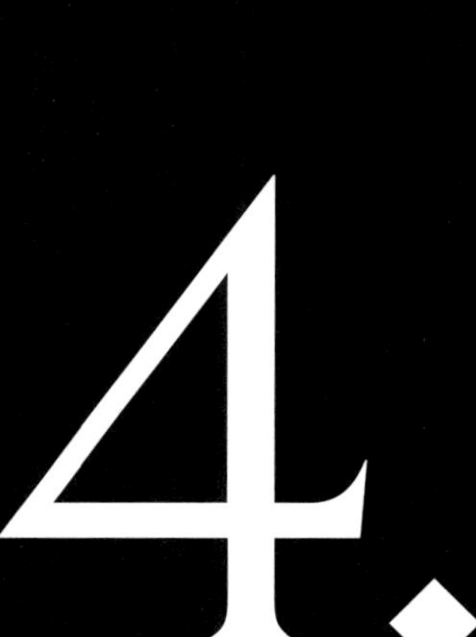

Mikkel Hansen still has the first artwork he bought. It hangs in a corner of his living room in Ordrup, to the north of Copenhagen: a photographic series by Danish photographer Asger Carlsen, depicting headless, naked bodies with limbs cut away, twisted and frozen as though metamorphosizing into sculpture. Hansen bought it more than a decade ago, when he was playing handball for Paris Saint-Germain. A friend who often visited his apartment in Paris would have the same reaction every time she saw it: "Oh God, you still have this up? You own so many beautiful works—how can you keep this on the wall?"

Hansen smiles at the memory. "That's the beauty of art," he says. "Something that I find super interesting and beautiful, she really couldn't stand. It triggered something in her. That immediate reaction is what makes art exciting."

At 37, Hansen is widely regarded as one of the greatest handball players of all time, helping Denmark to win both Olympic and World Championship titles—and being named World Player of the Year three times—before retiring in 2024. Off the court, however, he has been an avid art collector for years. "Art is a way of bringing out emotions," he says. "It gives me memories, feelings, it's something that sparks the imagination."

Growing up, Hansen's exposure to art was occasional and his passion really developed once he could afford to buy works. He began visiting exhibitions and attending openings in Paris, at first collecting photography and paintings before his tastes widened to include sculpture, ceramics, performance, even video art. "I don't think I've come across an art form I didn't find interesting," he says.

Collecting, for Hansen, is intuitive. He doesn't see himself as a systematic buyer and resists the word "collection": "When I hear that word, I imagine several hundred works," he says. He instead owns around a hundred pieces, and he likes them to be visible. "I have a hard time putting things in storage. I don't think artists make work to sit in a basement. I want it to be on the walls, or with friends and family who can enjoy it."

Hansen is quick to downplay the monetary side of his passion. "Of course no one buys something hoping it will lose value," he admits. "But for me it's not about investment. The value is the joy of living with it, what it gives me and my family." There are still pieces he admires that are beyond reach, but Hansen also relishes the subjectivity of the art market. "That's what makes it fascinating," he says. "Something people will pay fortunes for leaves others shaking their heads." That subjectivity extends to his own household, where his wife sometimes vetoes certain acquisitions. "If she doesn't think it's completely terrible, then maybe I can get it up on the wall," he says with a grin.

As with sports, Hansen believes collecting requires repetition. "If you want to be good at math, you do exercises," he explains. "If you want to be good at handball, you do drills. With art, you look and look and look." Recently he has been drawn to sculpture, reading detailed accounts of the technical challenges artists face in their production. "It's fun to nerd out a bit," he says, "to understand the problems artists try to solve." He dreams of installing works in his garden, where they might play against the architecture and the pool.

Hansen has already amassed an impressive collection indoors. Walking through his home, he points out works by Tal R, Emma Kohlmann, Anton Funck, Sara-Vide Ericson and Nicolai Howalt. There are series of photographs, several large paintings, small ceramic pieces. The juxtapositions delight him. "I like the way things work together—art, furniture, colors. It tells the story of how we want to live," he says.

He stops in front of two Howalt photographs of a young boxer—before and after his first fight—that hang in a corner of the dining room. The boy looks proud and frightened, jaw set in one image, softened in the next, eyes glistening. Hansen explains that there's a book accompanying the series revealing which boys won and which lost, but he has never sought it out. "I like not knowing," he says. "Some days, I'm sure he won—other days, I'm convinced he lost. It all depends on what mood I'm in. If I knew the result, it might kill the mystery. And for me, that's what art is about."

Philanthropy: The OBEL Foundation

5.

Henrik Frode Obel was only ever an amateur enthusiast of architecture, but he has come to have an outsize impact on the field. Born into a prominent and wealthy Danish family, he preferred to go abroad to make his fortune, rather than stay at home and inherit. The venture gave him financial freedom and—as a seasoned traveler, a bon vivant with a keen eye for aesthetics and a friend of the architect and Sydney Opera House designer, Jørn Utzon—an enduring love of architecture.

When he died in 2014, Obel left his fortune to the foundation that bears his name, with the goal of promoting architecture as a force for change, most notably through the annual OBEL Award.

"It was very important to him that architecture was not just seen as an aesthetic object, but as something of value for future generations," explains Jamiee Touveneau Williams, head of Projects and Partnerships at OBEL. "He wanted to reward and recognize the potential of architecture not only as a social construct or shaper, but also as something that preserves culture and heritage."

Unlike most prizes, the OBEL Award is not application-based. Instead, it relies on a network of around 50 anonymous scouts—architects, academics and climatologists, among others—who are spread across 30 countries. Each year, they are asked by OBEL's executive director, Jesper Eis Eriksen, to nominate projects or practices in line with a theme chosen by the jury. "We try to unfold what architecture is and understand its plurality," explains Monique Schröder, head of Brand and Communications. "Architecture is not just the design of a building. It can be an idea, an innovation, a process. We've never awarded simply a building or an architect."

The scope of the award is reflected in its recent winners. In 2023, landscape architect Kate Orff was honored for Living Breakwaters, a coastal defense project off Staten Island conceived after Hurricane Sandy. The project used oysters as natural breakwaters to buffer storm surges, and combined ecological restoration with political lobbying and deep community engagement. "She was in the trenches with lobbyists, trying to change policy to secure funding for climate resilience," Williams says. "It wasn't just about design—it was about mobilizing a community and shaping legislation."

In 2025, the award went to HouseEurope!, a nonprofit initiative campaigning to reform European legislation and make renovation more financially attractive than demolition. "It's urgent work," says Schröder, "because demolition has a huge impact on the environment, materials, people and neighborhoods." That urgency persuaded the jury even though the campaign's outcome remains uncertain: HouseEurope! needs one million signatures by the end of January 2026 to bring the issue to the European Parliament. "We are not afraid to award something unfinished," says Schröder. "It's about long-term impact and scalability."

In an industry awash with prizes for glittering, multimillion-dollar projects, the OBEL Foundation positions itself differently. "There are so many architecture awards, some for profit, some for media, some with different purposes," says Williams. "What's nice about ours is that you don't need to be a big name. You can win because you're trying to change something. It shows younger practices that it's okay to be purpose-driven."

Support extends beyond the €100,000 ($115,000) prize. Winners receive follow-up funding to advance their work, as well as practical help with communications and connections. Sam Draper and Barney Shanks, the material scientists who won in 2022, were developing carbon-neutral concrete. "The award enabled them to find funding and even set up a lab," Williams recalls. "We're not investors, but we can act like an early-stage supporter, building the network they need."

Architecture is becoming an increasingly interdisciplinary field—intertwining climatology, material science, activism and policy—and the foundation sees its role as connecting dots. "Every year we pick a focus that reflects what's most relevant at the time," Williams says. "In the future, we'll have an archive of these themes and submissions, mapping how architecture has responded to society's challenges."

For Schröder, communication is equally critical. "We don't want to speak only to architects. We want to shift the public perception of what architecture is. It's not just glossy buildings. It's something everyone lives in and shapes together."

That message, voiced through exhibitions, biennale events and fellowships, may unfold slowly, but OBEL believes it will endure. "You can't rush gentleness and care," Schröder says. "We're a modest foundation with a modest endowment. But we hope to create more relationships, more community and more impact—exactly as Henrik Frode Obel intended."

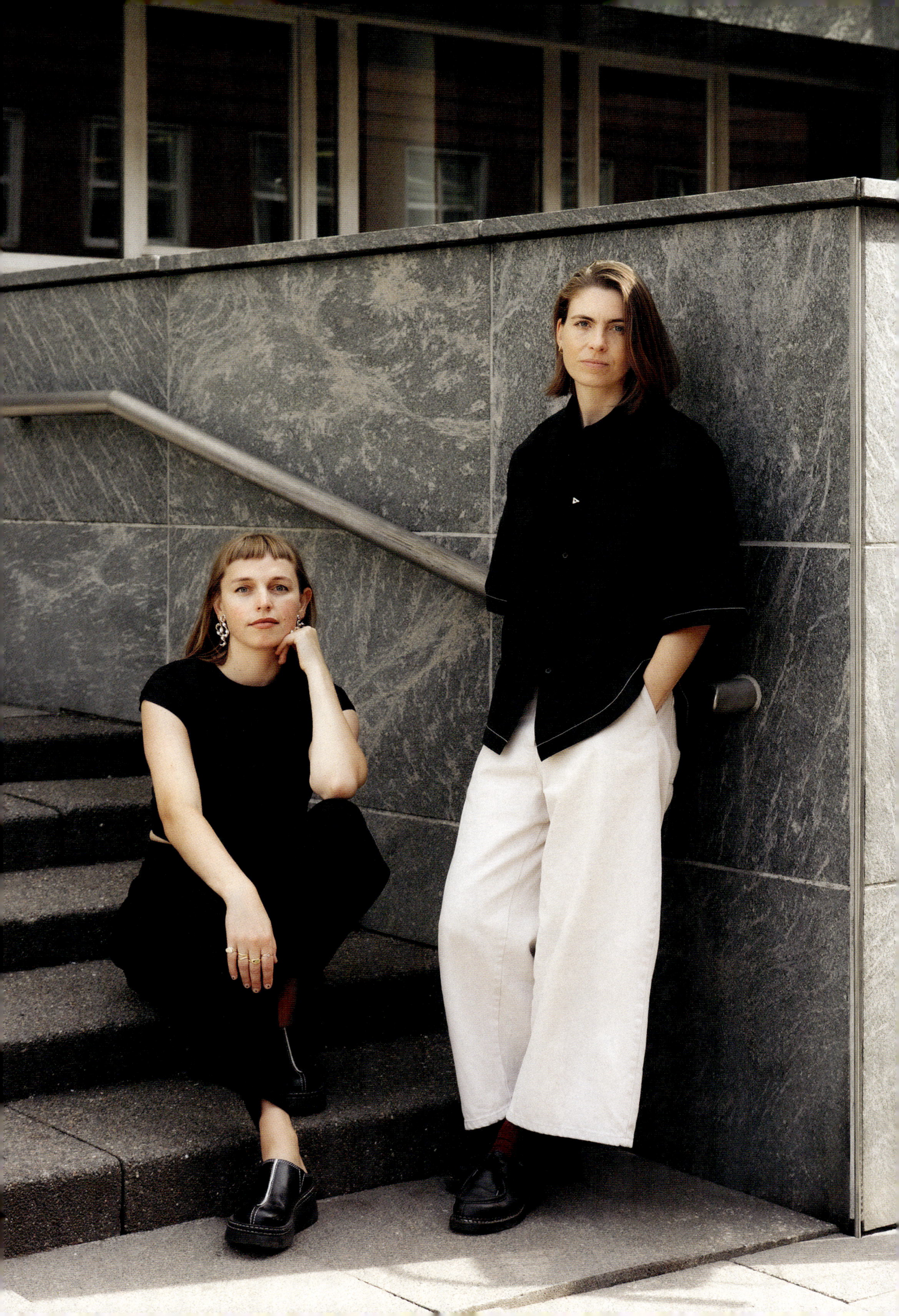

Tastemaker to the 1%: Behind the scenes with the editor of *HTSI* magazine.

JO ELLIS

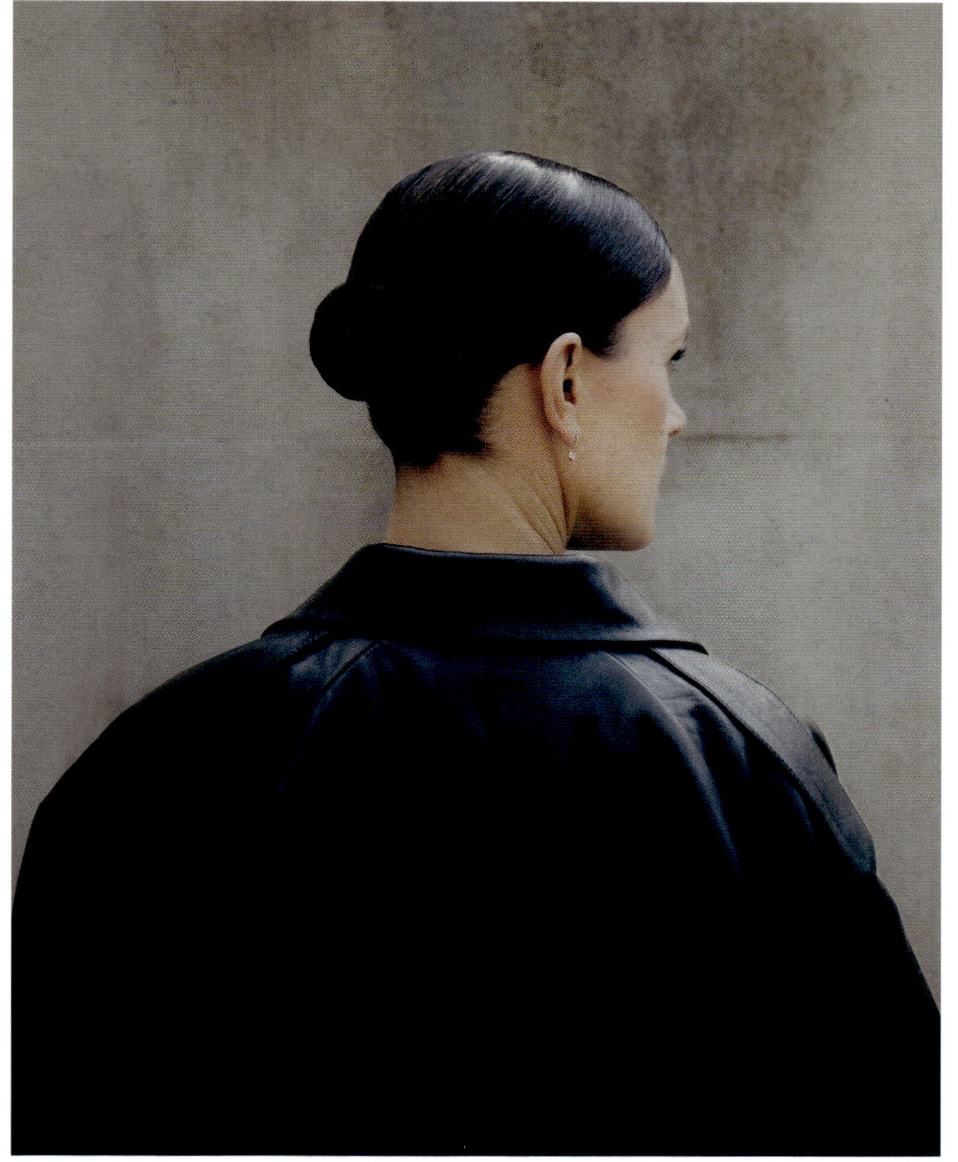

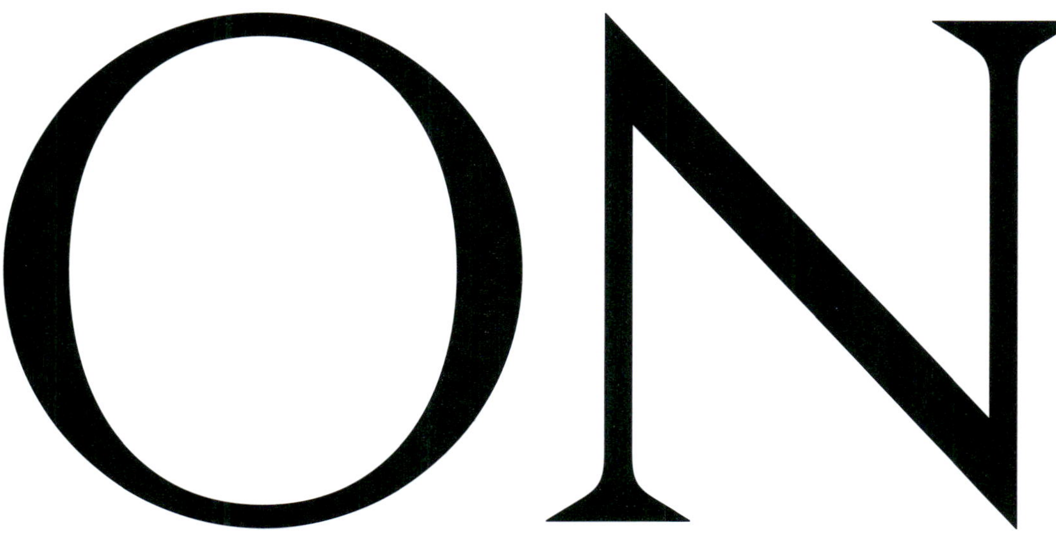

ON

Words
Fedora Abu

Photos
Alixe Lay

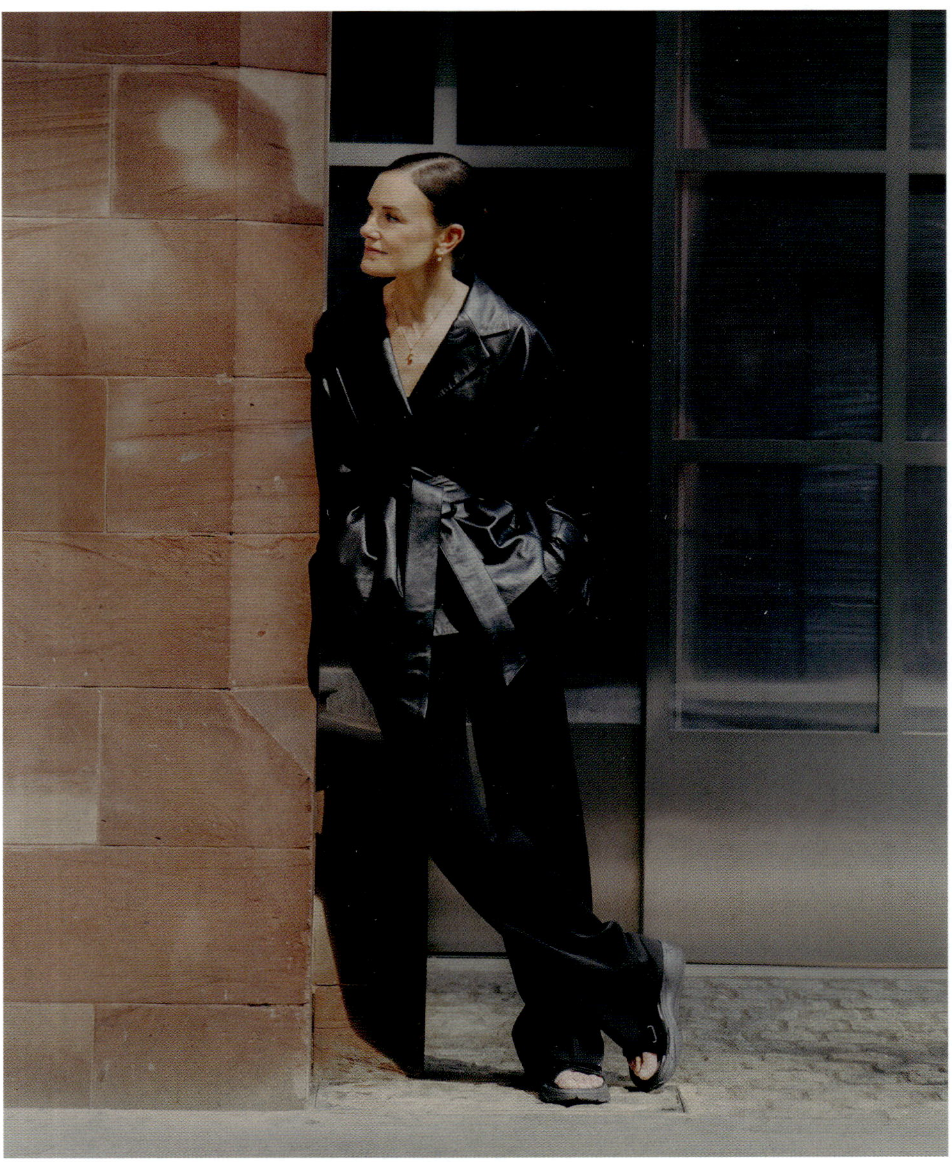

A month or so before this interview takes place, a bombshell drops. The world's most powerful magazine editor, a titan of the fashion industry, is stepping down after a 37-year tenure. The news breaks in tandem with a rare *Vogue* digital cover (you know, the one for *that* wedding in Venice). It's not long before a glut of hot takes roll in, heralding the final capitulation of good taste and editorial judgment to clicks and, ultimately, the twilight of the glossy print magazine. Besides, in the age of influencers, no one's really looking to be decreed to by glamorous women in glass towers anymore, even if they do happen to be Anna Wintour.

Jo Ellison's reign at *HTSI* flies in the face of all that. As the editor of the *Financial Times*' luxury supplement, she has transformed the magazine into a cultural force that reaches far beyond the newspaper it sits within, and established it as the new bible of good taste—*her* taste. "If I hate something, it's going to be hard to feature it in the magazine," Ellison says. In a media machine that seems to prioritize pundits and platforms who shout the loudest and react the fastest, the elusive idea of "good taste" can seem to be of diminishing value. *HTSI* has proven there's clearly still an appetite for it.

Ellison is at the *FT*'s headquarters in London on a late afternoon in August. Her office, which sits within the Life & Arts newsroom, is pretty sparse and down-to-business, save for a couple of family photos. She's not the media archetype of a luxury magazine editor but low-key, polished and practical, dressed in an oversized black turtleneck with her hair pulled back. "Brilliant," "a workhorse" and "slightly terrifying" are words used by people I know who've worked with Ellison or been in her orbit; she puts it in less delicate terms: "People have always thought I'm a dick."

Of course, the qualities that might intimidate some—her decisiveness and tendency to say it as it is—are precisely what have made her such a successful editor and journalist. "I think I was born with a confidence about what I liked," she says. "I am definitely one of those people who has very strong opinions." Her distinct point of view filters what makes it into the magazine, shapes her column in the Life & Arts section and accompanies her posts on Instagram (where she has over 100,000 followers), and is what makes her a respected figure in media and fashion circles. She's also a regular subject of street-style photographers, and seems happy to go out and be the face of the magazine.

Ellison joined the *FT* as fashion editor in 2014 from *British Vogue*, where she ran the features desk. "I was in a really weird position because I was at a newspaper which thought I had a tremendous authority over fashion and at the shows, people were like, 'Who the fuck is she?'" Then in 2019, the opportunity came about to lead the paper's luxury supplement when Gillian de Bono, her predecessor, announced she was stepping down. *How To Spend It*, as it was formerly known, began as a page within the paper in 1967, evolved into a magazine in 1994 and had come to be viewed by some as a symbol of the excesses of the City. A year before Ellison took the reins, *The Guardian* described it as "unashamedly ostentatious."

Though Ellison was already one of the *FT*'s star journalists and an obvious contender for the role, the job wasn't simply bestowed upon her. "I think there was an understanding that *HTSI* was a golden goose," she says. "Break it and the whole ecosystem of the *FT* will fall apart." By the final round of the hiring process, she was asked to present her vision for the magazine, and although she was keen to create something that she felt reflected the real "style arbiters" she was surrounded by in London, she didn't propose a radical reset. "I felt very confident that you could really massage the parameters in which luxury was being editorialized. I felt there was a lot of room to shape and rethink it, but I needed to present it in such a way that I didn't frighten anybody off.'"

H ow to describe Jo Ellison's *HTSI* rebrand? A magazine for the quiet luxury era would make it sound terribly beige but it's certainly more, well, tasteful. Yachts, supercars and helicopters don't frequent the cover as they used to; these days, it'll more likely be a newly restored palazzo in rural Puglia, or a model in chic tailoring dining alfresco in Athens. There are more celebrities, but the art direction is softer, cooler and the tone of voice inflected with humor.

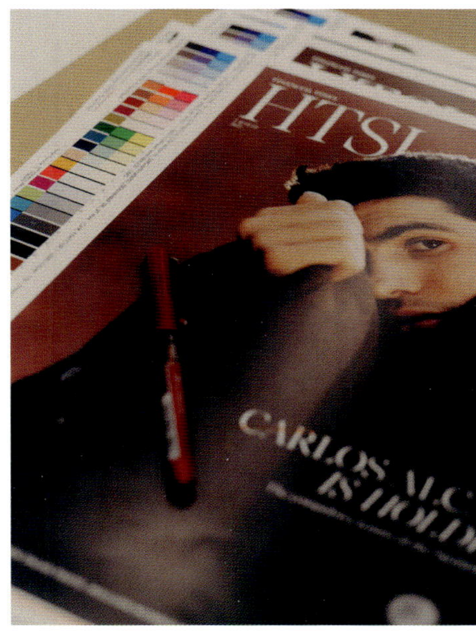

"I find her approach to be really interesting and not snobby," says Chris Black, an influential writer and creative director in New York who cohosts the cult podcast *How Long Gone* (on which Ellison has been a guest).[1] He has been a loyal subscriber to *HTSI* since Ellison took the reins. "It gets the point across in a way that is palatable, but I still learn something every issue. She doesn't take herself seriously, which really comes through in her writing and her editing, and it's refreshing when it's coming from a newspaper like the *Financial Times*, which has that level of stature."

There's still plenty of the eye-wateringly expensive stuff of the old days in *HTSI*. In August, the magazine offered a first look at London's Chancery Rosewood hotel (suites from $1,800 a night) and Louis Vuitton's beauty line ($160 for a lipstick), and shopping features include everything from a $8,800 Miele wine fridge to a $157,000 Van Cleef & Arpels watch. But Ellison's overall vision of luxury seems less beholden to the material trappings of wealth and more about relishing the finest that life has to offer. It's an approach that proved to be especially timely when COVID hit. "A lot of the stuff that was going to happen more gradually [with the magazine] then happened really quickly," she says. "It wasn't about expensive foreign holidays and safaris and building a kitchen to entertain in out of marble. It was about all these kinds of slightly smaller, more esoteric ideas."

Divining what will pique the interest of the luxury shopper (the media kit states its readers have an average net worth of £3 million [$4 million]) involves a combination of insights gleamed from conversations at dinners ("I have to do a lot of dinners"),

(1) *How Long Gone* billed itself as a "bicoastal elite podcast from old friends" in its inaugural episode, blurring water cooler talk, in-depth interviews and hot takes. When she appeared, Ellison spoke about British slang, car insurance, her teenage years in Dubai and watching *Euphoria* with her daughter.

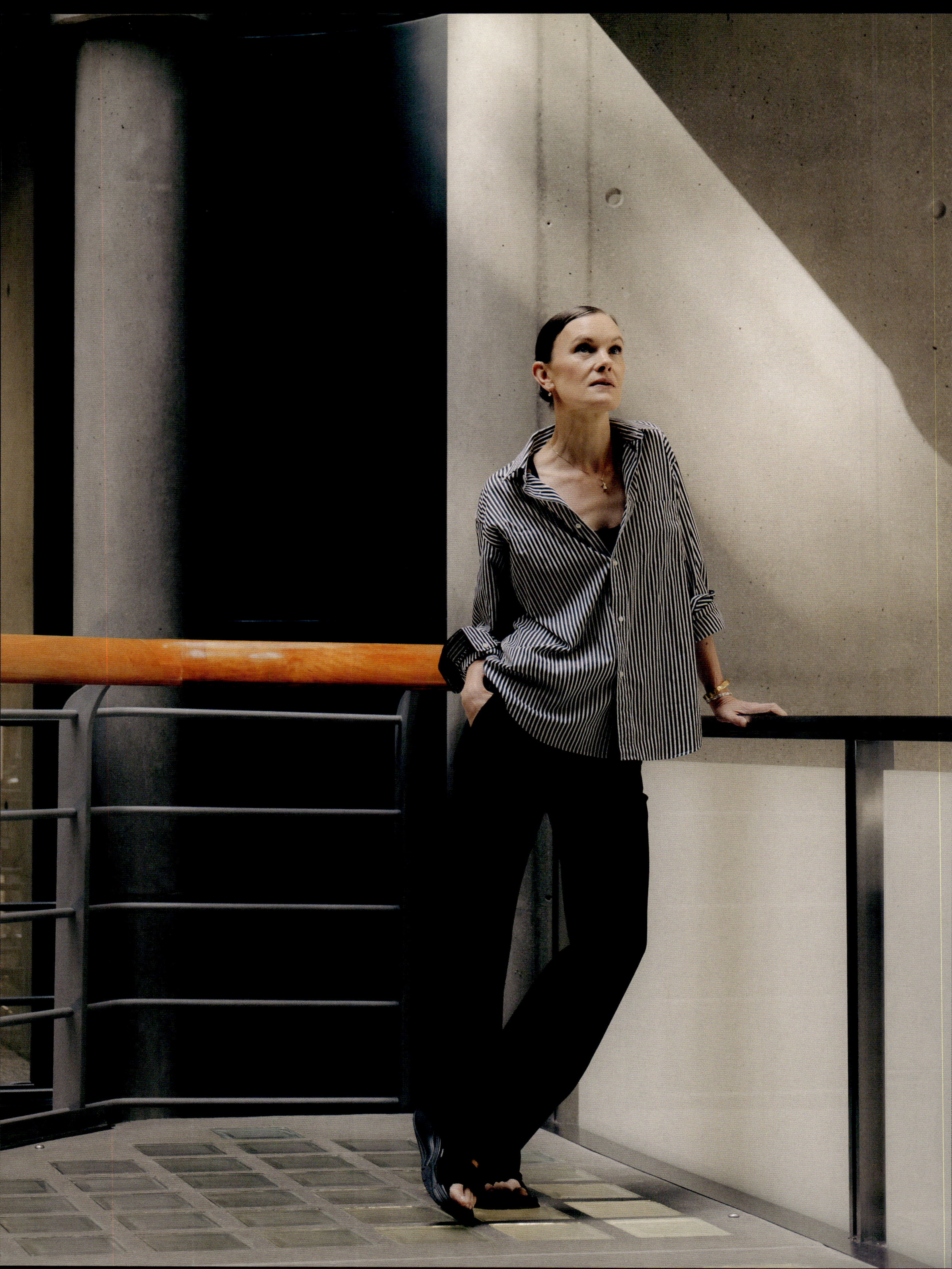

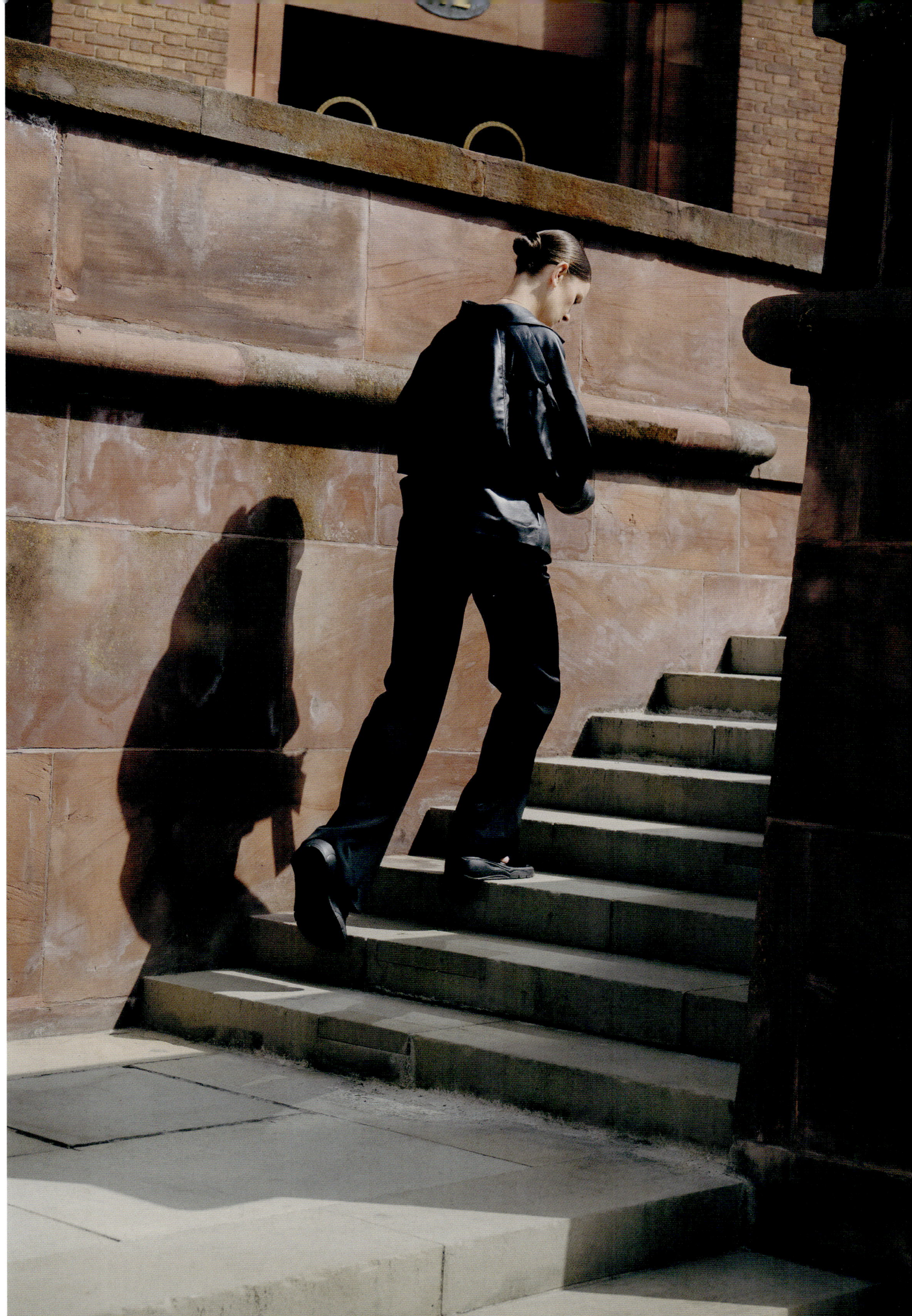

(2)   The City of London is a politically independent part of central London that follows the rough boundaries of the city's original Roman settlement. Often called the Square Mile—or simply "the City"—it serves as a metonym for London's financial district.

(3)   Founded in 1888, the *Financial Times* is a daily newspaper focused on business and economic current affairs. Printed on its distinctive salmon-pink paper, it has become the broadsheet of choice for a highly educated, financially literate and largely affluent readership.

in-the-know contributors and "a strong instinct" from years in the industry. And it was instinct, rather than any sort of market research or focus grouping, that prompted Ellison to make her boldest move with the brand. In 2022, in light of the pandemic, the war in Ukraine and the cost-of-living crisis, she announced that *How To Spend It* was becoming *HTSI*, where the "S" stood for whatever you wanted it to: savor, save, style.

"I think [in America], where the circulation and the readership have been growing, they found [the old name] quite obnoxious. It was tied to a slightly tongue-in-cheek, '90s, winky City-boy humor," she says.[2] "I was like, I just don't want to go out every weekend, especially not in a cost-of-living crisis, with 'How To Spend It' on my forehead." Higher-ups were immediately on board, but the decision was received with cynicism by some corners of the media (even derided as "woke"). "We didn't lose any advertising, we didn't lose any readers, we've carried on growing, we're bigger than we were, so I think it was the right thing to do," she says.

Ellison's editorship has by all measures been an undeniable success—so much so that when a "top job" over in New York is vacated, her name is whispered. However, her verdict on the magazine business isn't exactly favorable. "I think the Hearst and Condé Nast stables are really becoming increasingly reliant on the big events and the YouTube, memeable format and brands to sustain their relevance and it's pretty fucking sad," she says.

Though *HTSI* is facing the same headwinds, it appears to be defying the odds. Admittedly there's the privilege of being under the umbrella of a newspaper whose pink papers, Ellison believes, are a visual shorthand. "I've always thought the *FT* is such a status symbol. You walk around town with it on your arm. It's semaphoring a lot."[3] Still, she's well aware that the modern media ecosystem is fragile and is always thinking about how to evolve the magazine and stay relevant. Over the summer, *HTSI* hosted "The Brains of Wellbeing + Beauty," a series of wellness-themed talks sponsored by Clinique La Prairie, and more events are in the cards.

She's not blindly following the luxury brands and media titles rushing onto TikTok to capture Gen Z quite yet, but she does spend time on the platform herself. "At the moment, I don't see the return on investment particularly, but if someone wanted to give me five million quid tomorrow to develop one, that isn't to say I wouldn't be very happy to do so." Should anyone be ready to invest, Ellison's track record suggests she'd be more than capable of shepherding the next generation of readers toward *HTSI*, but only if it's on her terms.

> "I felt there was a lot of room to shape and rethink [luxury], but I needed to present it in such a way that I didn't frighten anybody off."

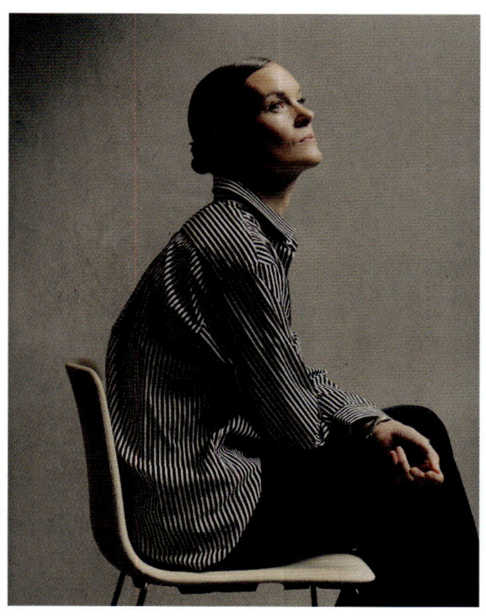

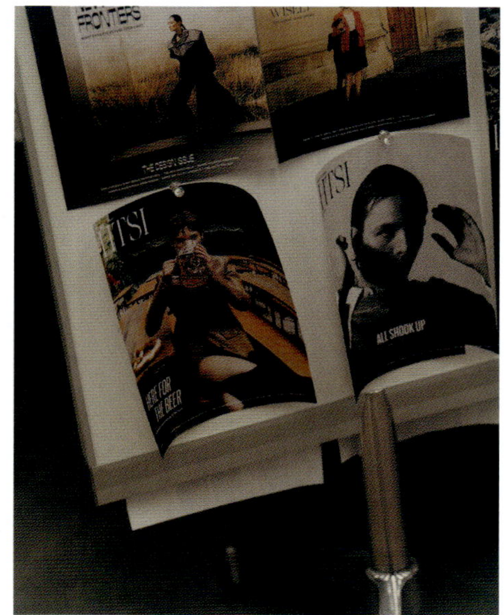

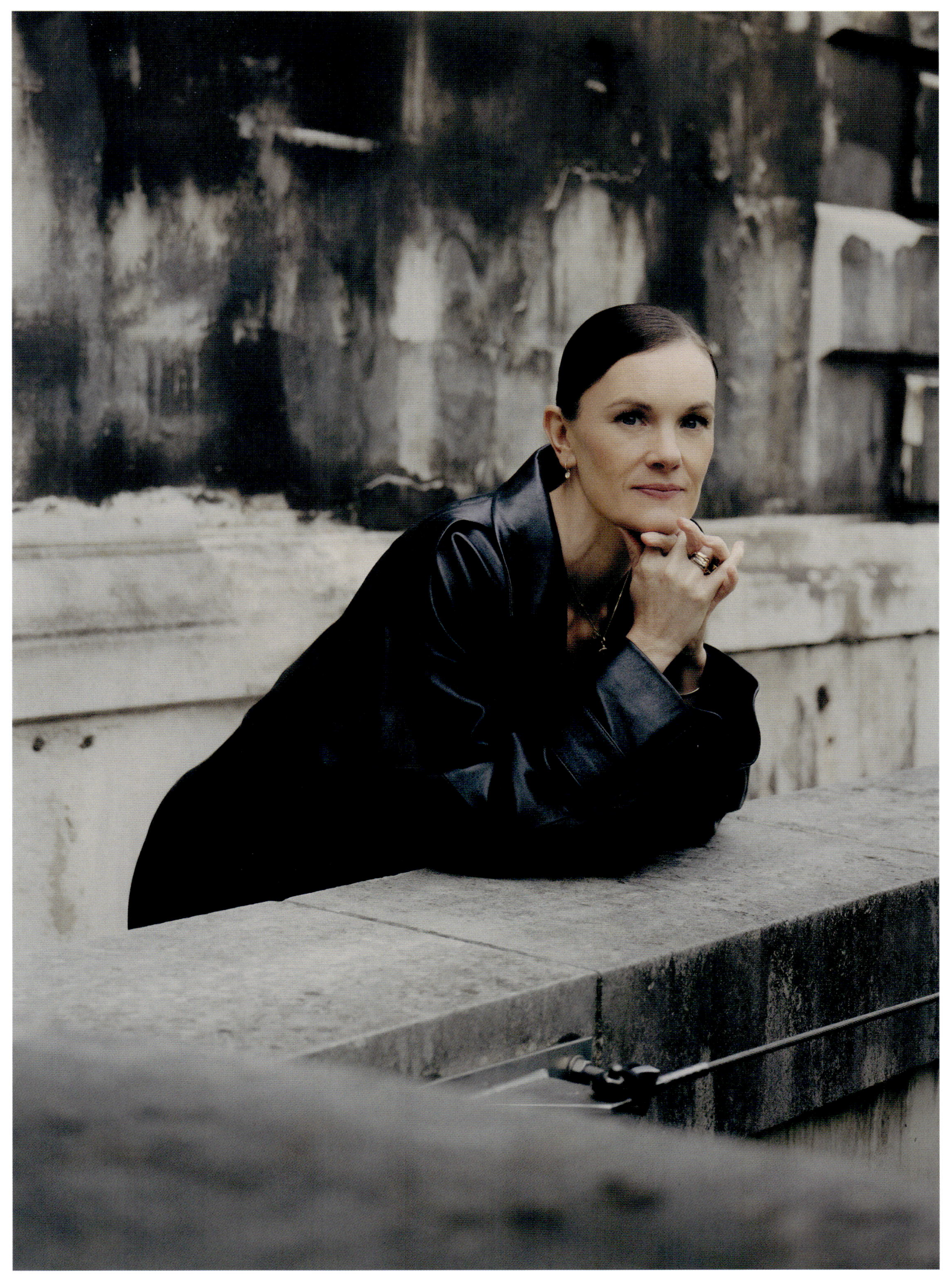

RI CH

Photos
Annika Kafcaloudis

Styling
Stephanie Stamatis

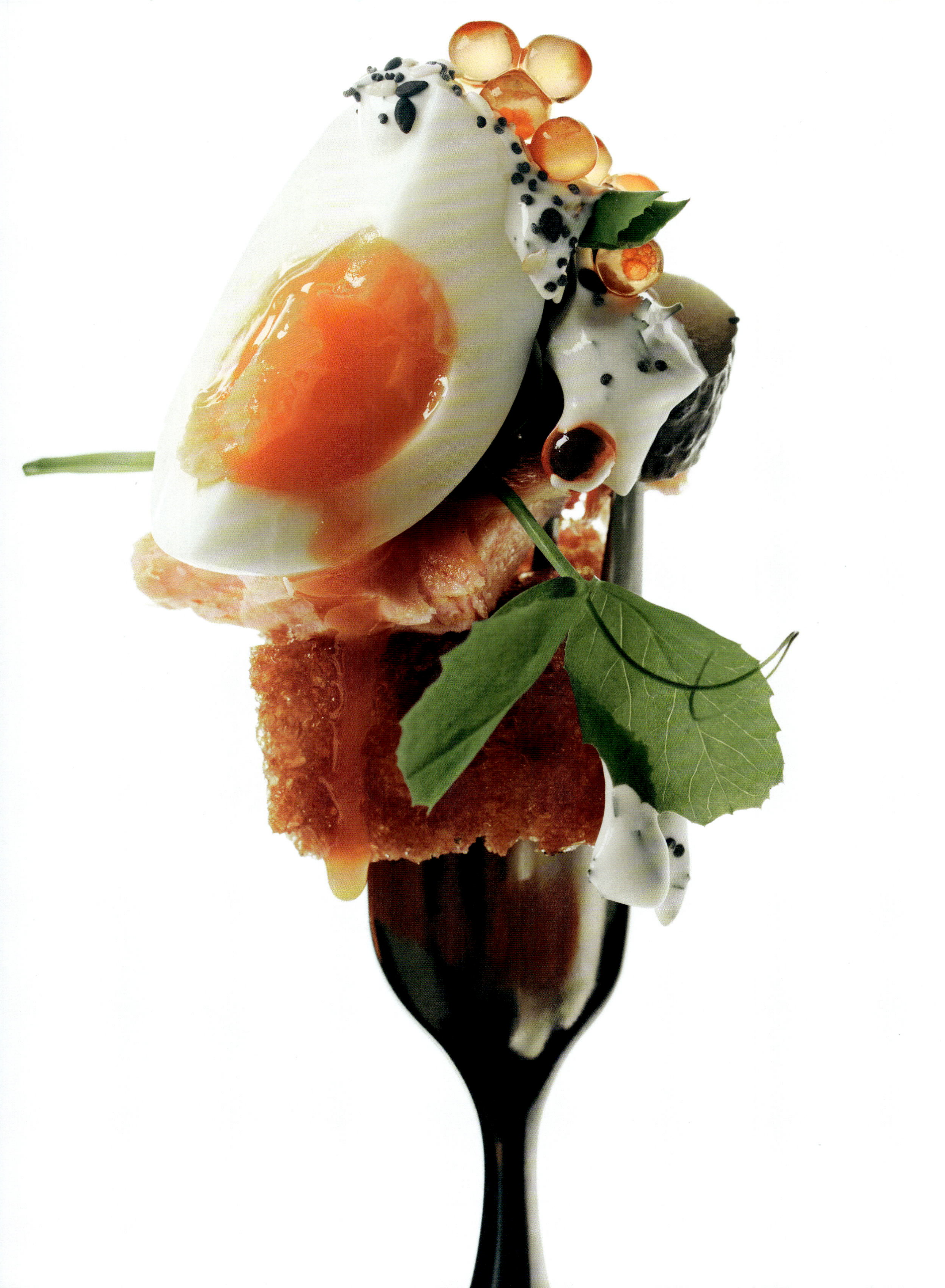

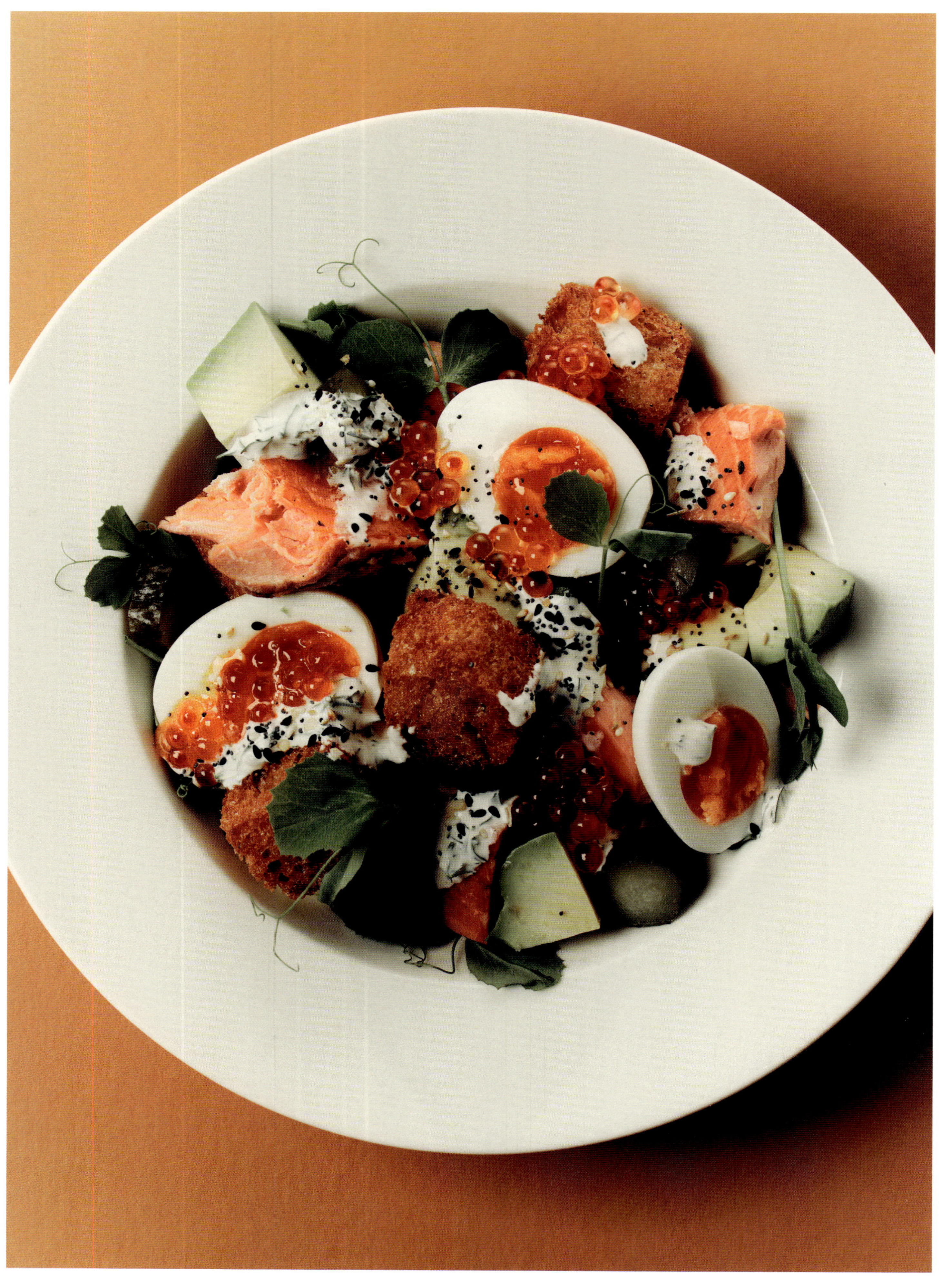

MONEY

HOT SMOKED SALMON EVERYTHING SALAD

SERVES 4 AS A MAIN, 8 AS A STARTER

For the everything seasoning:
1 tablespoon white sesame seeds
1 tablespoon black sesame seeds
1 tablespoon poppy seeds
1 teaspoon onion granules
½ teaspoon garlic granules
½ teaspoon flaky sea salt

For the salmon salad:
5 ounces (150g) sourdough bread
1 tablespoon olive oil
4 eggs
¼ cup (60g) mayonnaise
¼ cup (60g) plain Greek yogurt
Juice of 1 lemon
1 tablespoon chopped fresh dill
Flaky sea salt
2 ripe avocados
2 ounces (60g) pea shoots
12 ounces (340g) hot smoked salmon fillets
4 tablespoons salmon roe
2 tablespoons diced dill pickles

This is the kind of luxurious dish that would make a perfect starter for a dinner party, and it's a fresher way to eat your smoked salmon and everything seasoning than loading it onto a bagel. It oozes elegance (quite literally with the jammy egg yolks and creamy dressing), and the little pops of fish roe add a very classy finish.

To prepare the everything seasoning, add both types of sesame seeds and the poppy seeds to a pan and toast them over medium heat for a couple of minutes, until the white sesame seeds are lightly golden and fragrant. Tip into a medium-sized bowl and add the onion granules, garlic granules and salt. Give it a mix, then set aside.

To prepare the salmon salad, preheat the oven to 400°F/200°C/180°C fan. Cut the sourdough bread into chunky slices and dice them into 1-inch (2.5cm) cubes. Add these to a sheet pan, drizzle with the olive oil and toss. Bake for 10 minutes until crisp and golden, turning over halfway to ensure they cook evenly.

Meanwhile, bring a medium-sized pot of water to a boil. Turn down to a simmer, add the eggs and cook uncovered for 7 minutes. Prepare a bowl with ice water and once the eggs are cooked, place them in the bowl to cool down.

In a separate bowl, combine the mayonnaise, Greek yogurt, lemon juice and chopped dill, then season to taste with salt. Set the creamy dressing aside.

Halve the avocados, remove the pits and score the halves into strips before scooping out the flesh with a spoon. On a large serving platter, spread out the pea shoots. Dot the avocado around the platter, then break the hot smoked salmon into pieces and arrange. Peel and halve the eggs, and add these on top. Drizzle over the creamy dressing, then finish the salad with dollops of salmon roe, diced pickles and a good pinch of the everything seasoning.

For the arancini:
2 tablespoons olive oil
½ white onion, finely chopped
2 garlic cloves, finely chopped
1 tablespoon tomato puree
4 tablespoons 'nduja
½ teaspoon red pepper flakes
3 cups (700ml) chicken stock
¾ cup (150g) arborio rice
¼ cup (25g) grated Parmesan
Zest and juice of ½ lemon
Flaky sea salt and freshly ground black pepper
4 ounces (112g) fresh mozzarella
⅓ cup (40g) all-purpose flour
2 eggs
2 cups (90g) panko breadcrumbs
Vegetable oil, for frying

For the aioli:
Pinch of saffron
1 egg yolk
1 small garlic clove
6 tablespoons (50ml) olive oil
¾ cup (100ml) vegetable oil
½ lemon
1 tablespoon white wine vinegar
Flaky sea salt

'NDUJA ARANCINI WITH SAFFRON AIOLI

These arancini have all the makings of a great deep-fried treat—a crispy exterior and a gooey, cheesy middle with a silky saffron aioli to dip them in. The hit of spice from the 'nduja and the acidity from the lemon offsets the richness and makes for a very addictive canapé.

To prepare the arancini, heat a large shallow sauté pan over low-medium heat and add the olive oil. Tip in the onion and cook for 20 minutes, stirring occasionally, until tender but not colored. Add the garlic, tomato puree, 'nduja and red pepper flakes to the pan, and cook for 2 minutes, stirring occasionally.

Add the stock to a medium-sized saucepan and, over a high heat, bring to a gentle simmer before turning down to keep warm. Add the arborio rice to the pan with the onions and toast for 2 minutes. Add the stock a ladle at a time, stirring until the rice has absorbed the stock before adding another ladle. Continue like this for about 30 minutes, until all the liquid is absorbed and the rice is al dente.

Sprinkle in the Parmesan, then add the lemon zest and juice. Stir to combine, then season to taste with salt and pepper. Pour into a dish, cover with plastic wrap and let set in the refrigerator for at least 2 hours.

To prepare the aioli, soak the saffron in 1 tablespoon of freshly boiled water and leave to cool and steep for at least 30 minutes. Add the egg yolk to a medium-sized mixing bowl and grate in the garlic.

Wrap the bowl with a rolled-up kitchen towel to steady it, then gradually pour in the olive oil and vegetable oil, whisking continuously to emulsify it and loosening it with the saffron water and squeezes of lemon juice when it gets too thick. Add the vinegar, season with salt and squeeze in the remaining lemon juice. Keep in the refrigerator until you're ready to serve.

Cut the mozzarella into 1-inch (2.5cm) cubes.

Once the risotto feels firm to the touch, place the flour, eggs and breadcrumbs into 3 separate bowls. Season the flour with ½ teaspoon salt and beat the eggs together. Roll the risotto mixture into golf ball–sized balls. Make a hollow in the middle of each, then insert a piece of mozzarella. Seal the gap by pushing risotto into it and rolling the ball together with your hands again.

One at a time, dip the balls first in the flour, then in the eggs and finally in the breadcrumbs, and arrange them on a large sheet pan lined with parchment paper. Chill until ready to eat.

When you are ready to serve the arancini, heat a medium-sized saucepan one-third full of vegetable oil. Heat your oven to 350°F/180°C. When the temperature of the oil reaches 350°F/180°C, carefully add the arancini in batches and fry for 5 minutes until crisp and golden. Remove with a slotted spoon, keep warm in the oven and repeat with the remaining arancini. Serve with the saffron aioli.

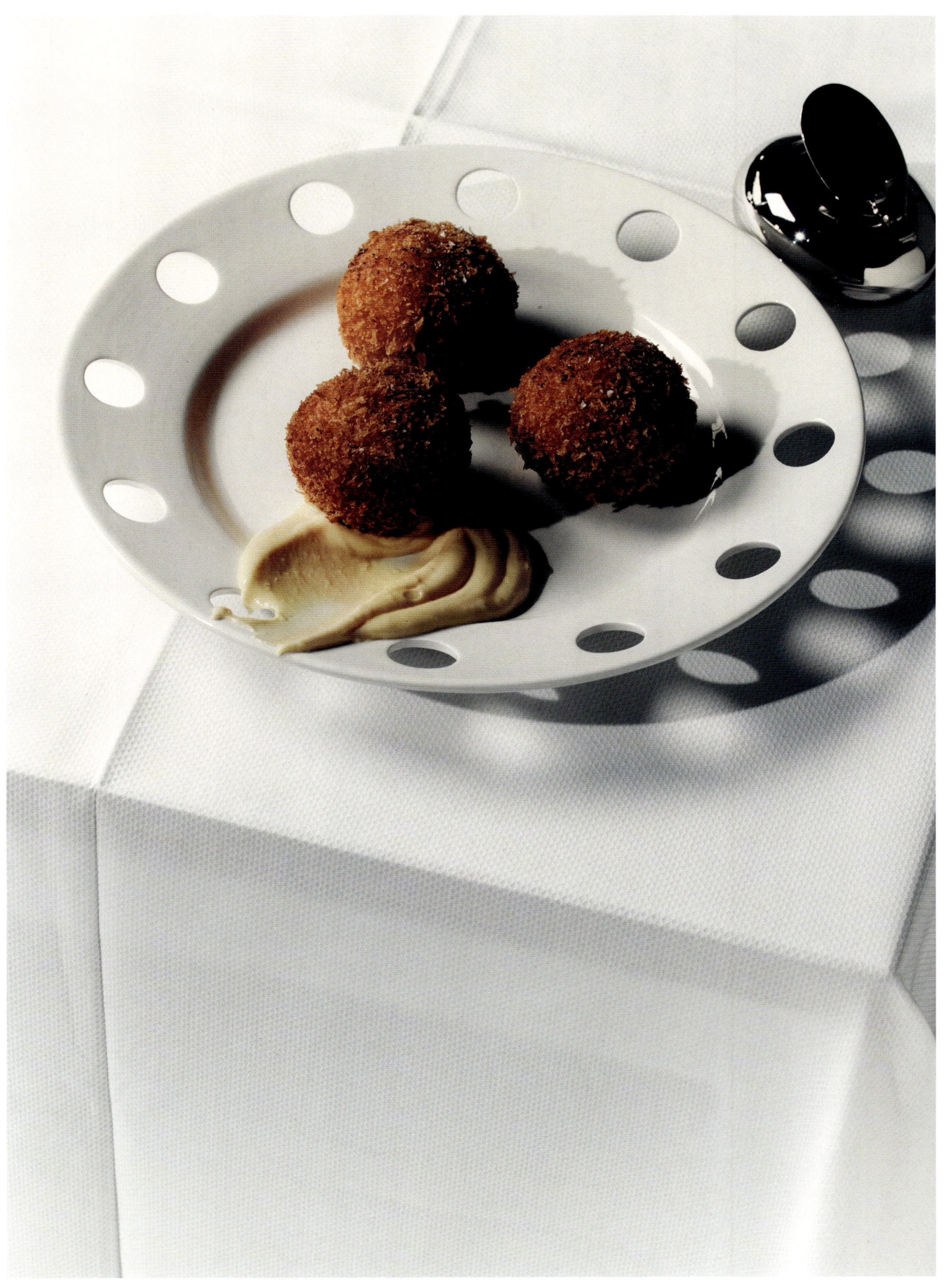

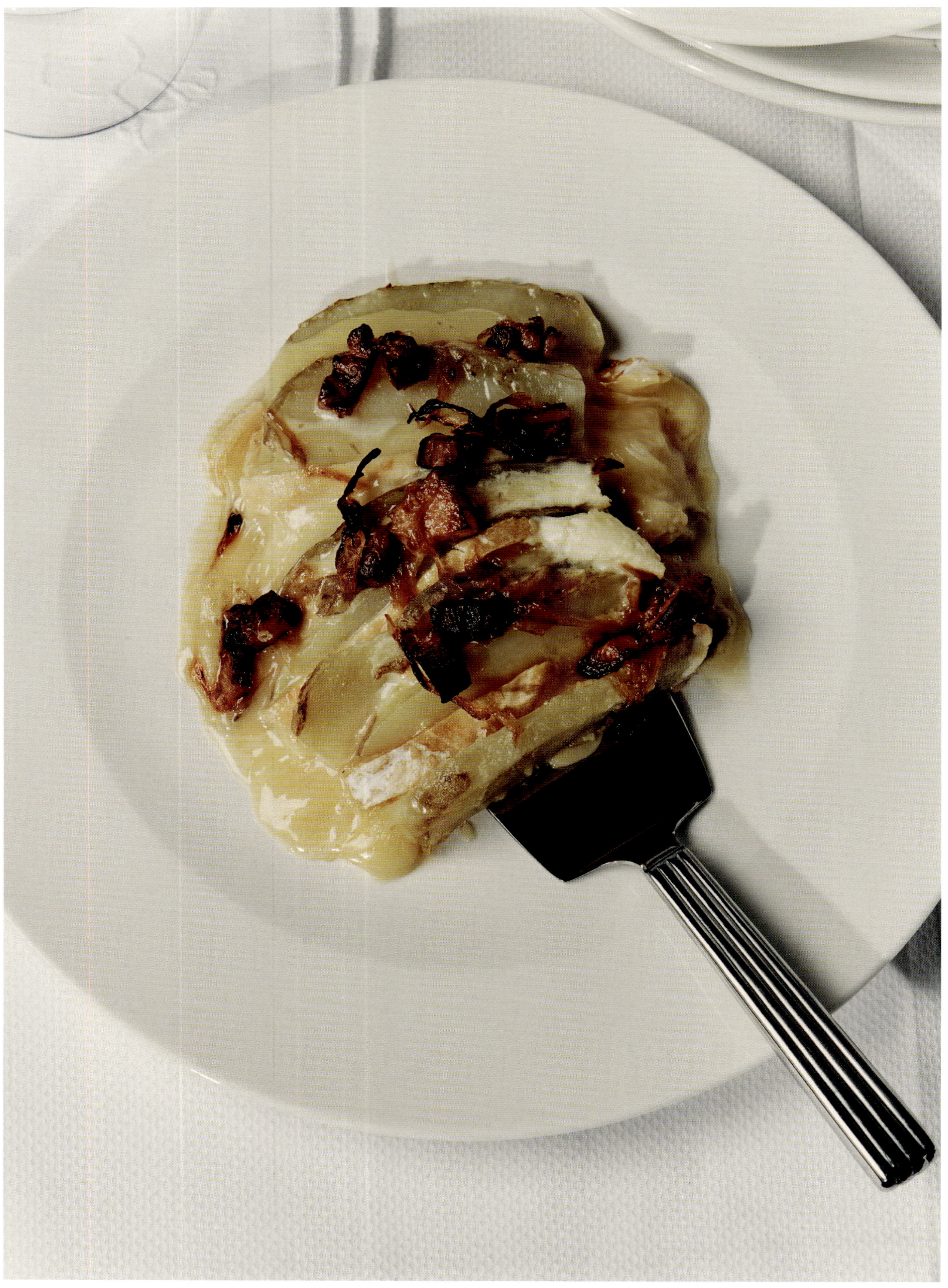

POTATO, REBLOCHON AND BACON CRINKLE PIE

SERVES 6

Flaky sea salt
10 ounces (300g) small waxy potatoes
5½ ounces (160g) diced pancetta
4 tablespoons (60g) salted butter
10 ounces (270g) phyllo pastry sheets
1 onion, finely sliced
5½ ounces (160g) Reblochon
2 large eggs
½ cup (120ml) whole milk
½ cup (120ml) heavy cream
¼ cup (25g) grated Parmesan
Black pepper

A tartiflette is a really gorgeous Alpine dish made from potatoes, bacon, lots of cream and Reblochon (a creamy, nutty soft cheese similar to Camembert). It is very rich, very lovely, and lends itself very well to becoming a pie.

Bring a medium-sized pot of salted water to a boil. Add the potatoes, lower the temperature to a simmer and cook for 15 to 20 minutes, or until tender. Drain in a colander, then let cool to room temperature.

Heat the oven to 375°F/175°C fan.

Heat a large sauté pan over medium heat, add the pancetta and fry for 5 minutes, or until the fat has rendered and the pancetta has crisped up.

Melt 2 tablespoons of the butter in the microwave, then brush a 13 x 9-inch (31 x 25cm) baking dish with it. Fold each piece of phyllo pastry from short edge to short edge like an accordion and nestle into the baking dish, repeating until the dish is filled, fanning out the layers to fill the space. Brush over the remaining melted butter, then bake for 10 minutes.

Add the remaining 2 tablespoons butter and the onion to the pancetta pan. Cook for 10 minutes over medium heat, until the onion is soft and starting to take on a little color. Remove from the heat.

Slice the potatoes and Reblochon into thin slices. In a glass measuring cup, whisk together the eggs, milk and heavy cream until combined. Stir in the Parmesan, then season to taste with salt and lots of black pepper. Nestle the pancetta, onions, potato and Reblochon into the ridges of the phyllo pastry, then pour the egg mixture over it. Bake for 30 minutes and serve hot with a crisp green salad.

SERVES 6

For the chicken:
1 whole chicken, 3½ pounds (1.5kg)
4 tablespoons (60g) salted butter,
softened
1 teaspoon ground cumin
1 teaspoon garam masala
½ teaspoon mild chile powder
2 garlic cloves
Flaky sea salt
1 tablespoon vegetable oil

For the sauce:
3 tablespoons vegetable oil
1 onion, diced
1 teaspoon ground cumin
1 teaspoon ground coriander
1 teaspoon garam masala
1 teaspoon mild chile powder, plus a pinch
8 garlic cloves, finely chopped
1 (2-inch/5-centimeter) knob of ginger,
peeled and finely chopped
6 tablespoons tomato puree
⅔ cup (150ml) heavy cream, plus 2 tablespoons
1 tablespoon fenugreek leaves
4 tablespoons (60g) salted butter
Flaky sea salt
1 tablespoon whole fresh cilantro leaves

BUTTER CURRY ROAST CHICKEN

It's with good reason that the curries from the north of India, packed with cream and butter, are some of the most popular around the world. The silkiness and depth of flavor that butter brings to sauces like a makhani make for a joyful eating experience. Butter comes into this recipe another way too, in a spiced butter to rub under the skin of chicken, which flavors it as it roasts.

To prepare the chicken, preheat the oven to 400°F/210°C fan. Place the chicken in a roasting pan. Combine the butter, cumin, garam masala and chile powder in a bowl, and grate in the garlic. Season to taste with salt.

Gently pull the skin away from the chicken by slipping your hand between the flesh and the skin, being careful not to tear it. Gently spread the spiced butter under the skin, and sprinkle the skin with a good pinch of salt and the vegetable oil.

Roast for 15 minutes, then turn down the heat to 350°F/180°C fan and roast for another 45 minutes. Insert a skewer into the thickest part of the chicken and check that the juices run clear.Meanwhile, prepare the sauce: Heat the vegetable oil in a large sauté pan over medium heat, then add the diced onion. Cook for 10 minutes until it has softened and is beginning to take on color, then add the cumin, coriander, garam masala and chile powder. Cook for 2 minutes. Add the garlic, ginger and tomato puree to the pan, and cook for 3 minutes, before pouring in ½ cup (100ml) water, ⅔ cup heavy cream and the fenugreek leaves. Simmer for 5 minutes.

Once the chicken is cooked, transfer it to a plate and let it rest for 30 minutes. Pour all the roasting juices into the sauce. Pour the sauce into a blender and blend until smooth. Pour back into the pan and season with salt. Keep warm until you're ready to serve.

Carve the chicken, arrange it on a plate and pour over the sauce. Drizzle with the 2 tablespoons of heavy cream and sprinkle on the cilantro leaves and an extra pinch of chile powder to serve.

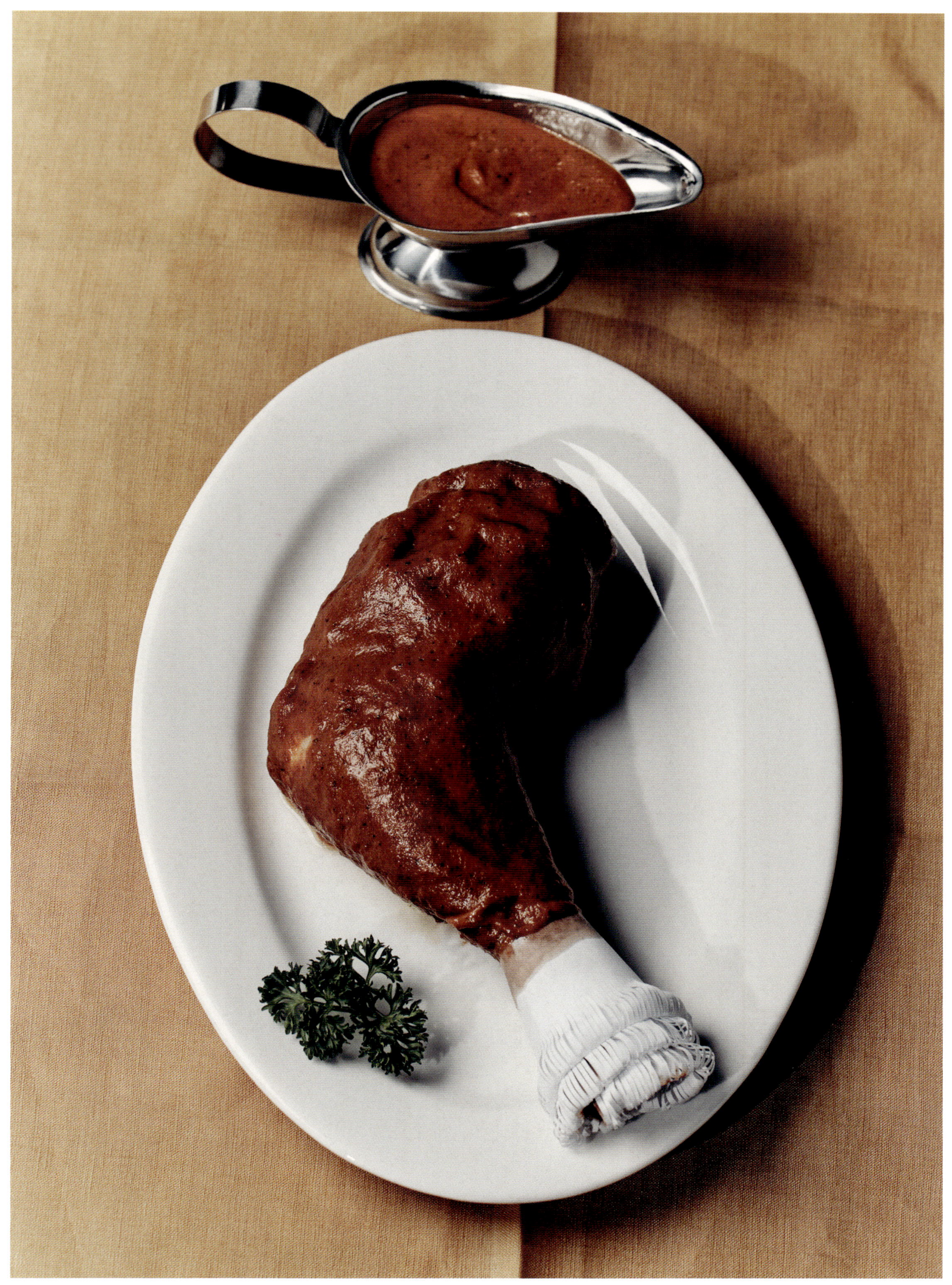

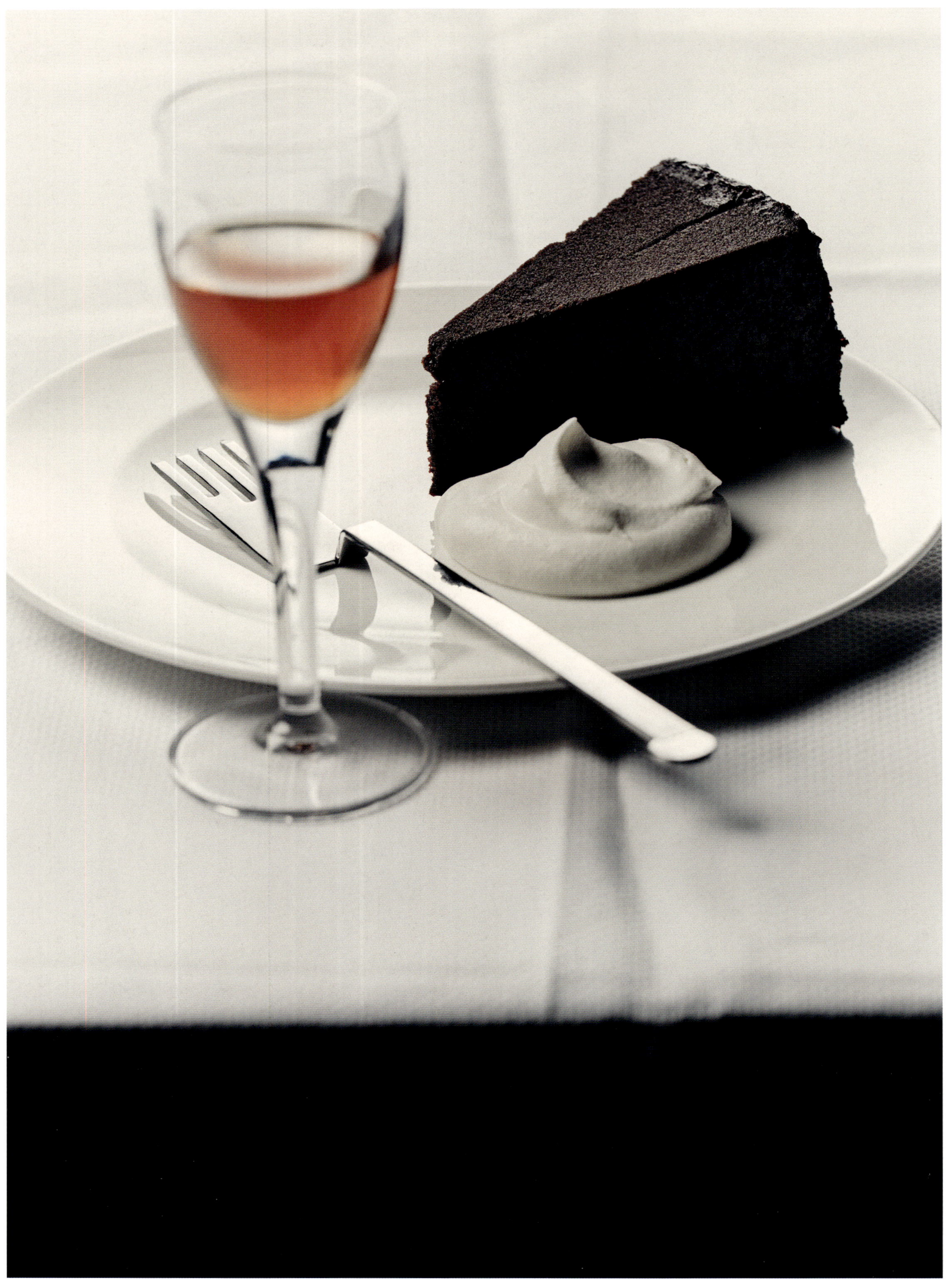

SALTED CHOCOLATE MOUSSE CAKE

SERVES 8

1 tablespoon softened butter, for greasing the pan
1½ cups (375ml) whole milk
2½ cups (600ml) heavy cream
¾ cup (160g) superfine sugar
6 eggs
3 tablespoons cornstarch
7 ounces (200g) 70% dark chocolate, finely chopped
1½ teaspoons sea salt
4 tablespoons maple syrup

This deluxe dessert falls somewhere between a flourless chocolate cake, a baked custard and a chocolate mousse. Egg yolks are used to create a rich salted chocolate custard, while the whipped whites lighten things up to give it the airiness of a cake. It is one of the more decadent desserts possible, especially when topped with pillowy mounds of maple whipped cream.

Grease a 9-inch (23cm) springform cake pan with the butter, then line with a large square of parchment paper. Preheat the oven to 350°F/175°C fan.

In a large saucepan over medium-high heat, add the milk, 1¼ cups of the heavy cream and half of the sugar. Heat gently until the mixture is steaming, stirring to dissolve the sugar. Remove from the heat.

Separate the egg whites and yolks, leaving the whites in a large bowl. Place the yolks in another large bowl with the cornstarch and whisk until smooth. While continuously mixing, slowly pour in the hot milk mixture in a thin stream. Mix until it is fully combined. Pour the mixture back into the same saucepan, and place over medium-low heat, stirring constantly so the bottom doesn't catch, until you can feel the mixture thicken enough to coat the back of a spoon, about 3 minutes. If it feels lumpy, remove the pan from the heat and whisk vigorously until smooth again.

Remove the pan from the heat. Add the chocolate and 1 teaspoon of salt to the custard and stir until fully melted. Leave to cool to room temperature.

Once the custard is cool, whisk the egg whites to soft peaks. Add the remaining sugar and continue whisking until it forms soft peaks once more. Whisk the custard until smooth to loosen it, then mix through one-third of the egg whites. Add the remaining egg whites and carefully fold in until combined.

Pour the mixture into the prepared cake pan and smooth the surface with a spatula. Bake for 1 hour on the middle rack—it should still be wobbly, but not liquid, when you pull it out of the oven. Allow to cool for 2 hours at room temperature.

When you're ready to serve, pour the remaining 1¼ cups heavy cream into a mixing bowl, and add the maple syrup and the remaining ½ teaspoon salt. Whisk into thick, soft peaks, being careful not to overwhip it (it will look fluffy when it has gone too far).

Remove the cake from its pan and slice into pieces. Dollop with the maple whipped cream and serve.

As Told To:
Lavender Au

EXPENSIVE MISTAKES

Three Shanghai creatives each reflect on a failing that shaped their futures.

Photos
Alex Li

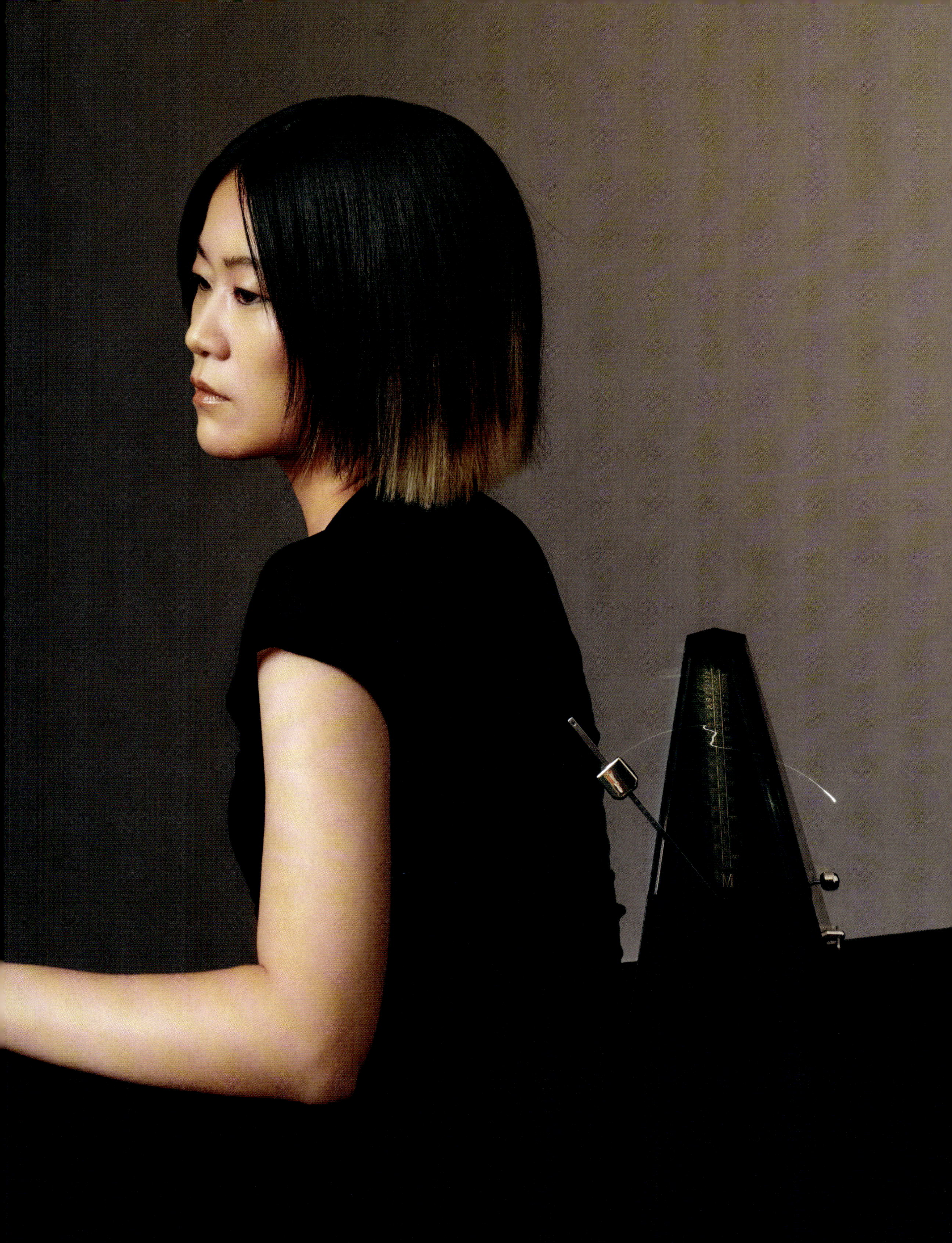

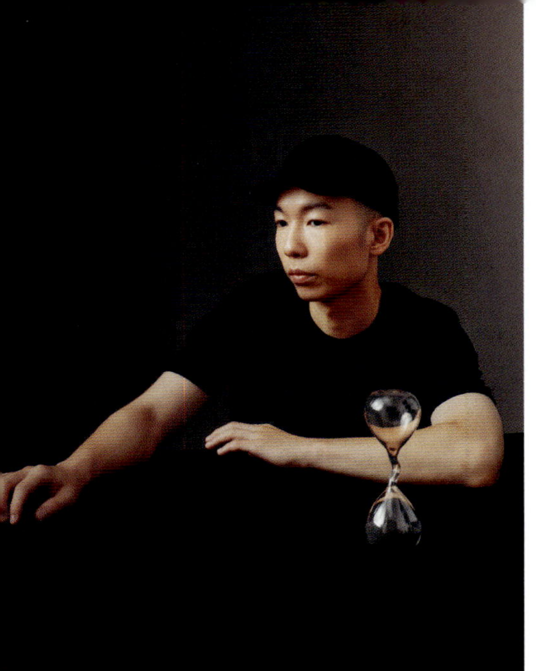

I founded Endo in 2021 with my brother and my ex-girlfriend. We offer a tasting menu of desserts, with tea and wine pairings. The goal is to not only celebrate ingredients from China but to integrate Chinese culture throughout the experience—the presentation, the pacing of the meal, how we interact with customers.

Creating a new menu is always very stressful, but even more so when you're tight on time. When we first started, we ran two daily services, which finished at 10 p.m., and then opened the doors to family and friends to have a glass of wine. After that we'd squeeze in R&D, usually tasting fruits, spices and herbs at the very start of the season, when they are more expensive, and stay until 1 or 2 a.m. It was exhausting and inefficient.

Eventually, we gave ourselves a break. The first of May marks the beginning of the Labor Day holiday in China, and the first of October is the National Day holiday; we decided to give our staff a vacation and keep the restaurant closed for another two weeks after those holidays so we could focus on R&D. Suddenly we had the time to be creative and revisit old ideas.

I grew up between Amsterdam, Taipei and Shanghai—my name, Friso, is Dutch—and as a child I ate a lot of seaweed with citrus fruit. It's something that's quite common if you live near the coast in Fujian, in southeastern China, or Taiwan. This summer, we worked with yuzu and *taitiao*, a sea moss from Ningbo, a port city south of Shanghai. It's creamier and sweeter than a savory Japanese nori. A lot of people in Shanghai were very impressed because they wouldn't expect to find taitiao in a dessert—it's usually served with peanuts or fried with yellow croaker fish.

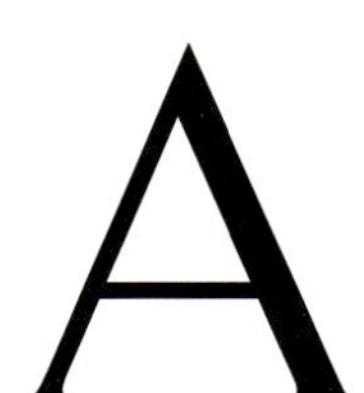

A nd in Quanzhou, which sits on the southeastern coast of China, there is something called *hai shihua*, a kind of jelly, like agar. I visited the city on a research trip over a year ago, and found that locals use hai shihua in cold sweet broths, the kind that come with tapioca and sweet potato. This year, we made a noodle out of hai shihua and kudzu, which we serve with yuzu and a taitiao crumble. The dish is a combination of my Quanzhou experience plus my Taiwanese background. It took us over 30 iterations.

I think its success comes from how it was created in calmer conditions. Some people like the stress or the rush of adrenaline, but it's important sometimes to go slower. Whenever we encountered a new idea we had this urge to create a dish on the spot, but it was only when we started to rest a little bit and allowed ourselves to be open to all sorts of ideas, and to let those ideas marinate, that this dish could truly take form.

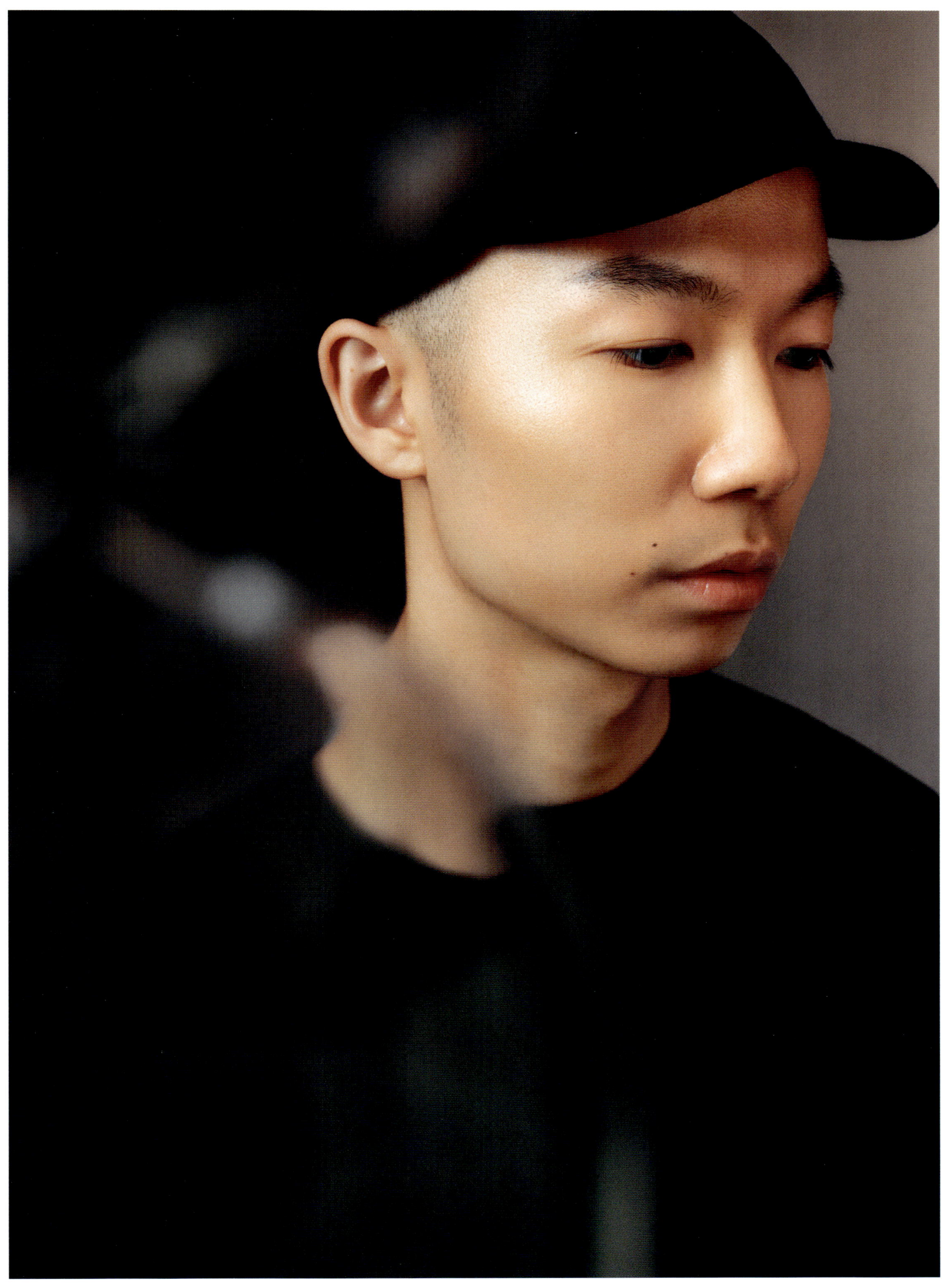

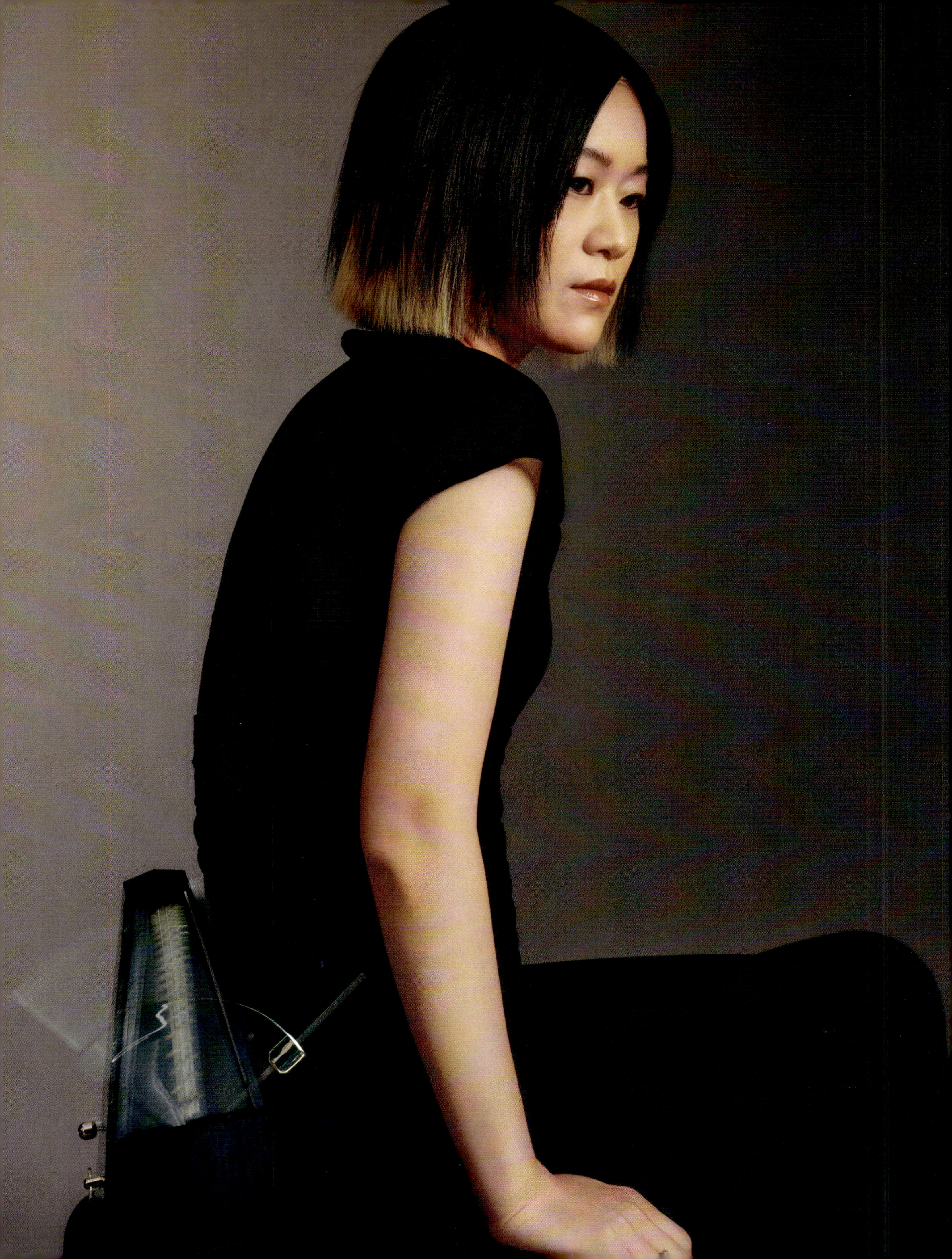

RUI ZHOU: FOUNDER OF FASHION BRAND RUIBUILT.

I started RUIbuilt after graduating from fashion school in New York. At the time, I didn't have a clear goal, like building a business that had a certain annual revenue or becoming someone well-known. It was much simpler: My graduation collection had received great feedback, many stylists and celebrities asked to borrow the clothes, and friends who had stores were asking to sell them. And so, I started making ready-to-wear.

At first, I did almost everything myself. I'd wake up, take fabric with me to school, head to the sewing machines and make samples. I'd deliver pieces to shoots myself because I was afraid they would get damaged—the fabrics are soft and they snag easily—and I'd fix tears myself. I had a few people to help me with beading or to sew simple pieces, but there wasn't any system, it was mostly just me. I even designed my own logo.

After spending two seasons traveling between Shanghai and New York, I returned to live in China permanently. I hired a few people who were skilled with their hands and started making pieces in my living room. But as the company grew, I found I couldn't work to my own rhythm anymore. I had to consider aspects of the business like marketing, public relations, my target audience, all of which took up more of my time.

I realized I had to learn to work with other people. When I was studying, I wouldn't draw at all; I would just have something in my mind and then make it. It was only after starting the brand that I started sketching. I had to find ways to explain what I'm thinking about to other people, to be more specific. I learned to put systems in place.

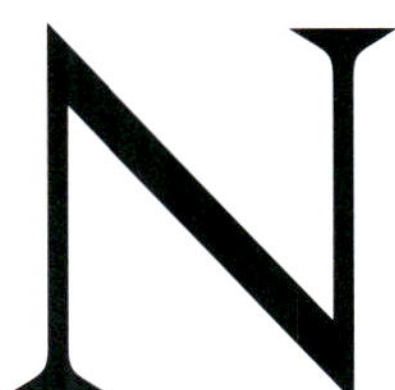

N ow I set the general direction, and I handle the most urgent tasks that have been escalated to me or things that are too difficult to assign. Otherwise, when I assign tasks to different people, I try to bear in mind that each person has a different personality, abilities and work style. It's a skill I'm constantly learning.

It's important to find your own rhythm, or rather the right rhythm. Each problem requires me to invest time, and reduces the time I have for other tasks. I'm always pursuing a balance, but I see it as dynamic—I know I can never achieve a perfect state—and I believe mistakes made at different times, big or small, can contribute to creating that balance. While I am continually adjusting my rhythms at work, I've maintained a stable rhythm at home. In New York, I was living alone but after returning to China, I married my husband and we got a cat and a dog. I stay at home for a while after getting up, walk my Shiba Inu, have a big breakfast and go to the office, and work until the evening.

Having such a stable routine allows me to focus on work, rather than constantly dealing with drama. Most of my time now is spent on communication, and I miss the early days when I made everything myself. But I still make time in the late evenings to create, when no one can disturb me. I want to devote as much of my time and energy to the fantasy world I'm creating through my brand as I can.

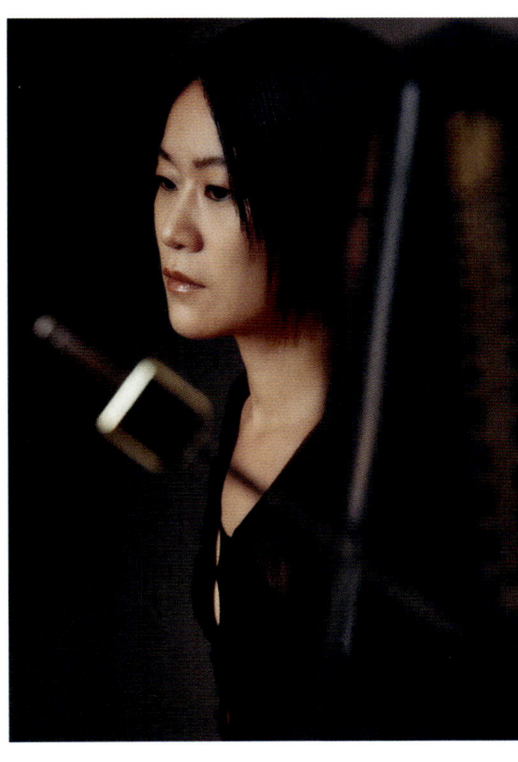

JILL GU: FOUNDER OF MADE IN HOUSE & SUHE HAUS.

I

*I saw the building that would become Suhe Haus during lockdown. I was living in an apart*ment right across the Huangpu River and would look at it every day from my desk. My business partner Chris Bryce and I asked around and found that the building was up for rent. We had started Made in House, a creative consultancy, six years ago, and in 2021 had hosted Design Miami in Shanghai, but it was only for one week. We wanted to build something that could last.

The building used to be China Industrial Bank's warehouse and is protected, so what you can do is very limited—it still had the wide stairs that was used to carry gold between the floors. We designed some of the public spaces but we also wanted to leave it as it was, using other corners of the building for exhibitions and installations. Currently we house eight different galleries and a non-profit art foundation, and we have our own projects collaborating with young artists and writers, a design studio, a material lab, our creative agency and a rooftop where we've just done a public installation.

t's a success, though in hindsight, I think I missed something essential when we were building Suhe Haus: the emotional and creative well-being of my team. I didn't always see the early signs of burnout or recognize when someone was struggling silently. I think I'm too logical—I didn't pay enough attention to how people felt along the way.

Over the years, some founding staff left the team and the creative process started to feel a bit stale. That was a wake-up call to slow down and really focus on the people we had around us. I read a lot of books about leadership and self-growth; about how the way you respond to the world and the people around you affects your brain, and about how we work, emotionally and psychologically.

I came to realize there was a miscommunication in our vision. When building the company, we had both short-term and long-term goals, but we were too focused on the short-term. It's something you witness in many companies in China because we are all so goal-driven. Everyone is under a lot of pressure, especially from themselves. Parents will often put pressure on their children to excel in school, and that pressure is brought into the workspace.

Now we focus on creating an environment where people can feel safe to take risks, make mistakes and shape their own path within the team. Instead of making direct decisions, I encourage the team to think. I can now sense when someone's under pressure or feeling anxious, and I'll take the time to talk to them. I've learned to invest in the pauses and the small moments that build team culture and momentum.

Ultimately, I've come to understand that the growth of a company mirrors the growth of its people. Creativity thrives when people are given space and shared ownership. Instilling that vision and confidence is so important. When people are free to collaborate and believe they're creating value together, it's exciting.

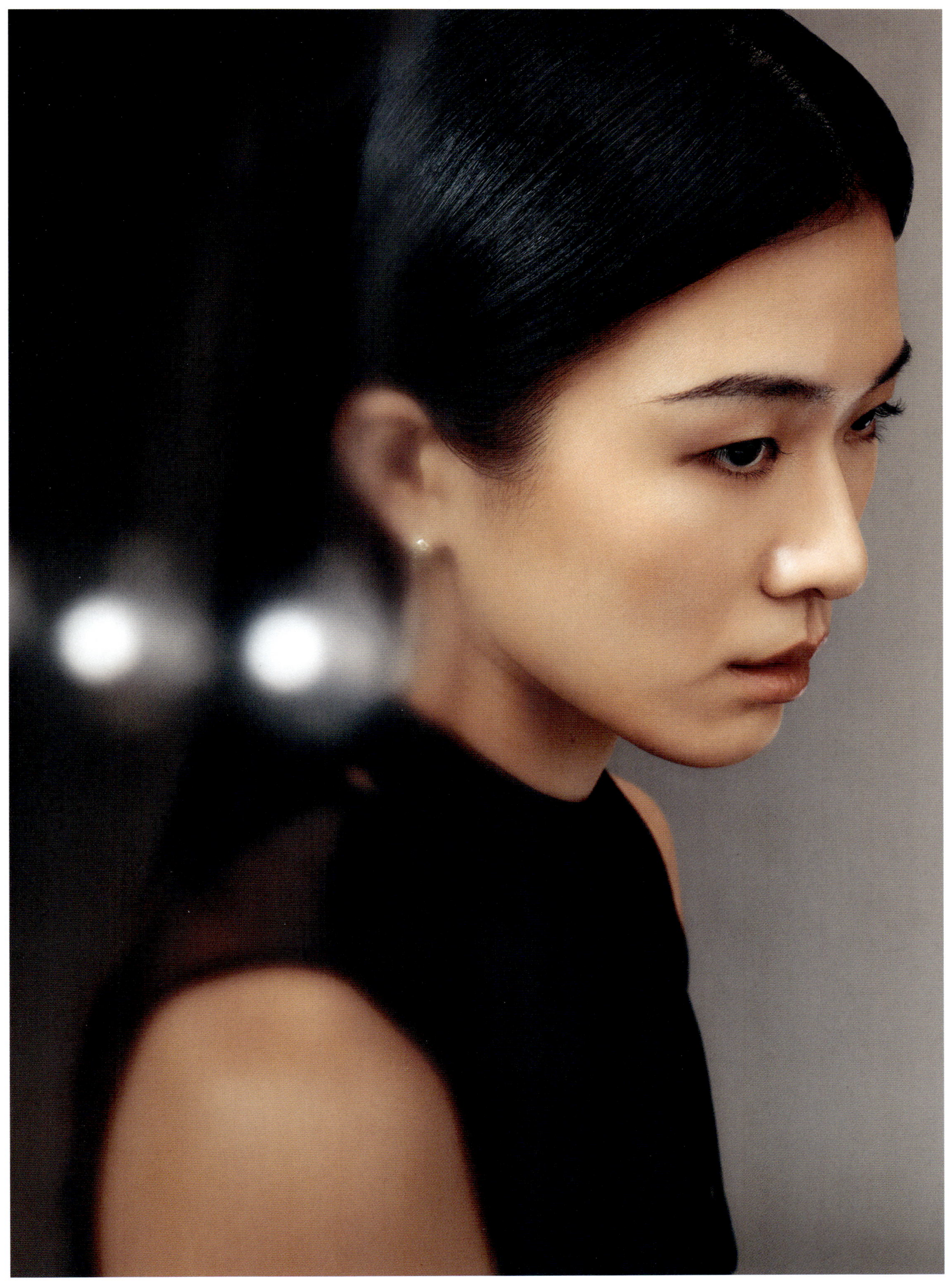

ACCOUNTABLE ASPIRATION

Can luxury prices be justified? Industry insiders crunch the numbers.

Photos
Aaron Tilley

Set Design
Sandy Suffield

As Told To:
Fedora Abu

LUXURY HANDBAGS
(TANNER LEATHERSTEIN, LEATHER EXPERT)
$1,000 to $5,000

There's so much that goes into the price of a leather bag—the raw materials, the labor, the overhead, the design, the distribution—but when I'm assessing quality and value, I look at just two things: the materials and the assembly. First, I'll estimate how much leather is needed, including the wastage—a bag could use about three square feet of leather, but you would need six to cut that out cleanly. Then I look at the craftsmanship and consider the labor costs where it was made. Three to four times the cost of materials and assembly is a typical markup for a sustainable, profitable operation. Anything lower is insane value for the customer. Anything more shows the premium you pay for a big brand.

Unless you're working with a specialty leather, like Togo leather, craftsmanship is usually the biggest determinant of cost. Leather prices are pretty standard around the world, but skill and expertise can demand a premium. No piece of raw leather is the same and every piece requires careful attention and a level of respect for the material. That's only possible with decades of experience.

It can be hard to find skilled labor, and usually it's focused in a particular area. In Ubrique in Spain, people have been working with leather for about 100 years. Florence, in Italy, has an important concentration of good leatherworkers, as does León in Mexico. But the Dongguan region in China has probably the biggest and best cluster today—the craftspeople are quick and proficient with their work and can create better value for their customers.

The most expensive leather is made of cleaner raw hides. Very few leathers are naturally clean—meaning it is without scratches or other deformations—and most require a lot of correction or "make-up." Clean hides also require minimal finishes, which helps give them that premium feel. Poor-quality hides, on the other hand, might be so full of scratches that you need to buff them off completely and cover the leather with a thick layer of finish.

The best way to figure out the quality of a bag yourself is to forget everything you know about the brand and rely on your senses. Look at it, touch it, smell it. If it feels good, it's a good leather; if it feels plastic and dead, then it's lower quality. Then you can assess the craftsmanship, which is all about the details: the stitches, the fold lines, the edges, the paints. Hardware, like the buckles, snaps and catches, is a tougher call, but usually you can feel the weight of it and see the quality of the finish—it's a good sign in leather if you see waves and imperfections, less so on hardware.

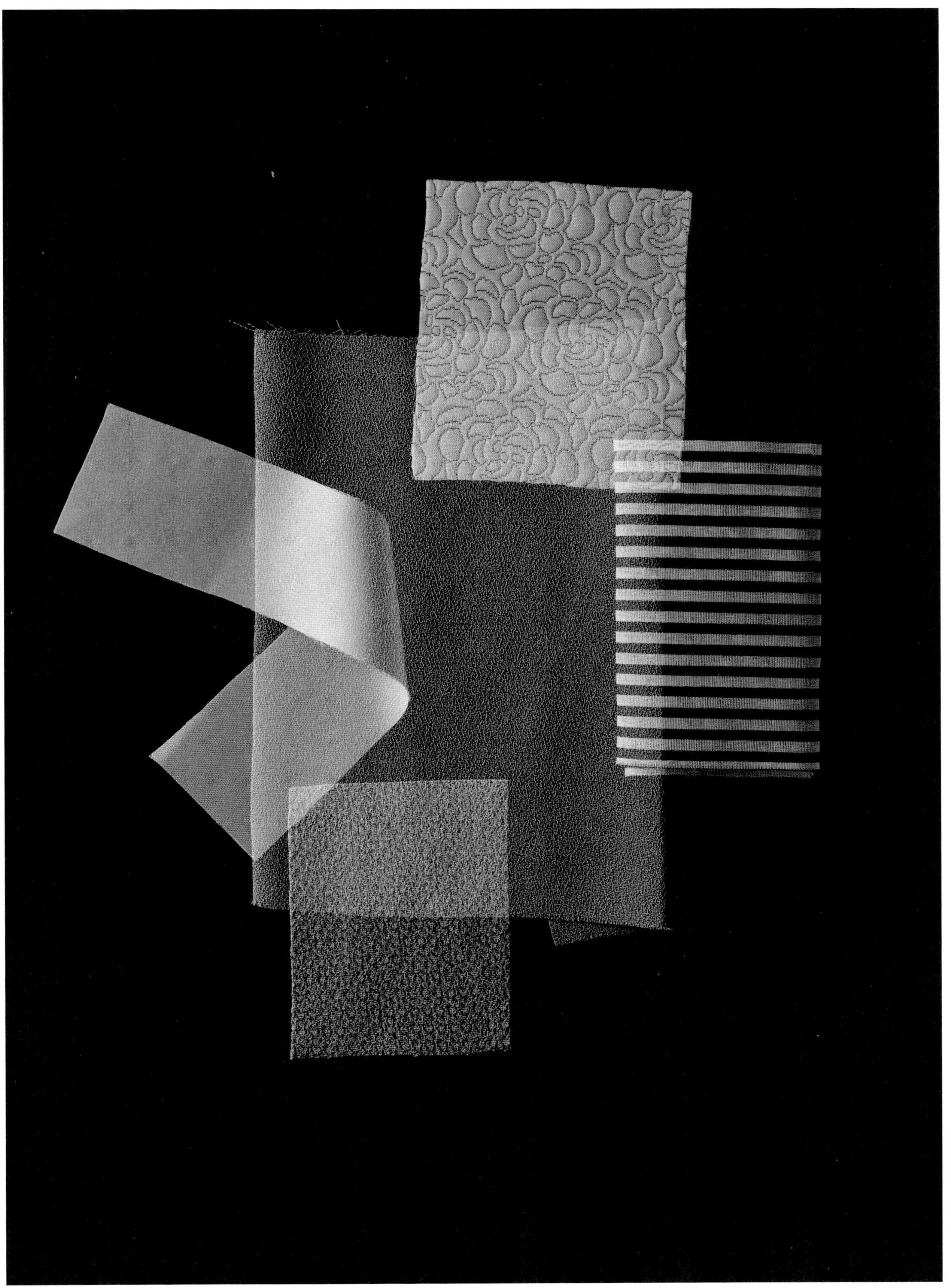

As Told To:
Francis Martin

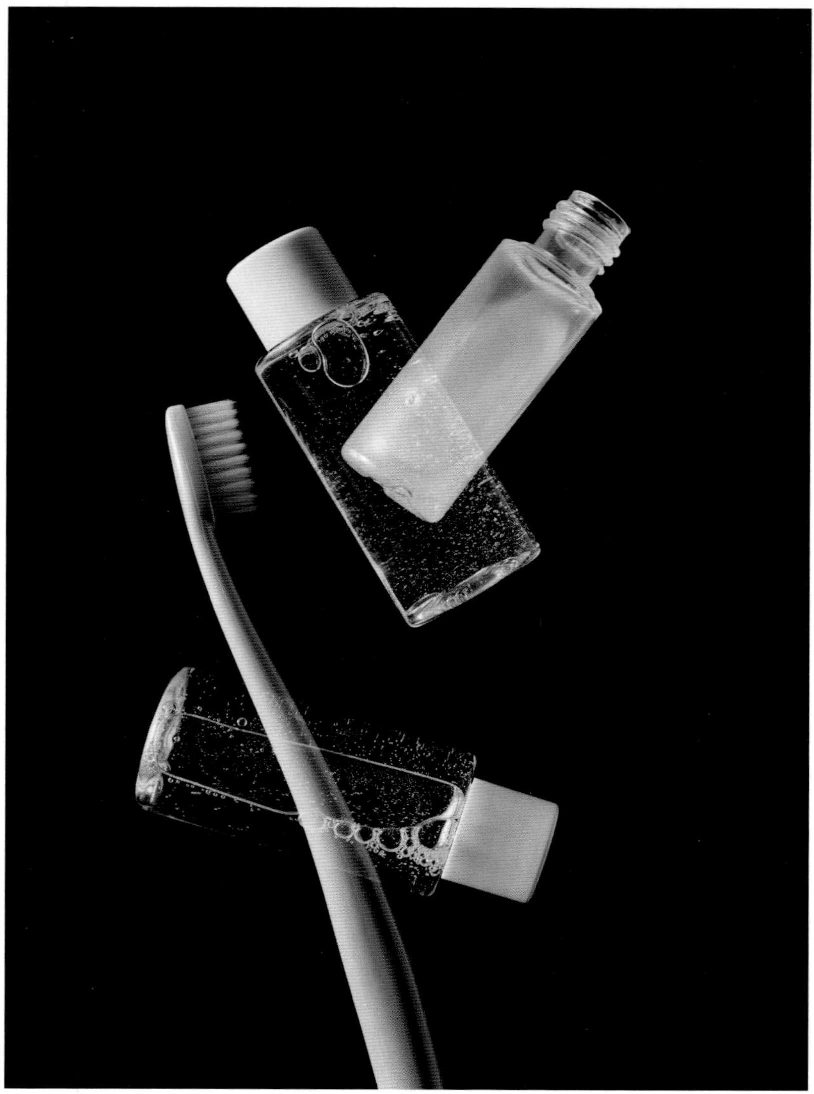

LUXURY TRAVEL
(JAMSHYD SETHNA, FOUNDER OF SHAKTI HIMALAYA)
$1,250+ per night

In India, land in the metro areas, where the luxury resorts are, is prohibitively expensive. Government taxes are phenomenal and vary from state to state, and these resorts are usually run as publicly limited companies: They have shareholders to support and need to give them returns. Prices have also gone up enormously since COVID.

With our walking tours in the Himalayas, we're trying to do things differently. It really started off as a kind of hobby. I went to a boarding school high up in the mountains and used to do a lot of walking at high altitudes. I wanted to be able to show visitors these magical spots in the Himalayas that are not normally accessible, and also offer comfort and great service.

Our guests stay in village houses that we've renovated with high-quality furnishings and the kind of bathroom you'd find in any great hotel. Such amenities are expensive, as are the services: Guests have access to a butler, a guide, a driver and a vehicle, and there is a chef and a chef's assistant. Lots of luxury travel clients are foodies, so we've gone to great expense bringing in chefs from different parts of the world, as well as from around India, to train our own chefs. Our head chef, Yeshi, was a follower and disciple of the Dalai Lama, and we have wonderful Indian home cooking as well as western cuisine at our properties.

Involving the local community was essential to maintaining the integrity of the business. Shakti Himalaya employs and trains villagers and has slowly been building up the team over the years. They are employed all year round, rather than seasonally, which is unusual in the Himalayas. We want it to be a symbiotic relationship. Before we set up Shakti, the regions in which we operate didn't have a wide range of vegetables, so to cater to our requirements, locals have started small businesses up growing vegetables for us with a guaranteed number of sales. We have also helped families invest in purchasing cattle to produce milk for our properties.

Our locations are remote. Recently we built Shakti Prana, a seven-suite lodge nestled in the mountains, right next to the Tibetan and Nepalese borders. It's an hour walk uphill from the nearest road—we had to carry 3,000 tons of stone up there through the monsoon season, on muleback. Despite all these challenges, if one was visiting a luxury hotel in Rajasthan, it would be much more expensive than what we offer in the mountains considering the daily spend on accommodation, meals and transport, and we haven't increased our prices for six years. One of the reasons we've been able to do this is because we quote in US dollars, and the Indian rupee has depreciated by about 6%, on average, per annum.

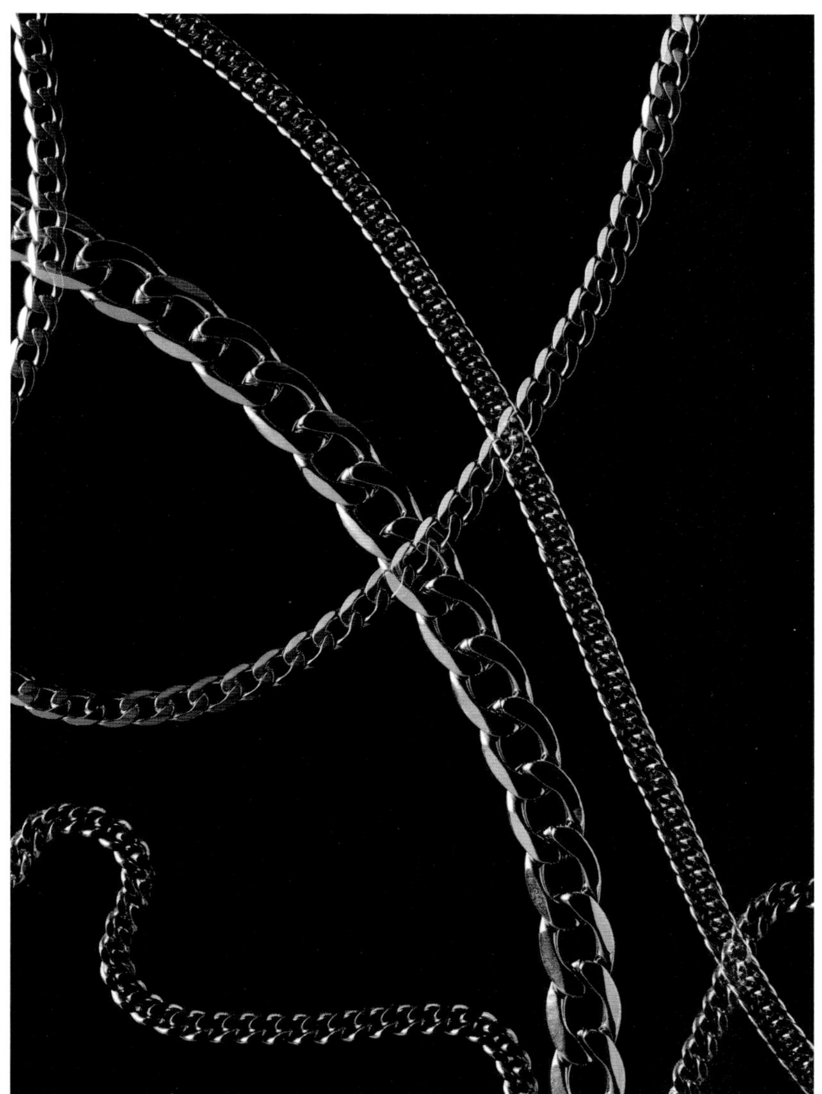

JEWELRY
(FERNANDO JORGE, DESIGNER)
$1,125 (Fine Jewelry) to $23,500 (High Jewelry)

Independent designers like me tend to use a pretty standard markup: double the manufacturing cost, which will then be doubled again by the retailer. Prices are high because the craftsmanship is demanding and time-consuming, and the materials are rare and sourced from the earth. But when you're talking about brands backed by investors and a luxury group, the markup is many times higher. They have to pay for advertising, events, VIP experiences—all to make people believe in the brand, so they can deliver bigger profits to investors, and make the owner the richest person in the world.

My brand is financially independent—I don't have investors. The revenue from sales has to cover my team, the after-sales care we provide, the showroom experience and growing the business, but I am also free to follow my own rules and expand the business as I choose. I've managed to maintain an ethical commitment to the craft community I've always depended on: the goldsmiths in Brazil that I've worked with since the beginning, and the ones in Italy I've found more recently; the miners, who I have a deep respect for. I've visited the mines and know that I use responsible suppliers with materials that are certified as single-mine origin. Meanwhile, luxury brands are buying up workshops to consolidate margins and control the industry, making it harder to find independent factories to work with.

My clients aren't buying a logo. I founded my brand in London in 2011, but I'm from Brazil, and that's always inspired my jewelry—the way it sits on your skin, its sinuousness, the way a fancy piece made of gold and gemstones can be worn both casually on the beach and to a Hollywood awards show. I want my pieces to be tactile, to be sensual, to be easy to wear. The goal is to capture the moment with enough beauty and thought to remain relevant long after the moment passes.

I don't aspire for my brand to be bought or to scale up. I want to keep doing what I do—experimenting with craft, supporting artisans and designing pieces that retain emotional and cultural value. A piece that depends on a logo will never gain value, but the pieces you wear every day, that you don't lock away in a vault—those are the ones that become precious. I'm making objects that become part of someone's life.

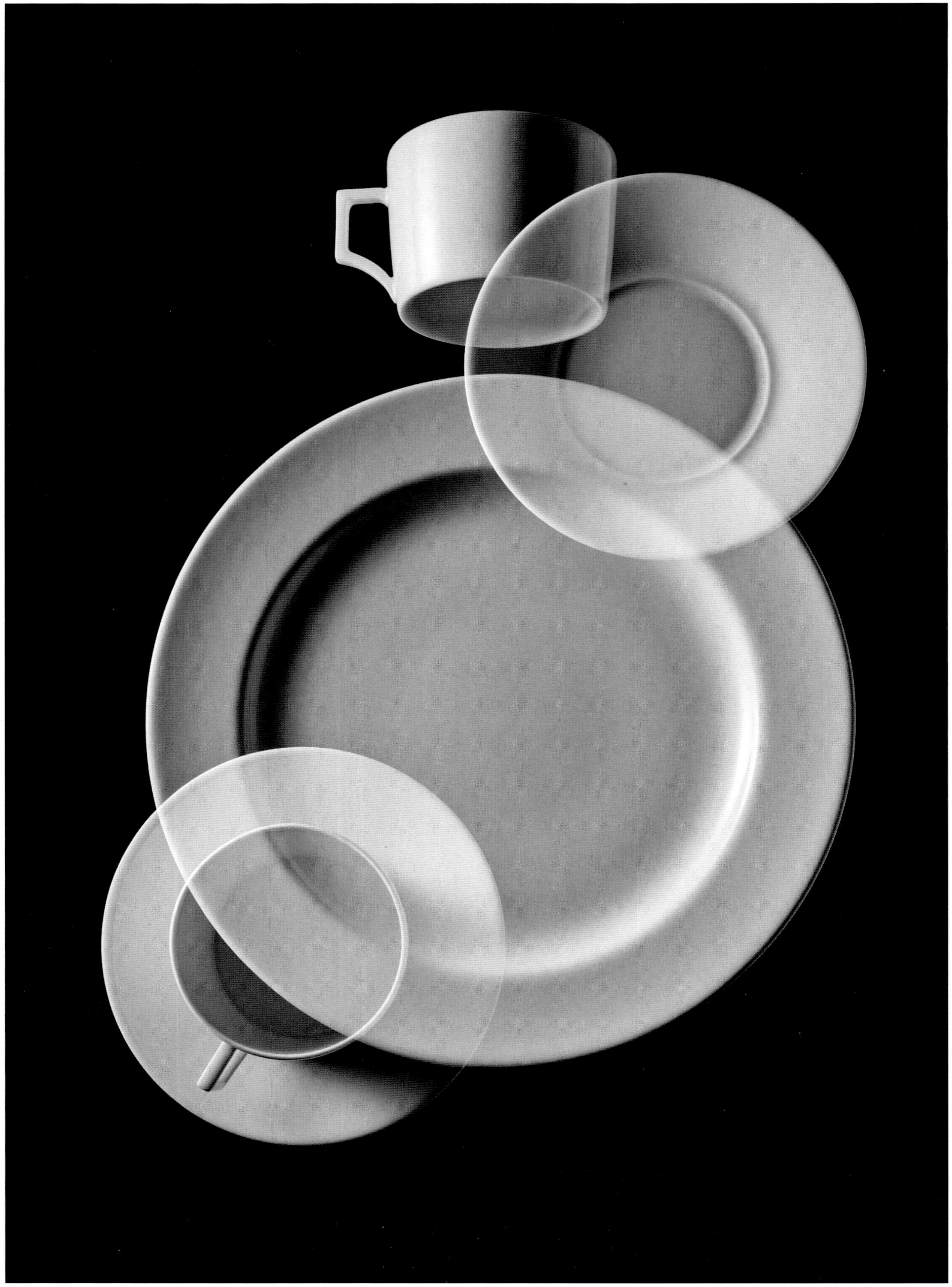

As Told To:
Ed Cumming

DINING OUT
(JACKSON BOXER, CHEF)
£60 to £70

The average spend at Brunswick House is about £60 per head, or £50 after VAT [value-added tax]. Dove is a bit higher, about £70. While London is a city of 8½ million, the proportion of people who can afford to spend 60 quid on dinner is vanishingly small, and those who can spend more than £100 is smaller still. It's an interesting game. We're always working hard to figure out the way to do the best thing possible while charging as little as possible.

The model has shifted a lot. Restaurants have gone from aiming to operate between 20% and 30% profitability to fluctuating between 2% and 10%—10% being a good month, 2% the bare minimum you need to be viable. Of our total revenues, 20% of the bill immediately goes to VAT, as we collect that on behalf of the government. Of the remaining four-fifths, about 20% is overheads, 30% to 35% is ingredients and 35% to 40% is labor, leaving you with about 5% profit, if things are going well.

One of the biggest price increases over the past five years has been labor. It has become necessary to pay people more, which is a good thing—for too long, people were paid too little, especially at supposedly unskilled jobs. In a restaurant it makes sense to pay people well, but pay fewer of them: One talented, skilled, organized and hardworking person can do the job of three unmotivated, underpaid and unengaged people.

Restaurants tend to buy their raw ingredients in a different way than other consumers. People often assume that if you buy wholesale, you pay less, but actually that's not true. Supermarkets are largely cheaper than wholesale suppliers, but only because supermarkets use economies of scale to put pressure on their suppliers, which in turn means the ingredients become lower quality. Restaurants aren't beholden to those supply chains: We can work directly with farmers, growers and fishermen. We pay more, but the product is of a much higher quality. Ingredients aren't necessarily discrete costs, however—we don't buy individual steaks; we buy a cow and butcher it, so it can be hard to work it all out once you've minced up all the trim to make a ragù. We try to keep it around 32% ingredients' cost to sale price.

Last year wine sales absolutely tanked. Pre-Brexit, there were decent wines you could get from France for five or six quid a bottle and put on a list for £20 to £30. None of those exist anymore. The cheapest bottle of decent wine you can buy is close to £10 now. That's an effect of climate change, Brexit and general inflation across Europe. We're always working hard to find bottles we can put on the list that aren't a rip-off, but there's very little out there. On the other hand, spirits haven't increased as much, so people are drinking more cocktails.

In Britain people assume restaurants are incredibly profitable—I think because they used to be and successful restaurateurs were quite flash. That hasn't been the case for a long time. But that doesn't mean it's a bad job; in some ways it makes it a better job. I really enjoy my work—it's valuable, nourishing and rewarding. Profit was never really the motivation.

At the time of publication, the approximate conversion rate was £1 = $1.35.

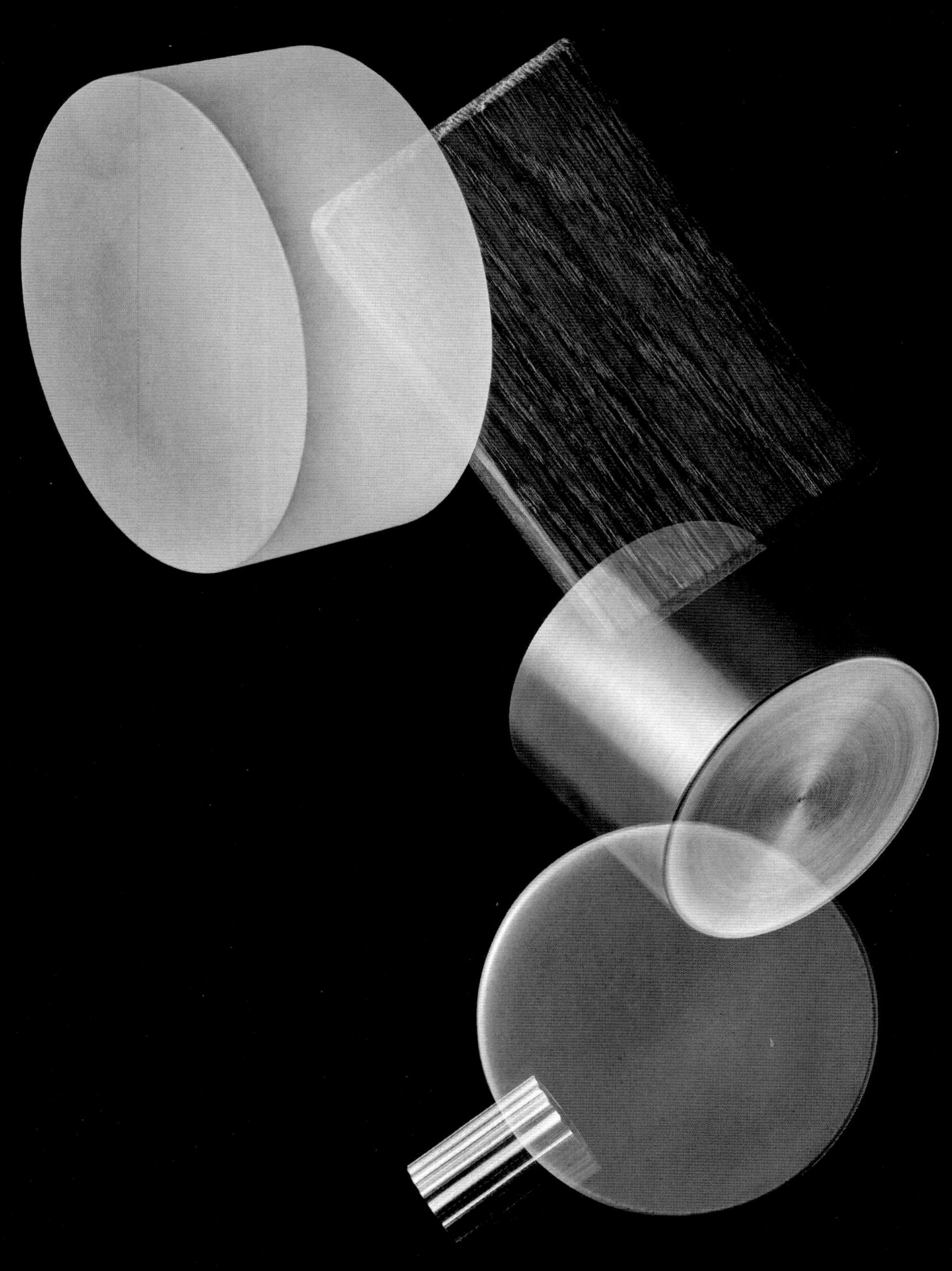

DIRECTORY:

163   Recipe Card
164   On the Shelf
166   Behind the Scenes
168   Crossword
169   Received Wisdom
172   Power Tool

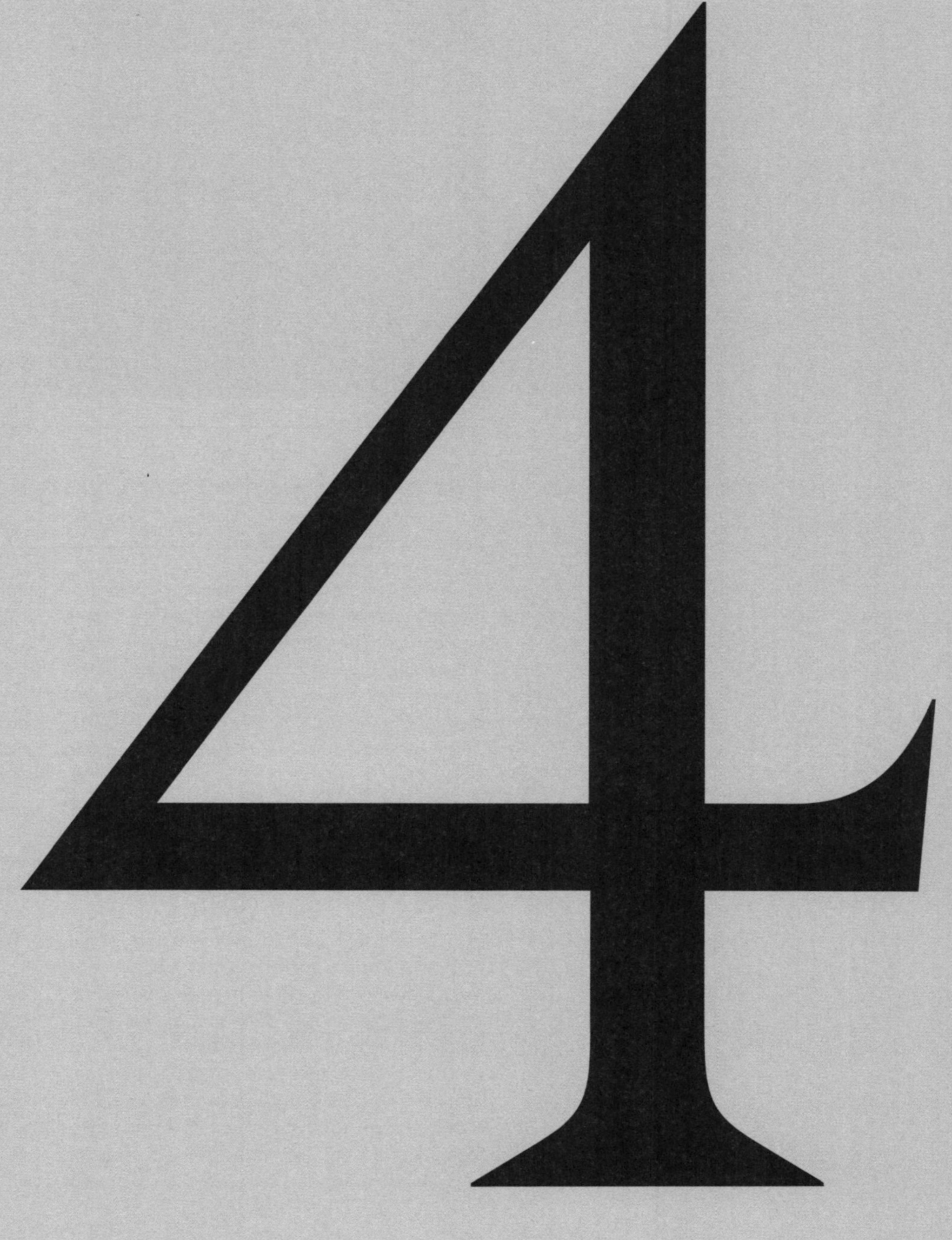

Words:
Benjamin Alva Polley

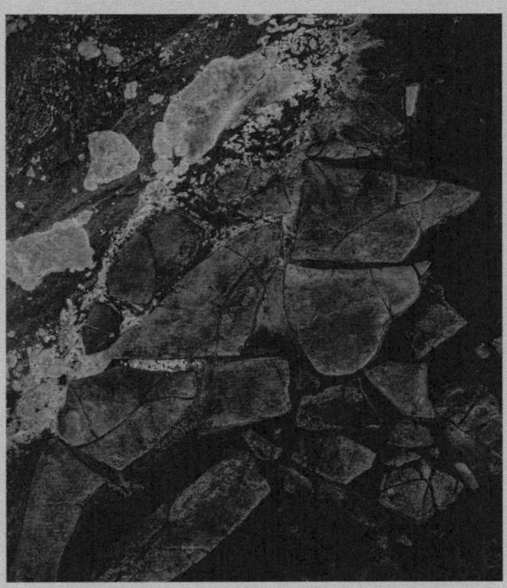

How to listen to the lake.

From a distance, the lake appears innocently blue, like open water. As you ski closer, however, a thin blanket of ice reveals itself. Nearer still, you hear strange noises from beneath the surface—grumbles, gurgles and moans that echo like an ancient language. They resonate like whale song, or a rumbling stomach.

These sounds have a rational explanation. During the day, the shifting temperature causes the ice to expand and contract. At night, the water cools, thickening the ice as hexagonal crystals align and form hydrogen bonds. Ice can form in various ways: Congelation ice forms on the surface and grows downward; superimposed ice is created from frozen rain or seepage; shelf ice is floating ice pushed ashore by the wind and waves; and candle ice, a form of "rotten ice," appears when ice begins to melt, creating a distinctive honeycomb structure. Sometimes small pools of water dot the surface, and pressure ridges—formed when sheets of ice are compressed and buckle upward—can run through it like scars.

If you fancy venturing out on the ice, bear in mind that its strength can vary significantly, even in the same body of water, so it's always best to err on the side of caution. Four solid inches of lake ice can typically support the weight of a single person but be cautious of slush, cracks or a grayish-white appearance that suggest the ice is weak, and avoid areas with currents, underwater springs, docks and incoming streams, where the ice is often thinner. If the ice is less than two inches thick, stay off it.

The sounds the ice makes are a memory of all these factors and fluctuations. Richard Nelson, a cultural anthropologist, writes that Koyukon people of Alaska believe the sounds are the lake asking the heavens for a blanket of snow to insulate it from the cold. It's a reminder to stop, listen and wonder about the stories this icy expanse holds.

—

NICOLE RUCKER'S comforting London Fog Brownies.

These are made with white chocolate—an uncommon move in brownie recipes, and I'm not sure why, because, wow, are they delicious. This recipe yields a cake that bakes into a variety of textures in one pan: chewy edge, extremely chewy corner and fudgelike center. The brownie is the only cake that's allowed to have so much textural variety in one pan.

This bar is flavored with Earl Grey tea—steeped in the melting butter—along with vanilla and the creamy dairy flavor of white chocolate in place of traditional dark chocolate. The result of these elements commingling is a "brownie" that's aromatic and elegant, and very delicious.

If your first question is "Can I use a different tea?" or "Can I leave the tea out?" Yes, of course.

MAKES ONE 13 X 9-INCH
TRAY OF BROWNIES

8 ounces (226g) unsalted butter
1 tablespoon (6g) Earl Grey tea, pulverized
¾ cup (127g) roughly chopped white
   chocolate
½ cup (106g) packed light brown sugar
1 cup (200g) granulated sugar
¾ teaspoon (2g) Diamond Crystal kosher
   salt
4 large eggs (200g)
2 teaspoons (10g) vanilla extract
1⅔ cups (200g) unbleached bread flour
1¼ cups (212g) roughly chopped 72%
   dark chocolate

Preheat your oven to 375°F (190°C). Lightly grease a 13 x 9 x 1-inch (31 x 25cm) quarter sheet pan, and line the bottom and sides with parchment paper.

Put the butter and pulverized tea into a small saucepan, and heat the mixture over medium heat. Stir every few minutes and watch it closely to prevent it from browning. While the butter is melting, put the white chocolate into a heatproof bowl. When the butter is melted, pour it over the chocolate, and stir gently until every piece of white chocolate has melted into the butter.

In a large mixing bowl, combine the brown sugar, granulated sugar, salt, eggs and vanilla. Use a hand mixer to beat vigorously for 1 minute, until the mixture is pale in color and very creamy looking. It is important to beat the eggs and sugar really well, because this is how you get a shiny, flaky top layer on your brownie. Add the melted white chocolate and butter to the egg mixture, and whisk until everything is combined. Add the flour, and use a spatula to incorporate it, mixing just until no dry bits of flour remain.

Transfer the batter to the prepared pan, and smooth the surface. Gently rap the pan on the counter to burst any air pockets in the batter. Scatter the chopped 72% chocolate over the top, and gently press it in a little (most pieces will sink into the batter). Bake for 10 minutes on the center rack of your oven, rotate the pan, and continue baking until a cake tester or toothpick inserted in the center comes out with very moist crumbs still clinging to it, about 15 minutes longer. The edges will show some browning and wrinkling, and the center will still appear a bit unset. If you have beaten the egg mixture enough, there will be a wonderful shiny surface to the brownies.

Remove the brownies from the oven, and allow them to cool in the pan. Eat immediately, or, if you enjoy a chewier brownie, put the pan in the freezer for ½ hour. Cutting the brownies while they are very cold will produce a densely packed, chewy texture and clean cuts. Store them in an airtight container at room temperature for 1 week or in the fridge for 2 weeks.

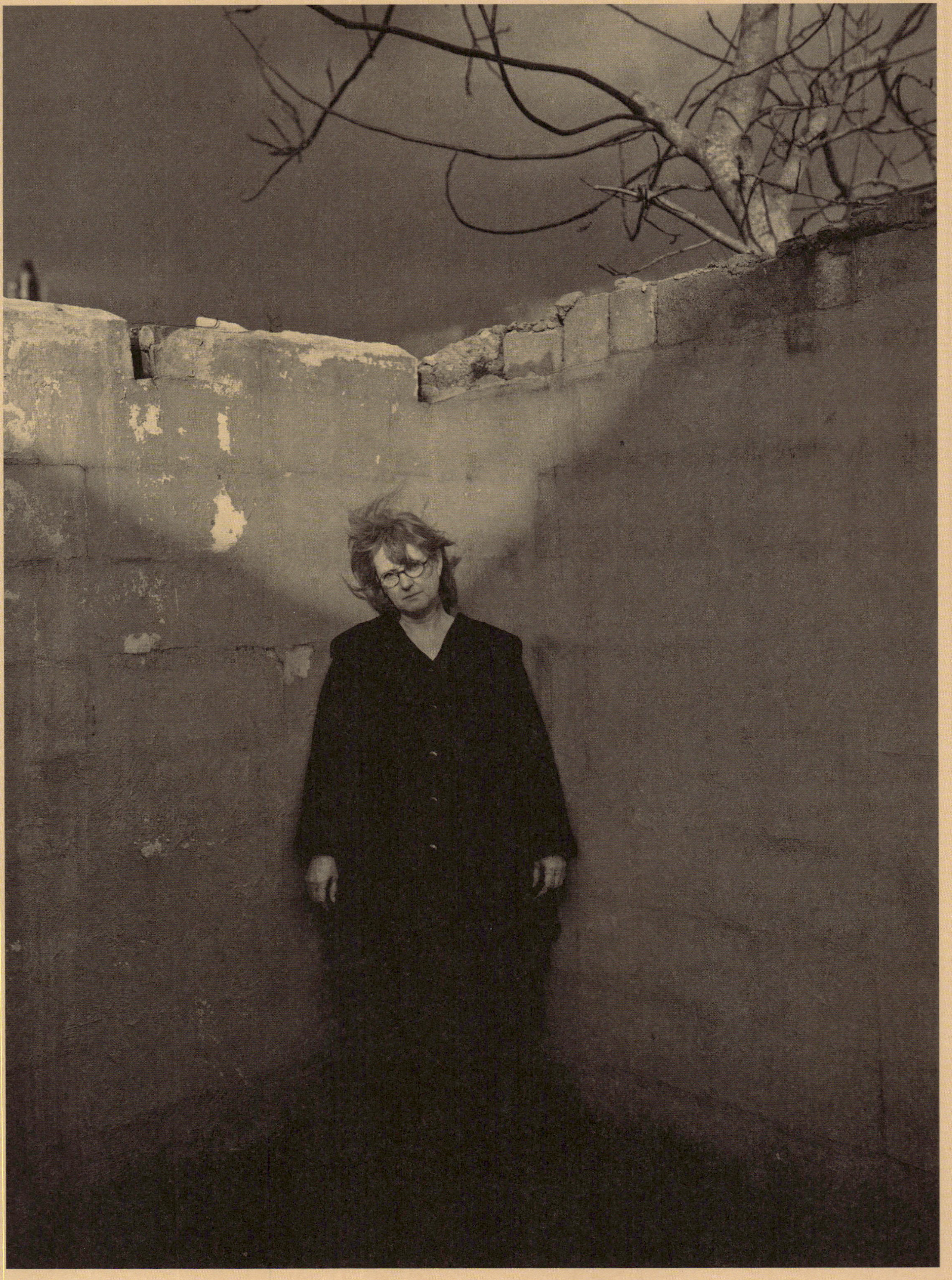

DIRECTORY

Photo: Sarah Hartvigsen Juncker.

SOLVEJ BALLE on her award-winning series of novels.

Danish author Solvej Balle is nearing the completion of her seven-book series of slim time-looping novels, *On the Calculation of Volume*. Its premise, at least on the surface, is simple: Tara Selter, an antiquarian book dealer living in France, finds herself reliving the same day, November 18, starting each day wherever she ended up the day before. What emerges is a mesmerizing account of a woman's ingenuity and resourcefulness and a profound meditation on the nature of our days and all they contain: relationships, injuries, domestic rituals and the infinite within the finite.

NATASHA STALLARD: You first had the idea for *On the Calculation of Volume* in the late 1980s, around the same time your debut novel, *Lyrebird*, was published.[1] How did you feel about the idea during the passing years?

SOLVEJ BALLE: Very up and down. I didn't know if it was a stupid idea, but it somehow kept clinging to me. At the time, there was a lot of talk about the novel being dead. I didn't feel I could write another one. I also realized that it was going to take me a long time if I started. So I was like, If I go in here, I'm going be stuck. I didn't want that for a while.

NS: Did you have to prepare to go into the novel?

SB: I now realize I had to get a bit older to write it. There were many things I simply didn't understand. Tara grows older in the books, and I had a very clichéd way of understanding age, as you do when you are young. I'm 63 now but then I had absolutely no idea about what one can do at 63—I imagined a grandma, with purple hair.

One's understanding of time becomes much more detailed and layered. I've had several boyfriends and I've been married twice, and over the years you go through lots of friendships and relationships. I needed a deeper understanding of many different aspects of these relationships before I could write it.

NS: After reading the second volume, I can't imagine Tara being caught in any other day than November 18. How did you choose that date?

SB: It's funny because for a long time it was October 17. But it didn't work, it was too clear and crisp. I wanted something more rainy and gloomy. I tried the 8th of November, because the number eight represents eternity. When I realized it should be the 18th, it was like, Yes, there we are! Now I can write the book.

NS: The series is self-published in Denmark, under your own imprint, Pelegraf. Do you enjoy publishing?

SB: Yes, it's great fun to have your fingers in the material, to be able to say that you want this paper or this cover. I was tired of the increasing commercialism of traditional publishing. I'm self-publishing, middle-aged and I live out in the sticks [on the island of Ærø]—three low-prestige elements! In Denmark, if you don't live in Copenhagen then you are a little bit weird. It's almost like you're dead.

NS: In the second volume, Tara travels to experience the changing weather of the seasons. Did you also travel or are the places written from memory?

SB: There's a mixture. I've been to Bergen and other places, but it's as if they became Tara's in a way. I've never been to Cornwall, but I read on the internet about how there are spring lambs in the autumn in Cornwall and I thought, "Oh my goodness! I need this." I had to get beyond my own experiences and make it more schematic.

NS: Do you have any advice for a writer or an artist who's been holding on to an idea for many years?

SB: Don't worry about the time it takes. Learn to live off nothing and don't worry about time. And move to an island—an island with cheap houses.

---

(1) Balle had already been planning the novel for several years when the iconic time-loop film *Groundhog Day* was released in 1993. Rather than disappointed, she was relieved: "I thought, 'Oh, that's nice—somebody's helped me do research and gone in a direction I wasn't going to go anyway.'"

Words:
Rebecca Thandi Norman

At MATTHEW COX, a furniture-making apprentice and her mentor.

For a brand that draws so heavily on the traditions of furniture making, the workshop at Matthew Cox has a refreshingly modern take on the concept of apprenticeship.[1] Started by antiques dealer Matthew Cox in 2017, the UK studio specializes in handcrafted furniture and lighting that are made to last a century, and to become more beautiful as time goes by.

Here Matthew Cox's creative development lead, Greg Stone, and his apprentice, Georgia Coyle, discuss what mentorship means to them, and how a time-honored approach to passing down knowledge and skills is being renewed for the 21st century.

REBECCA THANDI NORMAN: What drew you both to Matthew Cox?

GREG STONE: I've been at Matthew Cox for six years. I had been in business myself as a furniture maker but when I saw Matthew Cox's Instagram, I reached out. The day I came in to meet Matthew, I had a tour of the studio and his home. I saw a bench that had previously been outside for years—it was all grayed and weather-beaten. Matthew has always been interested in seeing how pieces and materials weather. Taking a weathered piece out of its usual context and bringing it inside really makes you appreciate how beautiful the weathered surface is.

GEORGIA COYLE: I've been an apprentice for nearly two years, and it's coming to a close. I first found out about the company through someone I knew; the way he talked about not only the products but also about the way Matthew Cox treats their team sounded good. I'd previously worked in furniture restoration but I wanted to get involved in making. Matthew Cox brought those things together.

RTN: Georgia, what's the first piece you worked on as an apprentice?

GC: The first piece I worked on from start to finish was a table. It took about 3½ weeks. That was a single project, meaning I worked on it myself. Recently, I worked on a group project building three large cupboards. The biggest difference between my work at the beginning and now is the confidence I have.

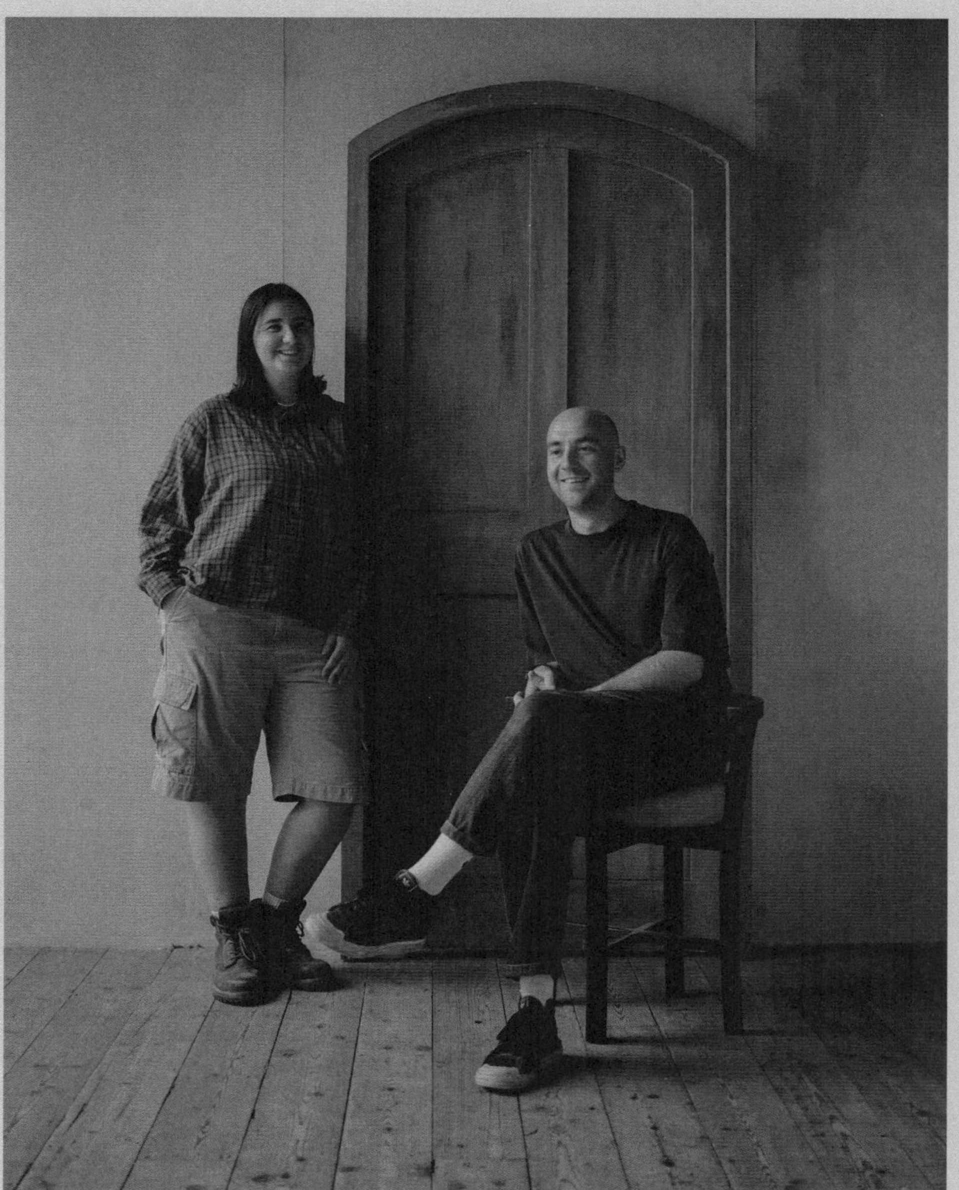

RTN: What does your working relationship look like day-to-day?

GS: We make sure that everything we do facilitates the mentorship/apprentice relationship, and we've added more structure to make that happen reliably, such as morning check-ins, debriefs and skill-specific tutorials.

GC: I find debriefs helpful—it's a chance to reflect on what went well and an opportunity to discuss where things could improve or could have been done differently. We are encouraged to be curious. When it comes to Greg, he believes in "one question, two suggestions," teaching us to problem-solve.

RTN: In what ways does Matthew Cox update the traditional apprenticeship?

GS: Within the first year of an apprenticeship, we get them to lead a project; the idea is that we want to give them exposure and experience in leadership as well as hands-on skills.

GC: Being given a client project early took me by surprise, but gave me the reassurance that my mentors believe I can do this. Building that trust from the beginning creates a strong bond.

RTN: Does the relationship continue once the apprenticeship is over?

GS: As mentors, we believe that there should be an ongoing relationship and dialogue even when our apprentices go out into the industry. It ensures people keep that high standard of craftsmanship.

GC: Even though the roles are related, the difference is that apprenticeship has a fixed term; there is an end point. Mentorship is an ongoing process. It has no end.

(1) Apprenticeships were a way to learn trades and crafts, such as goldsmithing, shoemaking, and tailoring, throughout the medieval and early modern periods. Apprentices were legally bound to a master, who typically provided room and board, and most began young. Leonardo da Vinci, for instance, started his apprenticeship with Andrea del Verrocchio at age 14.

FUNNY MONEY:
Who doesn't like fiscal comedy?

Mark Halpin

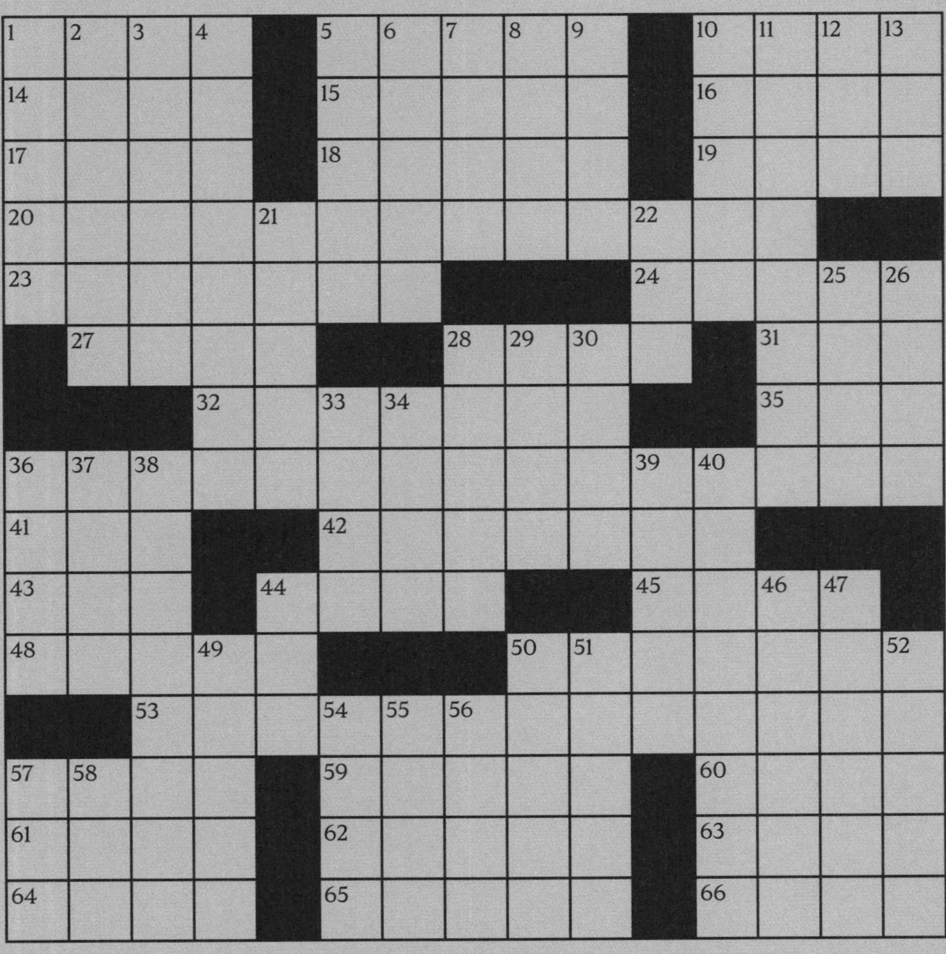

ACROSS

1. All-inclusive
5. Sluggish "Star Wars" character
10. Cut short
14. Trim
15. On the ball
16. What a tower does
17. Library catalog ID
18. Shakespearean compilation
19. Off-kilter
20. How the world's slowest currency moves?
23. Fruity, sugary drinks
24. "Way of the Sword" sport
27. Roe source
28. Alley division
31. Charged particle
32. Frequent Andrew Lloyd Webber collaborator
35. Corrida cheer
36. Facilities that no longer produce a Middle Eastern currency?
41. What you might be in Germany?
42. Queen of rap music
43. Journalist and activist ____ B. Wells
44. Miniscule
45. Acting company
48. Strong suit
50. "Sweeney Todd" prop
53. Some acting hysterical about a currency replaced by the euro?
57. Fever
59. What the next three clues form, read aloud
60. New York baseball team
61. A dark Oktoberfest beer
62. Cruising or confused
63. Falco of "The Sopranos"
64. Drunkards
65. Fingerprint feature
66. Nice negations?
—
—

DOWN

1. Like a hive-mind?
2. Samples
3. "Law & Order" actor Jerry who also voiced Lumiere
4. A Buddhist might be found in one
5. Disney villain with a parrot
6. Arnold Schwarzenegger's middle name
7. Slot machine symbol
8. Jewish rite
9. Surmounting
10. Run down
11. Cause of some eye watering
12. Couple's word
13. Wield
21. Lowest point
22. Scrape together, with "out"
25. Numbskull
26. Individuals
28. Like an unbrushed suit, maybe
29. "Superfood" berry

30. Make safer or easier
33. 1551, on a monument
34. "Knives Out" and "Glass Onion" director Johnson
36. "In your dreams!"
37. Classic dog name
38. Cause of some eye watering
39. Eastern gambling mecca
40. Misanthropic "Kiss Me, Kate" song
44. It might be black or green
46. Skimpy swimwear brand
47. Hergé's adventurous lad
49. Arduous journeys
50. Former
51. Congruent
52. This clue's answer has three of them
54. Tobacco plug
55. Old Testament verb
56. Soup served with sushi
57. Six-pack contents
58. Sticky stuff

RECEIVED WISDOM

As Told To:
Melissa Baksh

British painter MAGGI HAMBLING reflects on a life in art.

When I was a student at the Slade, my tutor, the painter Robyn Denny, said there will come a moment when you see yourself in your work, and that's what you've got to work with. He said a lot of people are so appalled or shocked when they see themselves that they pretend they're somebody else for the rest of their life.

That hasn't happened to me, though people seem to think I'm rather scary, which I don't understand—inside I feel like a Jelly Baby. I unwind by following the tennis and watching *Coronation Street*, which is addictive.[1] I'm absolutely devoted to it.

Life dictates what I paint. If someone I love very much dies, I know I'm painting

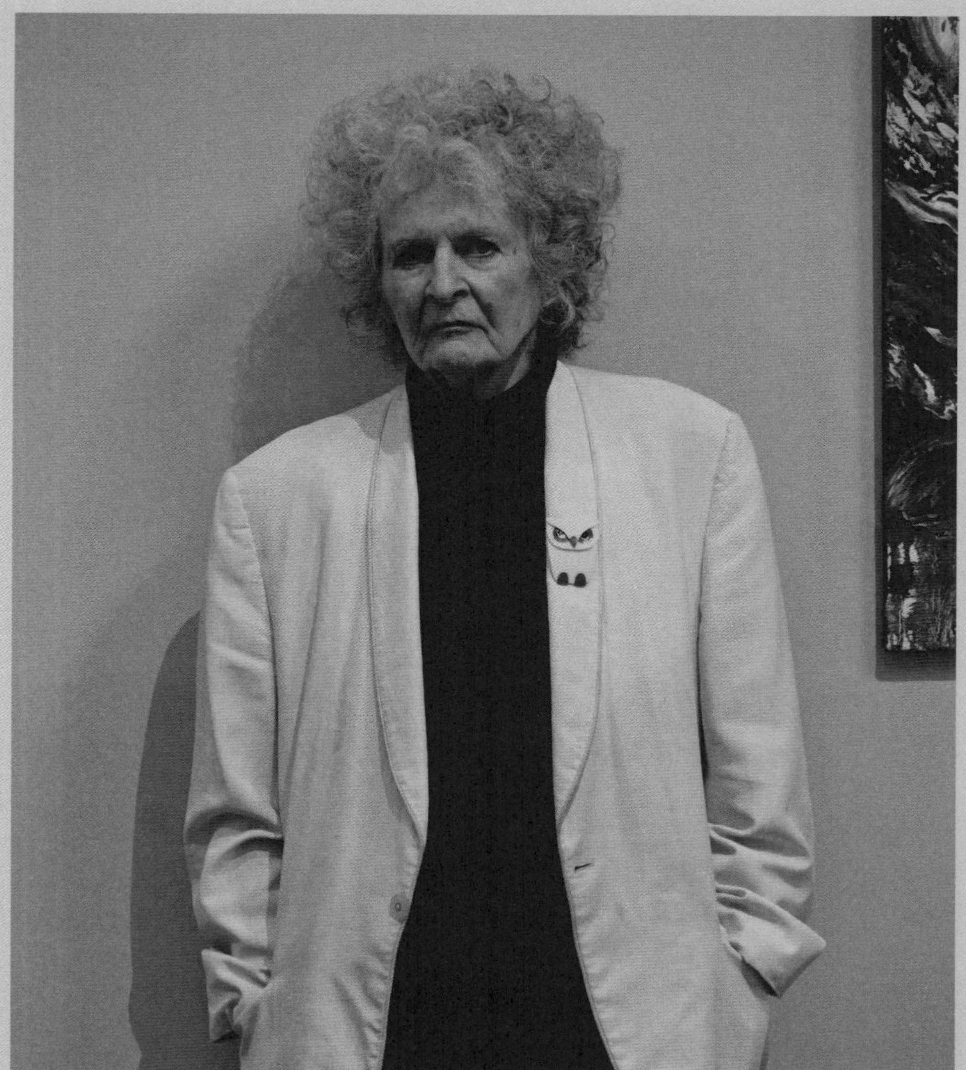

them after they're dead. The jazz singer George Melly said I should go down in art history as "Maggi Coffin Hambling." I would refuse to paint Mrs. Thatcher, because art is about the hand and the heart, but the heart is the most important, and what I felt about Mrs. Thatcher wasn't exactly love. If I could paint any living person, I think it would be the Dalai Lama—bring him here!

When I paint portraits, I try to channel the person in front of me. Likeness happens as a by-product of trying to paint the spirit of a person. Art should move people, and I think a piece can only move someone else insofar as the subject has moved the artist in the first place. As my first art teacher, Yvonne Drewry, said, "The subject chooses you, you don't choose the subject." So I try to be as moved as I can be by the subject, and then I hope the work moves other people.

One artwork I always return to is Rembrandt's *Self Portrait at the Age of 63* at the National Gallery in London. I call him "Ronnie Rembrandt" to bring him down to our level. It's his compassion. As somebody once said to me, unlike Goya, he didn't make judgments. I think this is true. The subject has to be in command of the artist, not the other way around.

The greatest thing anyone ever said to me is "If you're going to be an artist, you've got to make your work your best friend." In other words, you can go to the work with whatever it is you're feeling in the moment. If you're feeling tired, bold, happy or randy, you can go to it and have a conversation with it. And that is how I live my life, even if my outlook changed somewhat in 2022, when I had a heart attack in New York. Since then, I try to paint more with less.

Each new work is an experiment, otherwise what's the point? As for my proudest achievement, I don't think I've achieved it yet. It's still coming

(1) *Coronation Street* is a British soap opera set on a cobbled street in Greater Manchester. First aired in 1960, it holds the record as the world's longest-running TV soap. Its storylines often reflect contemporary social concerns, cementing its place in British popular culture.

As Told To:
Rebecca Thandi Norman

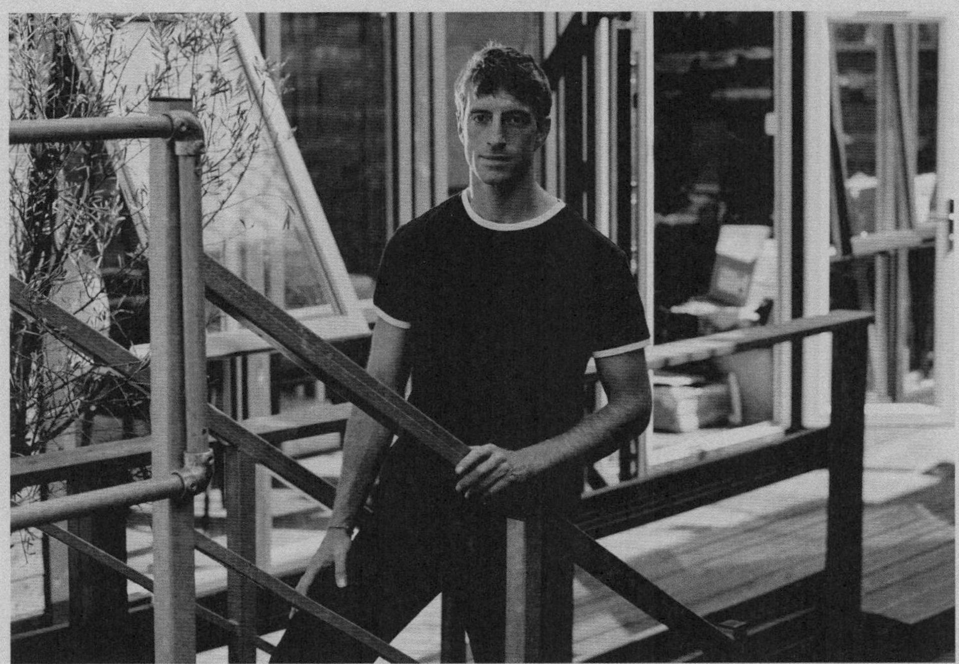

Artist ORFEO TAGIURI on the power of small rituals.

Growing up, the wishing part of blowing out your candles on a birthday cake was really important; once when I forgot to get my friend a cake for his birthday, I put a candle in a banana just so he could have that moment.

A wish makes us feel something beyond what's directly in front of us. I think any small ritual can offer the same. It allows us to rise above the mundane parts of our days and make a decision about how we want the world to look. With birthday candles, you're the center of attention but you also get this moment of stillness, and for the people watching, you're seeing someone really consider their own hopes and dreams.

A few years ago, after finishing art school, I was exploring small creative experiments in my studio, including one artwork that was meant to be burned after viewing. I pierced a piece of paper and threaded in a wick from a tea light, expecting it to ignite, but the wick fizzled out, leaving the paper intact. I set aside that "failed" attempt and moved on. The next day, seeing that half-burnt scrap in my studio, something clicked. I realized it would be a great way to gift someone a wish. So I set about adding a small amount of wax and a wick to some vintage postcards I'd collected from Portobello Market in London and taped on a match and a strike pad. After I posted them to Instagram, they became really popular, and I ended up partnering with Hani Asfari to launch a company devoted to producing them.

When people use a Wish Card, it's a very contemplative and present moment. I think it's similar to wishing on a shooting star, when you're lying on your back and looking up at the sky—there's a moment of awe and hope. Even if you spend only a short amount of your day doing something you love, adding positivity to the world, over time it will add up to something significant.

—

As Told To:
Tara Joshi

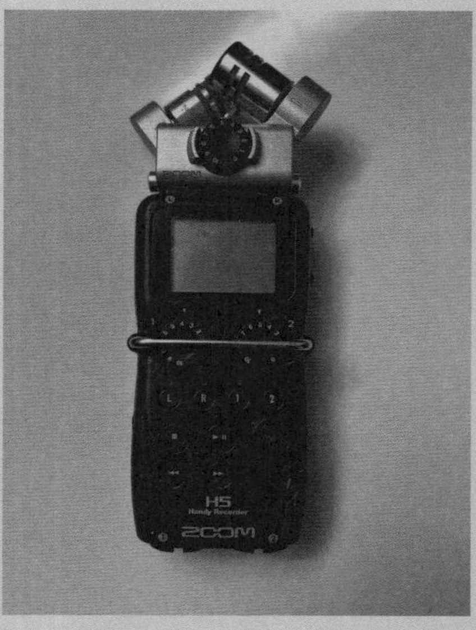

Musician CLAIRE ROUSAY on her field recorder.

I've always been into the confessional kind of songwriting. I used to play drums in church and toured with indie-rock and country bands, but I decided I wanted to step away and make my own music. Around the same time, I got into experimental, avant-garde sound art.

I was trying to figure out a way to do diaristic music that didn't depend on traditional songwriting. Field recordings felt like the best way to get something similar across. First, I was just using the voice memos on my iPhone, but the fidelity was not great and it was only recording in mono. So around four years ago I got a Zoom H5 audio recorder—an older, secondhand model. It's nothing fancy or expensive, and it's small enough that I can carry it with me most of the time.

Today I have thousands of hours of recordings on my computer. I'll usually start with a recording and then add more traditional harmonies and melodies on top, or I'll build a basic structure using the recording.

The initial inspiration often comes from the recording, or the general feeling I had when I made it. It could literally just be the sound of the air conditioner, but I'll remember what I was thinking about and going through and what that day was like. Somebody else listening to it without any context probably won't get that, but it will hold so much for me. Then I will start adding things musically that better evoke the feelings or emotions that I'm trying to convey or investigate.

My Zoom H5 is so fucked now: It has dents in it and you have to hold the SD card in. If I move at all while I'm holding it, what's meant to be minimizing the noise of you handling it now creates this sticky sound. It's been through so much, but even though it's completely busted I like the portability, and I don't have enough money to buy another one right now. I don't tend to use super expensive or complicated tech; it's important to me that it's accessible. It shows that anybody can make music.

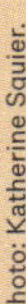
Photo: Katherine Squier.

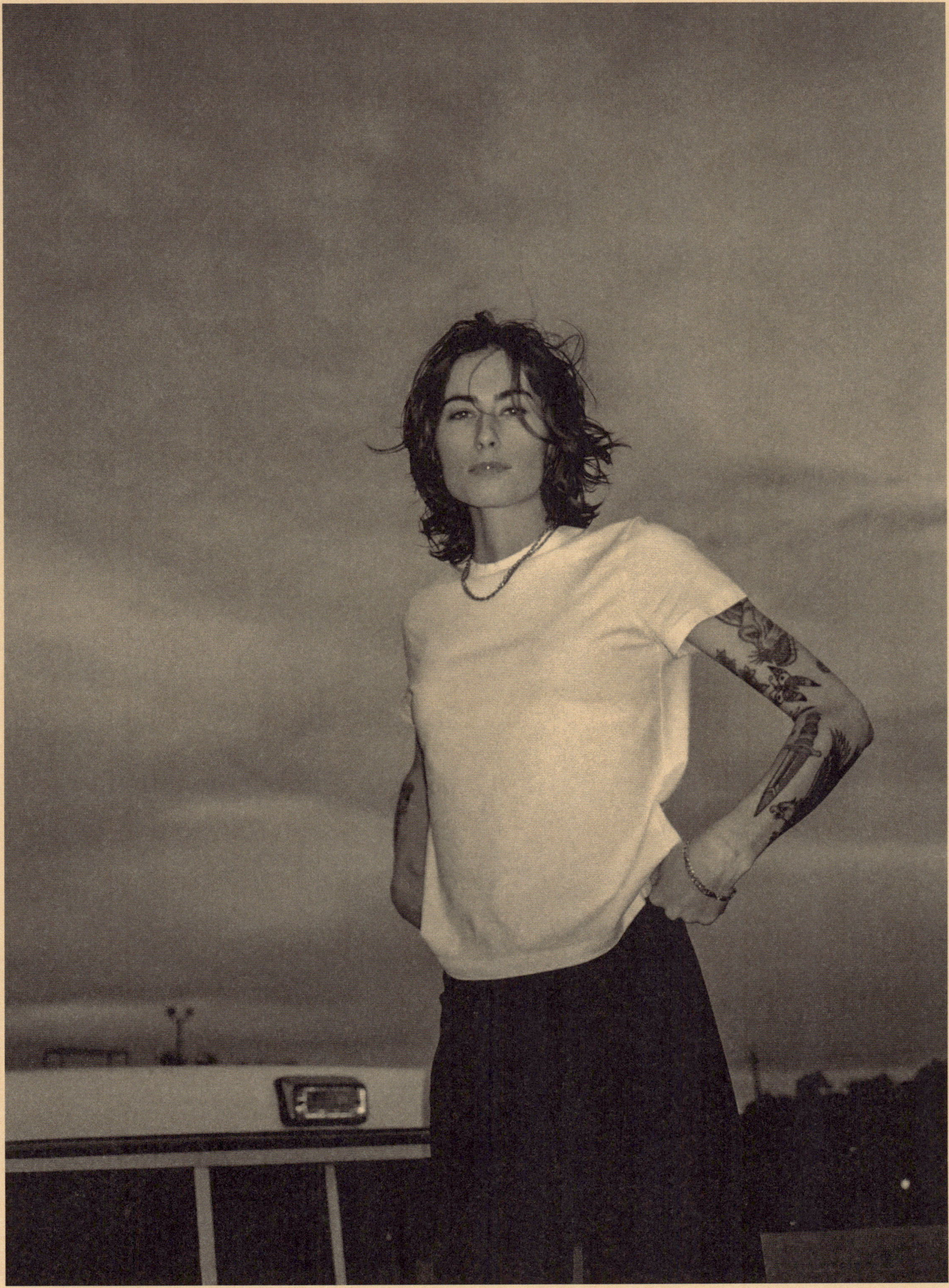

CREDITS

COVER:	PHOTOGRAPHER	Guillaume Garat
	ART DIRECTOR	Joséphine Daru
	STYLIST	Maureen Barbier
	MODEL	Emily Bennett
	MAKEUP	Ellen Walge

Emily wears a faux fur coat by Elie Saab.

AT WORK WITH:	PHOTOGRAPHY ASSISTANT	Ezra Evans

IT SHOULDN'T COST THE EARTH:	PHOTOGRAPHY ASSISTANT	Benjamin Meredith-Hardy
	STYLING ASSISTANT	Claire McKinstry
	STYLING INTERN	Nicole Alonzo

HEALTH IS WEALTH:	LIGHTING ASSISTANT	Clémence Justet
	STYLING ASSISTANT	Victoire Mottier
	SET DESIGN ASSISTANT	Jules Toso

SPECIAL THANKS:		Lavender Au
		Shannon Studios
		Smithsonian National Portrait Gallery
		Studio 18%
		Studio Zorse

A	ACNE STUDIOS	acnestudios.com
	AEYDE	aeyde.com
	ALIGHIERI	alighieri.com
	AMINA MUADDI	aminamuaddi.com
	ANUKA	anuka-jewellery.com
B	BAR JEWELLERY	barjewellery.com
	BITE STUDIOS	bitestudios.com
C	CECILIE BAHNSEN	ceciliebahnsen.com
	CELINE	celine.com
	CHANDON	chandon.com
	CHANEL	chanel.com
	COMPLETEDWORKS	completedworks.com
	COPIN	copin.fr
E	ELIE SAAB	eliesaab.com
F	FALKE	falke.com
	FILIPPA K	filippa-k.com
	FREDERICIA FURNITURE	fredericia.com
	FRITZ HANSEN	fritzhansen.com
G	GANNI	ganni.com
H	HECTOR MACLEAN	hectormaclean.london
	HOUSE OF FINN JUHL	finnjuhl.com
I	ISANGS	isangs.com
	ISSEY MIYAKE	isseymiyake.com
J	JOHN SMEDLEY	johnsmedley.com
K	KASSL EDITIONS	kassleditions.com
L	LUCY DELIUS	lucydelius.co
M	MATTHEW COX	matthewcox.com
	MEOLA INTERIORS	meolainteriors.com
N	NANUSHKA	nanushka.com
O	OMEGA	omegawatches.com
	ONEPLUS	oneplus.com
P	PATEK PHILIPPE	patek.com
	PAULINE DUJANCOURT	paulinedujancourt.com
	PHOEBE SCOT	@_phoebescot_
	PIERRE HARDY	pierrehardy.com
	POLA WIŚLICZ	@pola.wislicz
R	RACHEL BOSTON	rachelboston.co.uk
	RAQUEL DE CARVALHO	raqueldecarvalho.com
	RAY CHU	raychustudios.com
	REPOSSI	repossi.com
	RICHARD MILLE	richardmille.com
	RÓHE	roheframes.com
	RÓISÍN PIERCE	roisinpierce.com
	ROLEX	rolex.com
S	SAMSØE SAMSØE	samsoe.com
	SANDQVIST	sandqvist.com
	STRING	stringfurniture.com
	SVENSKT TENN	svensktten.com
T	TALLER MARMO	tallermarmo.com
	TAUS	tausstudio.com
	TINA FREY	tf.design
	TOGA	int.toga.jp
	TOM WOOD	tomwoodproject.com
	TOTEME	toteme.com
V	VANESSA SPOSI	vanessasposi.com
W	WENS	wensjewels.com
Y	YSSO	theysso.com

As Told To:
Ali Morris

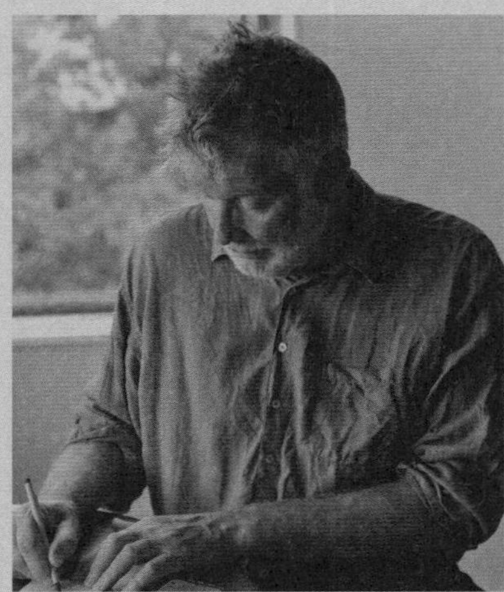

Architect PETER BARBER on the models that have shaped his practice.

I'm in the meeting room of our office in King's Cross, in London, which sits in an old Georgian terrace with a shopfront. It's small-ish, about the size of a living room; on three sides, the walls are covered with models, the fourth is the window onto the street, with shelves all the way up. You can peer through to see outside, and by the same token, people passing outside can look past the models into our meeting room. We get tourists, local people, residents from the homeless hostel around the corner. People come and press their noses against the glass. Sometimes they knock on the door, and we give them a little spiel about who we are and what we do. Sometimes it's a parent with their child. It makes the office a kind of gallery—a nice interface with the street, which feels appropriate because our projects are, in the first instance, about the street: street-based housing rather than apartment buildings behind high fences.

The models are an important part of what we do. Increasingly, architects use computers to test their ideas, but for me that is unsatisfactory and inadequate. Architecture is a three-dimensional, physical medium, and a scale model is really the only way to truly test an idea. So we are surrounded by them, hundreds of them: small ones showing areas of cities cut from blocks of foam, more detailed ones where you can look into the interiors of the houses we're making. They operate at different scales, and they go back through the whole history of the practice, from yellowing cardboard from the '90s to gleaming white ones made in recent months.

Everyone here is involved in making the models, even the directors. I'm really cack-handed, but I draw by hand, and my sketches work alongside them. They capture the spirit: people, trees, the atmosphere—together they are what make a building interesting. Looking around this room, I see the genesis of ideas, their elaboration, the way they've developed over the years. The sheer number of them is a good reminder, for an old bugger like me, of what one's done with one's life.

Occasionally, when we're not very busy, we make a model for its own sake. There's one of a theoretical project called 100-Mile City. It's five feet long and three feet wide and very detailed; a whole neighborhood with little curving, barrel-vaulted roofs. It took an enormous amount of time to make, but it's lovely.

That project was based on the idea that we need millions of new homes in London. Since then I've realized there are hundreds of thousands of empty homes across the country. Maybe we need to think about the housing crisis in the context of economic decline in coastal towns and northern cities in the UK. If we created new industries and moved people back into existing homes, the need for something like 100-Mile City might not be so pressing.

Today I'm not terribly optimistic about social [public] housing. When I was young, nearly half the population in this country lived inexpensively in social housing. That has been diminished through right-to-buy and demolitions. If we could build 50,000 social homes a year in the 1950s, surely we could do it now; we just need the political will. But the crisis is worsening.

I'm just a very small cog in the machine, but I'm not afraid of being critical of the system. I think some people keep their heads down and hope the work keeps coming in, and that's true of us too. But I'm not frightened of saying what I think is wrong. My hope is that as things get more difficult, it will become an increasingly pressing political issue—one which politicians can't ignore anymore. Democracy will kick in, and people will say: Enough.